Praise for Honk if you married Sonja

"Sonja has that rare ability to make you look at life (that's yours and mine, Brother, but hers too) and laugh as she has a capacity for insight and an enthusiasm that is belief in people based. A rare lady who can still wear pigtails and polka dots with grace and charm and see right through you with perfectly clear blue eyes. You'd just as well laugh, 'cause you know there are no secrets.

"If there was such a thing as the running of the bulls for females, it would be Sonja at the vanguard running from the bull (the kind most males put out), but laughing along the way and certainly from the hilltop as they lost their way below, never once thinking to look up . . . and not for lack of balls.

"Sonja has that special kind of vision to see humor, value and hope in folks and the knack to get 'er done when it comes to expressing it in a manner that you'll find readable, informative and entertaining. Thought provoking? I dunno, you'll have to answer that one for yourself, Pard.

"We're talking about a native here that has a Texas hideout any horse-riding outlaw would be proud to have had; once left a cobra behind when it didn't need spurs; a gal who has literally been all over the world; down rivers in rafts, slept on sand bars; made runs down parts of the Silk Road Marco Polo didn't know about in 'Stans' that neither you nor I could pronounce, let alone get a visa for; visited Chicken It'sa (it's NOT a fast food franchise) and Matza Peachoo (it's in the mountains, pretty far south; some even think it was built before the Alamo or the Internet); married a coupla fellers along the way; raised two great children; learned a lot. Now if she's willing to share ANY o' that with you—well, it's a bargain. She is also literate and a person you'd be better for knowin'. Get a lift and buy this book! Read it too!"

—Tracy Walsh, former Honda executive

Sonja Klein

"Sonja Klein has written numerous travel articles for the *Uvalde Leader-News* based on her trips throughout the world. Readers have enjoyed her humorous take on travel experiences coupled with pertinent and interesting facts about the countries she has visited.... Read her new book!"

—Carol Kothmann, managing editor, *Uvalde Leader-News*

"This book is as interesting as Sonja's life, racy and full of the wit and wisdom of a great Texas 'broad.' Buy several copies and treat your friends!"

—Roxanne Apple

"Sonja's . . . stories capture the true flavor and spirit of the people and land she calls home. She has a reporter's curiosity and writes with enthusiasm and flair."

—Willie Edwards, Public Information Officer,
Southwest Texas Junior College

"I first met Sonja Klein in Siberia. Not just a tourist but an adventure traveler, she seeks out those nooks and crannies that speak to culture beyond the 'must see' sites. Her numerous travel writings open up a world few of us in the western world experience. *Honk If You Married Sonja* is a guaranteed fascinating read, written by a individual with whom you'll fall in love."

—Ted Monkhouse, Educational Media Consultant
and Teacher (ret), Ontario, Canada

Honk if you married Sonja

Sonja Klein

Honk if you married Sonja
The travels and essays of Sonja Klein

Sonja Klein

Ambush Publishing
Barksdale, Texas

Honk if you married Sonja: the travels and essays of Sonja Klein
Copyright © 2011 by Sonja Rose Klein

Published by Ambush Publishing
PO Box 192
Barksdale, Texas 78828
1-830-234-3156

Library of Congress Control Number: 2011902135
Klein, Sonja 1942—
    Honk if you married Sonja: the travels and essays of Sonja Klein / by
Sonja Klein

ISBN 9780615446356 (trade paper)

9 8 7 6 5 4 3 2 1

Cover art designed by Chuck Roach, www.roach-art.com
Production by Castle Communications, www.castlecommunications.com

Printed in the United States of America

About the author

Sonja Rose Klein is a native Texan and graduate of The University of Texas. After retiring, she lives up a canyon in west Texas, where she gardens, writes and raises sheep and goats. She is active in the nearby communities of Barksdale and Camp Wood and has won awards for her poetry, essays and short stories. Sonja is an adventure traveler, having visited remote places around the world. She prefers the solitary journeys.

You can contact her by emailing <u>ambushhill@yahoo.com</u>

Acknowledgments

The encouragement of family and many friends saw me through the writing of these stories. I am grateful to all of you. Special thanks to my editor, Lana Castle, for her advice, counsel and encouragement. At times Lana led me where I didn't want to go, but the journey was the right one. I want to express appreciation for the talent of Chuck Roach, the artist who designed the cover. And thank you to my friend Linda Koehl. You are an extraordinary fine tuner. Most of all, deepest thanks to my children for putting up with my work-driven ways.

For my parents,
Alvin A. and Roberta T. Klein
and my brothers,
John, Allan and David.
Like trees planted, the roots are deep.
The branches are strong.

Contents

Preface

My brother David was the first in the door. "Well, here we are again on our yearly 'cruise.'"

I didn't hesitate to speak up. "Better than a cruise, we have no schedule and cook our own food."

My brother Allan was quick. "Mother would be proud of us."

David answered. "I sure do miss her."

The dialog continued among us three siblings. The sisters-in-law let us unwind. "She's with us. I feel her spirit."

"Can't believe she's been gone a year and a half."

"Not a day goes by that I don't think of her. Seems I always have a family question and realize I have no one to ask."

My brother David's ranch in New Mexico is the yearly setting for the family get together. My two other brothers and their spouses had flown from Houston that morning. I always made the ten-hour drive from my ranch in west Texas, cruising through Pecos to buy Pecos cantaloupes for our dining pleasure. This time the car was also loaded with a watermelon, cucumbers, squash and fresh shelled black-eyed peas.

The evening sunset found us on the deck overlooking David's 7,000-acre ranch. Tecalote Creek flowed in the valley below. David's wife Mary opened two bottles of white wine and Allan's wife Alma prepared a plate of cheese, crackers and sliced a cantaloupe.

"How's the writing, Sonja?"

"I think I've abandoned my career in writing after attending a writer's conference in Austin. I think I'll spend the rest of my life drinking, traveling and chasing men."

David was the first to speak. "If you just would listen to me. I've been telling you for years to charge off your trips and expenses."

"David, how can I charge expenses when there is no income?"

"You just do it and hope you're not audited."

I persisted. "At the conference I realized that 80 percent of the books being published are nonfiction. The odds of getting published are not good and then I have to write a sequel and have a website, blog, twitter, and establish a platform as well as hire a publicist. That's a job, and I don't want to work that hard. Besides I don't want to write a sequel."

Allan added, "Why don't you self-publish your essays and travel articles? Haven't you gotten awards for some of those?"

"Yes, it seems I do well at that, the short stuff."

Alma added, "You can't quit writing."

"Writing my travel articles for the Uvalde paper and having people tell me how much they enjoy them is enough satisfaction. I don't need the money, but the tax write-off is appealing."

David interrupted, "I don't know why you won't listen to me. You could have saved thousands of dollars by now. For heavens sake, publish a collection of stories and essays."

"I have enough material for a fair-sized book."

Allan agreed, "Then publish the book."

"I was thinking of calling it Beyond the Hills I Know.

David commented, "No, you need something more catchy."

"It won't be a best-seller; why write it?"

"Because if you do it, you've got to give it your best shot. What about that bumper sticker I was going to have made for you? One that said, honk if you married sonja.

Alma and Mary spoke at the same time. "That's a great title."

"Then I have to write a story so that the title makes sense."

"You can intersperse the essays with stories about your four husbands. They were quite a variety—the race car driver, the mafia enforcer, the South African Englishman and the west Texas rancher smuggler."

I became defensive. "You guys are no slouches on the marriage scene. Between the three of us and brother John we've been married 13 times. Pretty dysfunctional."

Allan grew serious. "Especially since our parents were married 38 years. What happened?"

David whispered. "Let's don't go there."

The wine worked.

"Okay, I write the book, self-publish and sell bumper stickers. Then I can start a line of dolls, outrageous clothing, cosmetics, tee shirts and stuff."

Honk if you married Sonja

"Hold it, just publish the book. You don't have to go off the deep end. Your imagination is unbelievable."

Mary stuck up for me. "David, that's why she's a writer."

Alma concurred. "Yeah, David. That's why she's a good writer."

Allan was thoughtful. "Just publish the book, Sonja."

"Mother always said, 'Go for it.' I think I will."

1

Husband number one— "Montgomery"

I met husband number one, "Montgomery," after graduating from the University of Texas. I had applied to the CIA for a job and, after undergoing a series of tests, I played the waiting and hoping game.

In the meantime my older brother John's wife had just given birth to their first child. John had dropped out of law school and obtained a job as a bank examiner in Louisiana. Since they owned only one car and John would be traveling, he asked me to stay with his wife and help take care of the baby.

Their apartment was in a large complex in Baton Rouge. I soon settled into a routine that often found me out by the pool. It was there that I met him as I pushed my niece's stroller around the pool area. He frequently visited friends that lived in the complex.

I thought him handsome, resembling James Dean. His hair was dark and he was slight of build and I watched him drive off in his burgundy MG sports car.

Days later he returned and seeing me without the stroller, sunbathing in a two-piece, asked, "Where's your kid?"

"Oh, that's not my child. That's my niece. I'm not married."

He was a junior majoring in business at L.S.U. At first I feared I was older, but he soon informed me that he had been in the service stationed in Germany and was attending college on the G.I. Bill, living at home with his parents. The romance blossomed; I met his parents. He was an only child. They drank a lot, and his father leered at me.

Within the next months, I had rented an apartment in a small cheaper complex and obtained a job teaching 7th grade history in St. Amant, a community east of Gonzales, 30 miles south of Baton Rouge. Birth control pills assured me of a safe sex life, and I was on my own, having been rejected by the CIA.

Before the school year was over I had convinced him to marry me the September before he began his last semester. I did not renew my teaching contract and found a job at L.S.U. in the accounting department. We moved into a new apartment close to the university campus.

During the months of courtship, I got to know his family. His father was a philanderer, a womanizer and often slapped his wife. She was not faithful. They drank to excess. I dreamed of saving Montgomery from his family.

We married early in September in Houston, the picture book wedding. My father and I cried as he walked me down the aisle. We honeymooned in Puerto Vallarta and stayed drunk most of the time. I was not impressed with his sexual performance, but having had little experience, had nothing with which to compare it.

He graduated and we moved to Pasadena, Texas, where he obtained a job with a savings and loan institution. I worked in the payroll department of a paper company. Our apartment was new and large. He traded his MG for a Plymouth. We purchased furniture with the funds in my savings account.

He wanted to race sports cars. We joined the SCCA (Sports Car Club of America), and spent the weekends going to local events, Gymkhanas and Rallies, making friends at the monthly meetings. Before long he convinced me to spend my savings on a 1963 AC Cobra, a powerful machine not suited for daily driving.

We rented a three-bedroom house. I went to work for a contractor at NASA, editing technical documents and making more money than him. We traded my Volkswagen for a Volvo P1800, a sleek little sports car.

The savings and loan sent him to a convention in St. Louis. I enjoyed being alone the week he was absent. When he returned he confessed that while drunk he had visited a whore in St. Louis and begged me to forgive him. I did, but in words only. I knew I had made a mistake, but divorce was not an option in the early 60's—not with my family.

He changed jobs, went to work for a bank in Houston. We purchased a house in West University. I went to work managing a real estate office. He continued to dabble with sports cars and soon bought a Formula Vee and trailer and began to race as an amateur. We traveled all over Texas, Arkansas and Louisiana. The Formula Vee was always breaking down. He spun out during the race. There was always an excuse. I became certified as a pit steward and worked the races for no pay. We partied a lot and were introduced to marijuana. He liked it. I didn't. It made me eat too much and feel out of control.

He changed jobs again, this time working for a larger bank in downtown Houston. Our salaries were almost equal. We saved money for his racing habit.

I wanted children. He didn't. I quit taking birth control pills. Nothing happened. I went to a fertility specialist. My ovaries did not ovulate. I had fibroid tumors and endometriosis. A varicose vein in his left testicle overheated the sperm as they were ejected. The motility was low. He went to a specialist at Baylor and insisted that the pills they gave him solved his problem. I believed him. I had surgery to remove the fibroids. It was painful. The doctor gave me fertility pills, put dye in my tubes. The procedure was humiliating. Nothing happened. He changed jobs, this time becoming a bank examiner, traveling all over Texas. I knew he was not faithful. I had an affair with a college student, another affair with a friend of his.

We purchased a Honda and Yamaha motorcycle dealership in Conroe, pledging some securities that my father had given me as collateral for the loan to buy the business. We sold our house in West University at a handsome profit and moved to Conroe, where we purchased a new home with the proceeds.

For four years I worked six days a week, keeping the books and running the parts department. He sold his Formula Vee and trailer and began racing dirt bikes. I learned to ride a motorcycle and raced a few cross-country Enduros. I wasn't very good, but I tried. We partied a lot. Our customers introduced him to cocaine. He liked it. I didn't. It was expensive.

We traveled to Baja in a motor home with three other couples and rode Baja on dirt bikes. We returned to Puerto Vallarta for a wedding anniversary. He continued to drink quite a bit. I had an affair with a mechanic at the motorcycle shop. From my point of view, the marriage was dissolving, but he was satisfied.

My younger brother David graduated from Rice University. It was the years of the Vietnam War. While awaiting a draft hearing, he invited me on a road trip to Colorado. I was happy to leave. We had traded the Volvo sports car for a Volvo sedan, and David and I left heading north through Taos. By the time we arrived in Grand Junction, Colorado, David had received a call from our father saying that his hearing was imminent. I put him on the plane and headed home south through Taos.

There were flyers at the hotel desk in Taos advertising a motocross the next day. I drove out to the dusty track and encountered some friends from Houston. With them was a tall handsome guy named John. I spent three months with him in Taos. We were both married. I told my family and husband I needed some time, that I wanted to write. I don't know what John told his wife back in Fort Worth, but every so often he went back there.

I rented a cabin outside Taos, took walks, wrote stories and loved John. I had discovered good sex, great sex. It was more addictive than drugs, though there was a lot of that in the early 70's in Taos. John was a user, and I suspected a junkie. I never saw him shoot up any drugs. We did our share of drugs, little alcohol except for beer. Music was important— Bob Dylan, Elton John, America, Neil Young, Gordon Lightfoot, Joan Baez.

Guilt finally drove us back to our spouses. My husband took me back without a question, and I continued to work six days a week at the motorcycle dealership. I had an affair with one of the sales reps. I didn't like myself, but I loved John, thought of him every day, expected him to come and rescue me. It didn't happen.

My husband had taken over the checkbook in my absence and, upon receiving a bill, I asked for the checkbook to see if the bill had been paid. Glancing through the check register, I found three checks a week apart to a doctor. When I questioned him, he replied, "Call the doctor; he wants to see you."

That was the last day I slept under the same roof with him. The doctor's nurse informed me that my husband was being treated for gonorrhea and that I should come in for treatment.

"I want a divorce. I'm going to stay at my parents."

"I don't want a divorce. I love you."

"I want you to move out of my house."

"It's my house too and I'm not moving."

"Goodbye."

My parents took the news quite well. I filed for divorce, let him keep the house. He kept the AC Cobra. I took the Mercedes that had replaced the Volvo sedan. He did manage to cheat me out of some assets and all the cash we had on hand. I kept the cabin we were building on Lake Livingston. When the cabin was finished I moved there, bitter and angry at the world. He promised to sell the dealership and return the securities I had pledged as collateral. In the meantime his girlfriend moved in my house and he continued to run and profit from the dealership. I was broke, relying on investment income to pay the bills.

I was 31. My world had collapsed. The next few months I spent clearing brush, planting a garden, working to the point of exhaustion. No matter how hard I worked the rage would not leave. Of course I blamed him. The dreams of being married, having children and living happily ever after were shattered. The marriage had lasted eight years.

The divorce became final. I contacted John. He was still married but came to visit. He was abusing drugs, so I asked him to leave. For the time, I remained alone.

2

Aunt Ella

" Little Aunt Ella. You remind me so much of my sister," my father said.

"Oh, Daddy. You're just saying that."

"You're more like her than her own daughters. You walk like her, have her mannerisms and even look like her."

Aunt Ella was one of a kind. She grew up north of Houston in a German farm community, one of eight children. She spoke German before English, married young to another German who sold insurance and died in his 40's of a heart attack, leaving her with four children. My father paid off her house. She managed to raise her children, working in cafés as a cook or waitress. At one time she owned her own café on Spring Creek. She later worked in the combination hardware, feed store, dry goods, meat and grocery store that her two sons owned in the town of Spring, Texas.

Spring had been a thriving railroad town, feeding the lumber industry before it dwindled to a small community with two grocery stores, a bar and several churches. It had been a trade center for local farmers until the oil strike in Tomball, to the northwest, attracted the farmers to the extra conveniences offered.

Aunt Ella bloomed like a flower in the town of Spring. She knew everyone and her neighbors loved her. The store stood a few blocks from her home. She never learned to drive but walked with a remarkable brisk rolling gait. Everyone knew that walk. She had two speeds: wide open and dead stop.

I spent my summers working in the grocery store, washing shelves at the age of 13, the raging hormone time of adolescence. Her old two-story wooden house in the center of town was my favorite. There were two staircases, and the back staircase was narrow, dark and twisting. Upstairs were three bedrooms and a large bathroom with a claw-footed bathtub. Her doors were never locked. She often rented out the upper bedrooms to railroad workers by the night or week. I slept upstairs in the back bedroom overlooking the shaded backyard. No fear of molestation

6

entered my mind. In complete innocence I shared the bathroom with the railroad men.

The summer months were my joy. We worked from 7 A.M. to 7 P.M. Sundays, the store was closed. The evenings were enchanting. Her yard was a jungle of flowers and shrubs. There was always something blooming, but Aunt Ella was the flower of the town. Her front screened porch lined with mismatched rockers of every size and shape contained a menagerie of living greenery. Her cousins, Alma and Dora, frequently visited in the evenings, sharing her Lone Star beer. Ivy covered the screens.

"Ella, I didn't know that ivy bloomed," said Dora. She was quite talkative. "Those little orange flowers are really pretty. You sure have a green thumb. My ivy has never bloomed."

"Dora, you just don't have the touch."

"I guess you're right. Nothing I plant ever grows."

Later that evening after Dora had gone home, I smelled the flowers. They were plastic.

Most days after work and returning home, she took off her shoes and sent me to the bar with a brown paper sack containing a dollar bill and a quarter. "Sonja, go to the back door of Viola's and hand this to her." No questions were asked, and I returned home with the cold beer. We rocked the evenings away, talking and reading True Secret, magazines about love and lust in the back seat of cars and unwanted teen pregnancies and unrequited romance—material I would never have been allowed to have or read at home.

Some Sunday afternoons, after church, her son Buddy drove us to Spring Creek for a few hours of fishing. Juicy fat worms from her compost pile in the backyard were our bait.

Once a month she called her brothers and relatives and cooked a chicken and dumpling dinner. No one ever denied her invitations for a day of dominoes and good food. I don't remember when I learned to play dominoes. An empty chair for one of us younger family members always beckoned.

She taught me to make sauerkraut and pickles in an open crock. We made sausage, wine and canned vegetables. I learned to sew on a pedal sewing machine. Aunt Ella never ran out of energy, but she did take her rests in the small alcove off the kitchen where she had a single iron bed, fluffed high with feather pillows and an overstuffed mattress. Before daylight I could hear her radio spewing out faith sermons and music. She lived close to God.

The house was cluttered with furniture. The walls were pasted with flowered wallpaper and covered with cards, letters and family pictures. Crocheted and embroidered fabrics covered every available surface.

She never gave her suitors any notice. She remained single for over 30 years, until her death at the age of 77. I loved her beyond comprehension. She was the aunt to best all others. I was her favorite companion.

When the wild grapes were ripe, she sent me up into the tree to gather them. I threw them down to her to be put in the bushel baskets. When we tired, we went home and made wine.

The highlight of the summer was our two-week vacation down on the creek. Her son Buddy drove us to the campsite. Aunt Ella and I strung a tarp between the trees for shelter and nailed wooden crates to the trees to store our food. For two weeks the woods were our home. Buddy and I waded up and down the creek to set out trotlines and baited the hooks with either bacon or minnows that we had seined from the clear water. Then he left us out in the woods.

We had no guns or fears. Twice a day we ran the trotlines and baited the hooks. Aunt Ella had never learned to swim, but she would stand on the bank to be sure I didn't drown. Whatever we caught, we cleaned and ate or put in the cooler. The days were spent reading our romance magazines or fishing for perch on the banks of the creek. She always caught fish. I could be right beside her and not get a bite, while she would be pulling in the perch. In the evenings we cooked over the open fire with black iron pots. Cushioned by quilts and blankets, we slept on the ground.

Buddy checked on us every three or four days. He replenished the beer, ice and magazines. Aunt Ella gave orders and I followed her. Whatever she told me to do, I did. It never occurred to me that I couldn't. She was fearless, independent and strong-minded.

One summer during our camping trip I found a troublesome splinter in the palm of my hand. We could not dig it out. "Sonja, you keep an eye on that splinter. If you see red streaks up your arm, let me know." When the streaks appeared, she removed a piece of bacon from the cooler, cut the lean away and put the fat on top of the splinter. She then wrapped a thin dishrag around my hand to keep the bacon in place. After three days, the bacon fat drew out the splinter. I knew she saved my life.

Honk if you married Sonja

Selfish years followed college and marriage. I saw Aunt Ella on family occasions. Then, as she was dying in the hospital, I visited. She was not conscious. When I entered the room, held her hand and spoke to her, her eyes opened wide. "Is that you Sonja? Am I back here in this old hospital?"

"Yes, Aunt Ella."

"I was having such a good time in heaven with Uncle Alec and Aunt Hannah." They were her brother and sister.

She took a deep breath and died.

The funeral was a sad one. Her children spoke words of comfort. "Sonja, she always loved you more than she did us." There was no room in the church for those that attended, and flowers lined the walls of the church from the front to the back. I had never seen so many flowers.

They gave me her desk, some dishes and some of her signature embroidered and lace-trimmed aprons. I treasure them.

As the years passed, my family often reminded me, "Here comes little Aunt Ella."

"I'm not Aunt Ella, I am my own person."

And then the time came when all women develop that extra sense— one of perception tempered with wisdom.

"You are more like Aunt Ella than you can imagine."

"If I am as well-loved as she was, then I consider that a great compliment. And by the way, send lots of flowers when I die."

Brother David became the father of twins. They were delivered by Caesarian. My mother was present. Later she said, "Sonja, when they held her up, she looked around with wide eyes just like you. Looks like we have another Sonja." They named her Shannon.

When Shannon began to walk, my brother called, "Sonja, she walks like you. I'd know that walk anywhere."

I smiled as I answered. "I think we have another Aunt Ella."

3

Husband number two— Raleigh

I met husband number two, Raleigh, while living on Lake Livingston, still angry at the world. The divorce from husband number one had cost me a few friends. A visit from a couple I had met while in the motorcycle business brought a surprise. He was tall, dark and handsome, with an old-world mustache. He was from Louisiana. The visit was friendly, and they left.

Weeks later the phone rang. It was him, and he had come to visit but was lost. I drove to Sandy Creek Marina and led him home, fixed dinner and visited. He slept in the guest room, manners personified. After breakfast the next morning he left.

His visits became regular. Every week or so he called, drove up in his black Lincoln and took me out to dinner. Sometimes I cooked. I learned very little about him. He owned a nightclub in Lafayette, Louisiana, next to the racetrack. He was single, several years older than me and divorced. He wined and dined me in a manner that was unfamiliar. I had run with the race and motorcycle crowd too long.

We drove into Houston to the Galleria. As we strolled through the levels I admired a ruby and diamond ring in the window of a jewelry store. He persuaded me to go in with him and asked the price. It was in the $5,000 price range. He pulled out a roll of hundreds and proceeded to buy me the ring. I would not let him; the salesman pulled me aside. "Let the man buy you the ring." I left the store without it.

We dined in splendor. He always dressed in a three-piece suit and wore a silk tie. His shoes shined. He drank only Dom Pérignon champagne. He made no demands on my body. His manners were impeccable, and the aura of his mystery was intriguing. He made me feel like a woman, a pretty woman.

Honk if you married Sonja

I began to dress like a woman, curled my long hair, wore jewelry. We visited Neiman Marcus. I let him buy me designer clothing. The wad of bills in his pocket was always big.

He invited me to visit him in Lafayette. A suite was reserved at a nice hotel. The bucket of champagne greeted me. His nightclub was called "The Galloping Jugs." There were go-go dancers and a card game in the back room. The rooms upstairs were left to the imagination. We went to the horse races, sat in a box. I wore a hat and fancy dress. He gave me money to bet and told me which horse to pick. I won over $500. I kept it. What was not to like?

We drove to Vegas and stayed in a lavish complimentary suite. I wore my long gowns to the casino. We saw Elvis, played blackjack. He knew everyone. He stood behind me and told me when to hit and when to stay. I won almost $1,000. I kept it too. We dined and drank. Sex didn't seem to interest him. We did some drugs.

My father was in M.D. Anderson, losing his battle with cancer. I spent time with him and my mother. The courtship continued. My father died. Raleigh attended the funeral with me.

Two months later we were married privately by the family Lutheran preacher. We spent our honeymoon night at the Warwick in Houston and left the next day in my cobalt blue Mercedes driving to Puerto Vallarta, a long drive through the heart of Mexico to the Pacific Coast. We spent the first night in Monterrey and the second in Durango. When we drove into Vallarta, the hotels were booked. He followed a Mercedes with Canadian plates up a steep hill to a condominium complex, parked beside them and left me in the car while he spoke with them. Moments later he returned to the car with the keys to a condo across the courtyard.

We spent a week in the luxury condo overlooking the Pacific Ocean. Nights, we visited the fancy nightclubs and restaurants. He bought champagne for everyone. He connected for some drugs—marijuana and cocaine. We partied hard. I dressed fancy; he wore his three-piece suits.

And then he left me in Livingston, coming to visit several times a month. Sex was not frequent and then only perfunctory. He preferred blow jobs. I wanted more, nagged him about moving to Lafayette. He remained mysterious. I ignored the clues.

John, my Taos love, called. He came to visit me in Livingston, asked me to divorce Raleigh and marry him. He was single. I refused, yet I drove to John's ranch in Brownwood every chance I had. We slept under the stars; we plowed and planted wheat. John was doing heavy drugs. He tried to hide it from me but failed. I returned to Livingston, waited.

Raleigh and I moved to New Orleans on Royal Street in the French Quarter, an apartment with three balconies, four bedrooms and three baths. He gave me money to furnish it. I shopped the French Quarter and purchased some nice pieces. It was fun. We dined at restaurants where he was known. The chefs came to our table. The owners would not let us see the menu. They served wonderful food; and when the valet brought our car around, there was always a bucket of Dom Pérignon iced down between the seats. He tipped the maitre de' with a gold and sapphire watch. I never saw money change hands.

He was absent most of the time. I would tell him that I needed to go and check on my house on the lake and visit the family. Instead I went to see John in Brownwood. The sex with John was fantastic, but John was abusing drugs in the worst way.

After a year we left New Orleans. I returned to my home on the lake. He rarely visited. "Your friend John is dead, killed in a drug deal gone bad." He had known of the affair all along. I mourned silently, living on the lake, fishing from the dock and working in the yard. I read a lot of books.

The phone rang. "You might not remember me, but my Uncle Bob married your first cousin Laverne. I have two babies. Welfare is going to take them away and put them in foster homes. I don't want that. Do you want them? I'll sign all the papers. I don't want any money, just want to know they're in a good home."

My life had become flat. In that moment my dreams came true, what I had always wanted. There was no hesitation. "Yes, I want them. How old are they?"

"The boy is 18 months; the girl is five months. They're brother and sister. My boyfriend left me. Do you want to see a picture of them?"

"No, it doesn't matter." I didn't care what they looked like; I knew they were beautiful.

I called Raleigh. He arrived the next day, met with her, took her to an attorney in Houston and the next night we met her outside a bar in Willis, Texas. She handed two babies to us. We drove to my mother's in Spring. She had resurrected the crib from the attic. The girl slept in the crib. I named her Molly after my grandmother. We slept with the boy between us. I named him Joseph. They never cried. The adoption was final the following year.

Raleigh purchased a brick home in Lafayette. I rented out the lake house and moved to Lafayette with the children. He was gone most of the time. I wanted more. With inherited funds, I purchased an old plantation home outside New Iberia. His family lived there.

The home was on three acres on the Bayou Teche. I remodeled the house and guesthouses, put in a swimming pool and enrolled the children in a private Episcopal school and joined the church. Soon I was active in the community. I was on the school board, church treasurer and a docent guide at an antebellum home. My life was full. My children were a joy. He was home maybe five nights a month.

And then my life was shattered. The swat team arrived in the middle of the night, surrounded the house and led him off in handcuffs. The newspaper headlines read SCARFACE, DRUG KINGPIN, ARRESTED IN NEW IBERIA. He was released on bail. A year later he was sentenced to 10 years hard labor. The children and I visited him every other Sunday, traveling 120 miles one way to the south of Baton Rouge. We never missed a visiting day.

Three and a half years into his sentence, he was diagnosed with kidney cancer. They removed his kidney and the tumor. He was released and came home to undergo radiation therapy. He recovered, stayed home, grew fat and waited to die.

"You need to do something," I said. "The cancer isn't coming back. I want a divorce."

"I don't have anyplace to go."

"Why don't you take your club back? It's not the same without you."

"I can't break the lease."

"I'm going to move your clothes to the guest house."

"Do what you want."

I moved his clothes to the guesthouse, put the house up for sale and filed for divorce. He came and went; mostly he was gone. The divorce became final.

I moved to Houston, built a home near my mother and went to work with my brother as a property tax consultant. The children began high school. The marriage had lasted 15 years. We remained friends.

4

Husband number three— "Rodney"

I met husband number three, "Rodney," while still living in New Iberia, waiting for my house to sell following the divorce. I met him through mutual friends in community service work. He was from South Africa and of English extraction, and with his blonde hair and charming accent, I thought him a handsome version of Prince Charles.

How he ended up in New Iberia is an interesting story. His family of English nobility and owners of sugar cane plantations in South Africa sent him to Louisiana State University to obtain a degree in sugar engineering. While there, he met his wife-to-be, who hailed from Oklahoma. They eloped and upon graduation returned to South Africa, where she was miserable. From there they went to Brazil, where he engineered and built a sugar refinery with his cousin. After the birth of their daughter, they returned to Louisiana, where he currently ran two sugar plantations in the St. Martinville area. His wife contracted lymphatic cancer and committed suicide when the disease progressed beyond hope.

We were both 48. He courted me, and when I moved to Houston, he continued to visit. I convinced him to marry me and move in and begin consulting, using his sugar engineering credentials. He was successful. My children hated him, but other family members loved him. I had proven that I could marry a normal educated man.

His ordinary habits annoyed me. He didn't like spoons left in the pot. His underwear were folded a certain way. The roll of toilet paper on the holder was always placed in the same rollout position. He was always playing with his hair. The signal for sex was a washrag on his end table. He didn't French kiss, thought it nasty.

Shortly after the marriage we traveled with his 23-year-old daughter to South Africa to visit his family, about the time of the unraveling of Apartheid. They were stuffy, heavy drinkers and lived in fancy homes with lots of Zulu house servants. They treated them as children and slaves and were extremely prejudiced. The familiarity he exhibited with his daughter made me uncomfortable. I was certain of yet another mistake. He no longer appealed to me. I quit having sex with him, using all sorts of excuses.

When he received an offer of a two-year contract in Hawaii, the marriage disintegrated. His pleasures were fishing and golf. He read only the sports section of the newspaper and was boring as an earthworm. I divorced him gladly after a miserable four years. I don't know why I married a man who wouldn't French kiss.

I devoted the next few years to meditation and hard work, making money with my brother in the property tax consulting business. My children finished high school and were poised for college.

I dreamed of John and one morning in meditation, I saw him in a room dressed in white with two other men. I believed him on the other side. On a whim I called his mother in Brownwood. He was in prison, had been for over four years and was due to be released the following month to a halfway house in San Antonio. I gave her my number.

John called collect. His first words were, "I thought you were dead. Some friends of Raleigh's told me you had been killed in a car crash." The world of drugs was a small fraternity.

My heart was pounding at the sound of his familiar voice. "Raleigh told me you were dead."

We talked for a while. I can't remember the words, just the emotion of the moment. He continued the conversation with, "Can I call you again? You sound great. I had a dream about you."

I remember answering, "I dreamed about you too. Our souls must have been searching for each other."

Fate had set the stage for husband number four.

5

Husband number four—John

Meditation kept me sane. I became convinced that I would not live long enough to see John again. He called me collect every few days. It was as if the 18 years had never passed.

When he was released to the halfway house in San Antonio, I drove to see him. He could only be absent for the afternoon and had to provide a phone number where he could be reached. I reserved a room at the Hilton and drove up to the shoddy frame house, an obvious firetrap, where he was confined. He was waiting on the porch. He walked down the steps and I thought I would die. He looked the same, over six feet four inches, dark hair now sprinkled with gray, sparkling blue eyes and that wonderful sly grin. His shirt was blue. I got out of the car to greet him. We hugged. He folded himself into the car, and I drove to the Hilton, checked in and we entered the elevator and stood there looking at each other, words frozen.

John broke the silence. "I guess it might be nice if you pushed the elevator button. What floor?"

I had to look at the key.

We entered the room. He sat on the bed, propped his back against the headboard bolstered by pillows and motioned for me to join him.

I sat beside him. He put his arm around me and began to talk. He spoke of the years that had passed, told his stories. I told mine. There was no regret, just revelation. As the time drew near for us to part he changed the mood. "We'll never forgive ourselves if we don't get naked under the covers."

With no embarrassment we undressed, rolled back the covers and climbed bare under the sheet. The feel of our skin touching was sublime, not sexual, more like a homecoming. We moaned in pleasure as our bodies reunited, and continued talking. Time tore us apart.

I continued to visit every weekend that I could. Through the halfway house, he obtained a job at a plant nursery. We wrote letters, talked on the phone and when his months had passed, he moved in with me. My family accepted him, my children likewise. They were emerging into adults soon to be on their own. He was on federal parole, having been sent to prison for the same reasons as husband number two, a sting operation with no dope or money, a setup.

He submitted to weekly urinalysis, counseling at the parole office. His parole officer visited the house. I continued to work.

"Sonja, what do you plan to do with the rest of your life?"

"I think I'd like to buy a ranch in west Texas and live the rest of my life with you."

"Then let's play it out."

We began spending the weekends west of San Antonio, looking at property for sale. Being with him was heaven. We had fun, laughed a lot, loved even more. I purchased a ranch in Real County, smaller than I had envisioned, but the flowing water of Bullhead Creek was beautiful and the land and water sang to us.

The three houses on the ranch were in poor repair. We began remodeling. His ideas were innovative. I quit my job, put the house up for sale and we spent the weekends at the ranch, painting in our underwear, sleeping in front of the fire, overcooking steaks on the grill.

The house sold; we moved to the ranch for good. His case was transferred to a parole officer in Del Rio. The urine tests continued, random now. He never failed. He was clean. I was happy.

"Are you ever going to ask me to marry you?" I asked.

"No, I asked you once. You turned me down. I'll not ask again. Besides, I can't put you in jeopardy. The state of Texas has a judgment against me, a marijuana tax for over $300,000. Heaven knows what it is by now with interest."

"Well, then, we'll just have an east Texas wedding. We'll jump over the broomstick."

And that is what we did. He laid the broomstick over the threshold and we jumped it together.

I included him on my hospitalization policy as my common-law husband and we spent the days walking fences, cutting cedar and remodeling the modest house on the ranch. We listened to music, read books and spent our days and nights together. He was 52; I was 55. Friends and family visited. We bought some sheep and goats. He taught me about them. He had grown up in a ranching family from around San Angelo. We fixed fences, worked side by side. He continued on parole.

Three years passed. We drove to Del Rio, visited his parole officer and drove across the border to spend Valentine's Day at Ma Crosby's. He gave me roses purchased from a street vendor. We dined on steak and enchiladas. We drove home. He was sick all night, throwing up with diarrhea.

The following week we drove to Spring to visit my mother and children and brothers. My mother took one look at John and said, "John, you're sick. You are yellow."

She called her internist and made an appointment for the next morning. The doctor took one look at John and said, "You have cirrhosis of the liver. You are an alcoholic."

"No, I'm not an alcoholic."

"I'm sending you down the hall for some blood work. Come back tomorrow for the results."

The following morning we met with the doctor. "You're not an alcoholic. You have Hepatitis C. Your liver is failing. You have about six months to live."

We drove directly to the bookstore and purchased books on Hepatitis C, studied them, adhered to a recommended diet. I began to research the disease, finding it common among Vietnam vets.

He continued to deteriorate. Flesh hung from his once-firm arms. A few months later a biopsy of his liver was performed. Liver cancer was advanced; they gave him three weeks. He said his goodbyes to family and friends. He sent me to town for supplies and while I was gone, called and bought a Mercedes over the phone, arranging to have it delivered the following day. When I returned from town, he smiled. "Sonja, I bought you a new Mercedes."

"You what?"

"They're delivering it tomorrow."

"What color is it?"

"I don't remember."

"How am I going to pay for it?"

"You have the money. Sell the sheep to help pay for it."

"Why did you do that?"

"Because you always drove a Mercedes, you deserve it and you're too tight to buy one yourself. This is my final gift to you."

"John, I can't do this."

Honk if you married Sonja

"You've always been strong. You can do this. You have to help me die. I want to be cremated, no memorial service, no embalming, no obituary. I don't want anyone to know you're out here alone."

"What do you want me to do with the ashes?"

"Scatter them off the cliff where we always watched the sunset."

"I don't think I can do that. I think I'll just put them in that Mercedes you bought and let you ride around with me."

"That sounds good."

Hospice helped that last week. He died in my arms at the ranch.

And that's what I did with his ashes. Whether I drove the Mercedes or the pickup, his ashes went with me. Two years later I emptied them off the cliff. A sudden breeze dusted me with his ashes, a final caress. A cloud of blue dragonflies kept me company. He's with me here at the ranch.

I loved him the best.

6

Valentine's Day

Having lived over half a century, I can honestly recall one singular Valentine's Day which I suppose exposes me as not being prone to the marketing hype that encompasses Valentine's Day. Over the years I have purchased cards, candy and flowers for family, children and friends and done my share of dollar spending, but as for memorable Valentine's Days, I can remember only one.

Valentine's Day 1997 in Texas I awoke on a cold gray day lying in my four-poster bed snuggled under Grandpa Klein's down comforter, next to John, the love of my life, at my ranch in west Texas.

"John, I slept so well I feel like a new person."

"You're not." I loved his dry wit.

John left the security of the warm comforter and carefully and consistently measured the coffee in the coffee maker before turning it on and returning into the bedroom to dress. John had assumed the coffee duties because I could never make the same coffee twice.

"How hard is it Sonja to measure 4 scoops of coffee grounds and fill the pot with water to the 8 level line?

"Very hard, John, because some days are plus and some are minus, and I never know which until I make the coffee."

"Let's go to Acuna and have lunch at Ma Crosby's."

"Great idea," I said, as I dressed in my usual jeans and shirt.

John drove the pickup through the winding roads to Bracketville, where he turned south on the highway that led to the border with Mexico and our favorite restaurant.

The signs were auspicious as we sailed through customs on the Mexican side, receiving the green light that randomly allowed us to coast through the narrow lane without stopping for inspection.

The parking lot at Lando's was almost empty as we parked against the concrete wall and received the numbered ticket. John paid the attendant the usual $3 before we walked to the uneven sidewalk along the main shopping district, unresponsive to the peddlers and store clerks attempting to lure us into their shops.

Our destination was Ma Crosby's Bar and Restaurant, family owned and operated since 1938. We walked into a dark and inviting room and seated ourselves at the empty bar and surveyed our surroundings: old pictures of bandits and revolutionaries in black and white, family groups dressed in their best attire from the 1930's and 40's and the familiar bartender in his green cotton jacket. The bar was empty, the clock on the wall showed not yet 11 A.M. and John sighed with approval.

"Good, we made it before 11:00; the margaritas are all doubles before 11:00."

We sipped our drinks in silence, letting the atmosphere of the years soak into our being, gathering our spirits to be in that place. I lit a cigar as John left the room, savoring the aroma, taking me back to the years as a little girl when I would sit on my father's knee and watch him blow smoke rings from the occasional cigar he enjoyed.

John returned to the bar with a dozen red roses and very formally handed them to me.

"These are for you. I love you. Happy Valentine's Day, Sonja."

Tears fell from my eyes as I thanked him and regathered myself, willing the tears to cease. I looked away as a few remnants drained my tear glands and we returned to our drinks. The morning droned on, the bar became noisy and we adjourned to the restaurant, ordered steak and enchiladas and snacked on the chips and sauces the waiter had brought to our table, continuing to sip the margaritas from the bar.

The musicians wandered to our table, John slipped them some money and I was serenaded with "La Paloma" as our food was served. Our hunger stifled the conversation as we cleaned our plates, paid the bill and walked hand in hand back to the car. We left Mexico before the line at U.S. Customs had become intolerable, and with our margarita buzz drove back to Ambush Hill before the day ended.

Home safely at the ranch, John lit a fire in the fireplace, put on some music and we snuggled on the comfortable leather sofa, calm in each other's presence before John became seized with diarrhea and vomiting that persisted through the night.

"It was the sauce at Ma Crosby's; I'm never going back there again."

"But John, I ate the same thing and I'm not sick."

John was better but weak and pale the following morning, and three days later he was given the death sentence, diagnosed with Hepatitis C and liver cancer. He died the same year after Valentine's Day 1997. He was 52. John never returned to Ma Crosby's.

Months later I returned to Ma Crosby's with friends and family. John and I were still there, our spirits lingering over enchiladas and margaritas —my favorite Valentine's Day.

7

Dancing

My first fragmented memories of dancing take place in a studio in The Village, the first urban shopping center in Houston, near Rice University and the now massive world-famous medical center. Mirrors lined the walls. I learned acrobatics, tap dancing and ballet. I don't think I was more than three years old, but I did manage to stand on my head and do a poor cartwheel as well as to make noise with my tap shoes and attempt to stand on my toes with my hands spread wide.

Later I was driven to The Heights, an older residential area north of downtown Houston, where I climbed old wooden stairs to another dance studio. I must have been older because the recital at the end of the class year took place in the Houston Music Hall on the banks of Buffalo Bayou. My father and mother and I suppose my brothers sat near the front. I saw their beaming faces in spite of the floodlights. I remember a dusty stage.

I disliked people messing with my hair and face. The photos reveal a small girl in a silly costume made up for a beauty pageant. One of the costumes was short and yellow, the other longer with orange sequins. I was neither excited nor nervous about the entire production. I merely did as I was told. To me it was no big deal.

I suppose when it was discovered that I would not become a world-famous ballerina, the dance lessons ended and I danced no more until junior high. Being a Missouri Synod Lutheran excluded ballroom dancing, but the young people's church group called the Walther League held monthly circle and square dancing. In a church gymnasium, I learned the circle dances—The Cotton Eye Joe, The Herr Schmidt, Put Your Little Foot, The Hokey Pokey—and basic square dancing. I loved it and had crushes on all the boys.

In later years I danced with my brother Allan. We jitterbugged well together. Since I was not allowed to date until my senior year of high school, I didn't attend many dances. Those I attended were mostly non-dance events; that is to say there was music, but we were all too shy to dance until usually the last few dances. Everyone was too self-conscious to be on the dance floor. What fools we were.

Attending college at the University of Texas in Austin was not a very social time for me. Mainly I studied and remained chaste, the time period being before birth control pills. The worst fate imaginable in the late 1950's and early 1960's was to be pregnant and have to get married. I remained chaste not out of predilection but simply out of fear. Beer drinking and folk music dominated the parties. The fancy fraternity and sorority balls again found me on the sidelines. The twist was popular and I wasn't, still too shy to be seen in the middle of the floor. Slow dances were mainly designed to allow free feels and rubbing bodies. Rhythm was not important. Dancing to the music didn't count.

Then I married four times. Dancing was not on the agenda with any of my husbands. My last and best husband wasn't much of a dancer. On one occasion during our short marriage we were invited to a Hispanic wedding in Robstown. John was best friends with the father of the bride, and our attendance was compulsory. The reception was held in a local hall. Food and drink flowed generously. John overindulged. We were the only gringos among hundreds of brown-skinned revelers. When the music began, everyone migrated to the dance floor, young and old alike, dancing with abandon to the Tejano music. Little English was spoken.

Our host, nicknamed Buckwheat, encouraged us to dance, insisted we dance. He became adamant. He instructed the band to play a country and western song. "John, they're playing this song just for us. We have to dance or Buckwheat will be insulted."

The floor was empty except for us. We stumbled all over each other. "Sonja, I thought you could dance."

"I thought I could, but my feet won't work with all those people watching."

Our solo performance became an embarrassing disaster, but Buckwheat was satisfied and the party continued into the night.

John died of cancer the next year at the age of 52. Dancing was not foremost in my mind; grief prevailed for a year. It was my rural mail carrier who lured me from the ranch. "We're going dancing Friday night at the Lone Star Saloon in Uvalde. Why don't you go with us? You need to get out. You can't sit out there on that rocky hill forever."

"I'm not a good dancer. Haven't danced in years and then it was a nightmare."

Honk if you married Sonja

"Anyone can dance the two step. It's easy. We'll teach you."

And that's how it all started. Having encountered death and cancer, I wasn't threatened by the dance floor. I danced with all the men and found I could follow any of them. I danced with abandon because I no longer cared. I was complimented on my dancing ability, was even popular. There were not many dances I sat out. I two-stepped, waltzed, jitterbugged, executed the Cumbia, and stood and shook it all. Most of all I smiled a lot. I was in love with dance.

My friend Vercia Lee invited me to Lajitas, the resort outside Big Bend in far west Texas. Her sister owned a ranch nearby, as well as a drugstore/café at the resort. We soon fell into the habit of working in the drugstore when there were conventions and dancing at night. Waitressing was almost as much fun as dancing. With my children and husband gone, I had no one to feed and nurture. Waiting tables satisfied that yearning.

Working from 6 A.M. until 4 P.M., constantly on my feet, proved to be tiring. "I'm not too excited about going dancing tonight. I'm worn out and my feet hurt."

"We'll take a sort nap, freshen up and trust me, when the music starts the pain goes away." Vercia Lee was right.

We danced to Mexican music, fast and slow. One night I danced with a fat Hispanic man who spoke no English. "Sonja, I can't believe you danced with a Mexican."

"Hell, I came to dance, not to get married. I don't care what they look like as long as they can dance." Soon she and her sister followed suit. They were hooked on dancing too.

Our friendship evolved over the next few years until they invited me to attend the Terlingua Chili Cookoff, promising there would be three nights of dancing and lots of men who were good dancers. The Terlingua Chili Cookoff attracted a cast of thousands.

Surprisingly, I was not a wallflower. I danced with drunks, smelly old men, cute young cowboys and anyone that asked. "You are a great dancer. Are you a professional?"

"Not in this lifetime but maybe in another."

"I believe you."

Friends made during the nights of dancing welcomed me back over the years. I pitched my tent beside theirs for the four-day celebration. I found a few boyfriends that didn't last long but were good dancers. Every year we reunited for the days of revelry and dancing.

Sonja Klein

Dancing became a part of my life. I attended conferences all over Texas and danced with county judges and commissioners. I continued to dance at the Lone Star with a group of friends and good dancers. The waltz was my favorite. As long as I could dance the waltz at least once a month I remained satisfied. One county commissioner from Loving County told me, "Sonja, you could win dances with the waltz. You make anyone that dances with you look good."

I traveled the world, danced with the Greeks, the Irish, the Uzbeks and stepped the Latin dances on cruise ships with men from all over the world. Dancing came so easy except for one thing. In my studies of religions, I had come across a form of meditation that recommended dancing against the music as a form of changing awareness. I couldn't do it successfully, until one year at the Chili Cookoff. I had danced so many nights and so many hours that my feet could not follow the music. They moved of their own accord to another beat. I was danced out and found that indeed it was another form of awareness.

Only one other time did it happen. I had danced the night away at the Lone Star Saloon in Uvalde, moving vigorously for hours. My feet went to another tune. No amount of will could change them. Once again I was danced outside myself. The good news—tomorrow was another day to dance.

8

Numbers

Someone asks, "What's your phone number?"

"Wait a minute. Let me think. I don't dial my own number that often."

Numbers have always fascinated me. When I travel the roads of Texas, I am always calculating. How many more miles can I get on this tank of gas? What time will I arrive? How many miles per hour am I averaging?

And then there's the coincidence of numbers. My phone number from when I lived in Louisiana has the same digits as my Texas number. The farm road on which I lived on Lake Livingston is the exact reverse of the farm road on which I now live in west Texas.

My brother David prides himself on remembering phone numbers, always questioning me why I don't commit familiar numbers to memory. "I choose not to clutter my brain disk drive with something as simple as phone numbers. I can write them down and have them handy."

I do pride myself on being able to rapidly add columns of numbers without error and now at a ripe age can recall my social security number and driver's license without referring to the scribed numbers. I have a landline phone number, a fax line number and a cell phone number. My family members all have three numbers too—a lot to remember. My passport number, bank account numbers and license plate numbers have not yet been mind-stored.

A code on my driver's license contains 12 digits. I was once told that those numbers reveal a plethora of information and 12 digits are capable of telling a life history.

When I call and order catalog items or make plane or hotel reservations, I am always given a confirmation code that usually consists of letters and digits, lots of them. I always wonder if some day they might run out of numbers and codes and have to wipe the slate clean and start all over again.

Sonja Klein

Credit card numbers are long enough, but now cards also have a security code. Will they ever run out of credit card numbers? I suppose the combinations are infinitesimal. Passwords complicate codes. Some codes require numbers, letters and even signs or symbols. Banks and shipping companies have tracking codes. Everything is digital. There might come a time when people are unable to read a clock.

Calculators have replaced simple mathematics. Cashiers are unable to make change the old-fashioned way, and the cash register tells them how much change to return. When I attended school we were not allowed to use a calculator. In fact pocket calculators were not in existence. I can remember my father's old adding machine. It was not electric but manual; you had to crank each entry like pulling the arm on a slot machine and the sound it made was comforting. You really knew the machine was working.

An accounting course in college taught me how to set up ledgers and balance the books. At year's end I relished sitting down and making entries in the heavy black books and balancing to the penny and then posting the totals. Today the Quicken software does the job for me, but I still post the results in my old set of black books.

Perhaps I'll be like Andy Rooney and remain old-fashioned and cling to the ways of the past. I still don't know how to store numbers on my cell phone. I have entered the 21st century—not completely—but at least I'm trying.

9

Central and South America

Two years had passed since John died. I scattered his ashes on the ranch, aptly named Ambush Hill, on the second anniversary of his death. I was tired of missing him and was gradually recovering from the acute pain of his dying of Hepatitis C and liver cancer in a short five-month period where we shared his ride on a runaway train to death. He was a Texan and died like a Texan, on the ranch in view of the land he loved. I was there with him to the end.

Now it was time to have some fun, and for the first time I realized my life was not defined by relationships with my family, my children or my spouse. I could live selfishly for my own enjoyment, and at 58 that wasn't a bad situation. After three husbands and finally reuniting with John, my kindred spirit, after 18 years, I thought I had found my happiness; but fate doesn't always let you know the cards you will be dealt. It was time to play a new hand.

I had always been a searcher and an avid reader, was fascinated with Central and South America. I had read Shirley McLaine at an impressionable time of my life and was intrigued by the adventure of traveling alone and visiting Macchu Pichu and ancient Mayan ruins in Honduras.

Months earlier, I had spent hours researching cruises and freighters and had decided to go first class. I found a six-star rated cruise going from Los Angeles south on the Pacific, along the coast of Mexico and Central and South America for a 21-day leg of a longer cruise where I could disembark in Valparaiso, Chile, and fly back home to Texas.

The attraction of this particular cruise had been that it was on a small-capacity ship, was very expensive and offered some interesting optional extravagant side trips. In Guatemala I could disembark and fly to Honduras to see the ruins at Copan; in Ecuador I could fly to Quito; in Peru I could fly to Cusco and visit Macchu Pichu. I had booked myself on the cruise, paying a premium for traveling alone and had even splurged for a stateroom on the promenade deck.

Sonja Klein

The only problem with booking a cruise was waiting for the date of departure, a long three months hence, during which I spent a lot of time thinking about what I planned to do. I disliked knowing of a commitment far in advance and felt the anticipation of that event clouded my daily life and kept me from living each day in its entirety. Somehow I was living in the future and not in the present, and it opened up a whole series of worries.

What if my mother became ill? What if I caught the flu? Maybe my children might need me. Most of all, why was I spending so much money on myself? Mentally I went over each outfit I would pack and what shoes and jewelry I would wear and how many suitcases I would take and how I would wear my hair and all sorts of stupid thoughts that kept my mind full of daily chatter. I had to increase meditating to still my anxious thoughts. I was learning to self-soothe.

Somehow the time passed and I didn't catch the flu, the low water crossings didn't flood, and my pickup didn't break down on my predawn trip of three and a half hours to the San Antonio airport to catch the plane to Los Angeles, where I would embark on the ship for a solo adventure.

I hated flying; I loved taking off and landing, but the minutes suspended thousands of feet in the air were pure misery to me. I believed there was a chance of surviving mishaps on the take off and landing, but up in the air the chances were nil. Every sound high above the clouds was a cause for alarm, and then there was always the added fear of a collision.

I dressed with care, wearing a fine wool brown plaid skirt and a cream long-sleeved silk blouse gathered by a wide cream leather belt sporting an elaborate silver buckle. My shoes were sensible flats. I topped off the outfit with a blue straw Stetson circled by a snake hatband in the same colors of the soft wool skirt. First impressions always counted. For luck I wore the 20-carat amethyst ring that my mother had designed for me, and on my right pinkie finger I wore a two-carat heart-cut diamond set in platinum, a gift from my second husband. Around my neck was a huge amber hunk that I had purchased in Poland. Amber earrings completed the outfit.

One thing I had learned over the years was that you can never be thinner or smarter than you were on the first encounter, and I wanted to start this 21-day cruise in the right mode. My purse revealed a flash of gold; nothing wrong with a bit of glitz. On my shoulder hung a small navy carry-on containing my jewelry, a religious book by Max Lucado and a few other essentials in case my luggage was lost.

Three large suitcases were packed with two outfits a day for 21 days. I was prepared to pay extra for the third bag, but the porter outside the airport in San Antonio checked all three bags without blinking an eye.

The plane left on schedule and landed on time in Dallas, where I had been allotted forty minutes to change terminals to connect with the flight to Los Angeles. That too had been another cause for anxiety, but fortunately the flight from San Antonio to Dallas was too short to allow much worry time. I negotiated the terminal transfer and arrived at the departure gate with adequate time to go to the bathroom and buy a cup of cappuccino and settle down with the religious book to comfort my fears.

The announcement that the departure was delayed due to mechanical problems did not surprise me. That possibility had been high on my anxiety list. I knew then that I would miss the ship and looked around for a sympathetic soul. I had no luck; everyone seemed nonchalant, and when I challenged them to join me in my fears, I had no takers. I just had to sit there alone in terror and wait like an idiot. Finally, however, the flight was announced and departed 45 minutes late. I knew then that my luggage had probably made the flight, but I struggled with the knowledge that the plane would land late and maybe the ship's representatives would not be there to escort me to the ship.

I settled into my cramped seat on the plane, ate a little of the cold snack the airline provided and dozed through most of the flight. The plane landed in Los Angeles, where the ship's people were smiling and holding up a sign with the name of the ship. It appeared I would at least make it onto the ship. I looked around to see if I could spot some fellow passenger, and my eyes settled on a man with gray hair, perhaps 50, who looked lost and insecure and stood off to himself. He was a possibility, and there were a few other obvious passengers who had congregated with the lady holding the sign. All were significantly older than me—or older than I thought I was—and they were linked in pairs. We were herded down to the baggage claim area, where we pointed out our suitcases and observed them being loaded onto carts. We were then directed to a large bus and boarded it for the drive to the docks, where we waited in a hospitality room until boarding time at 3 P.M.

Sonja Klein

It was 1 P.M. and I was hungry and feeling insecure because as I looked around in the hospitality room at the Hilton, I saw mainly people over 65—and lots of them. They had walkers, canes and wheelchairs and were all eating cookies and drinking coffee and complaining of hunger, most of them not having had lunch while in transit to Los Angeles.

I sat down at a large round table for 10 and went for a glass of water. No cookies for me. I had been dieting for a month to achieve a slim size 8, and I wasn't going to swell up on my first day. Seated at the table were two sisters from Dallas—Marcie and Betty; a couple in which the wife was outspoken and introduced herself and her husband as Jane and Tarzan from Seattle; and a large man in a wheelchair with his wife—John and Carolyn from Florida. I was Sonja from Texas and Jane quickly shortened that to Tex. I liked Jane because she seemed to have a sense of humor, and somehow we sat and made small talk while the room quickly became crowded and the cookies disappeared. In two hours I never saw anyone my age.

Being an intense person whose every action was done with extreme passion, I immersed myself and became one with the time and place. I lived the moment fully. I could be anyone and mirrored others with an uncanny ability. I had never meet a stranger and was usually the life of the party, and in this situation I was prepared to be what I had to be in order to have the most fun on the trip. I could surrender to any situation and ride it out for the full duration. In this case 21 days.

After three glasses of water and a trip to the bathroom, the magic hour of 3 P.M. arrived, and we were loaded onto buses for a short five-minute ride to the luxurious cruise liner. I boarded the ship greeted by pasted-on smiling faces and was directed to my room on the promenade deck. It was large with a picture window, two single beds, a love seat, a coffee table, a large walk-in closet and a full bath. My luggage had not arrived, but there were fresh flowers, a silver bowl of fresh fruit and a small icebox with cold drinks. I freshened up out of my purse contents and emerged from the room to do a bit of exploring.

The ship was convenient and mid-sized, as far as cruise ships go, with a maximum passenger capacity of about 700. I had heard that the ship would not be completely full until we reached Santiago, Chile, and that there would be about 500 of us on this 21-day leg of the journey around South America to the final destination of Ft. Lauderdale some 56 days hence.

Honk if you married Sonja

The dining room was on the same deck as my stateroom, and on one floor I found the lounge and theater as well as a bar. There was a dark espresso bar and a sun-lit lounge named the Midnight Sun. I also discovered a card room, library, computer lab, picture gallery and the all-important purser's desk—the center of information dissemination. I wandered around, muttering to myself and spreading smiling hellos before returning to my room to check if my luggage had arrived.

Having lost two hours on the flight to California, I was now hungry. I peeled myself a fresh pear and read the daily newsletter that announced dinner would be served informally at 7 P.M., and that the welcome aboard show would begin at 9:45. How I would manage to be alert at 11:45 Texas time when my usual bedtime was 9:00?

A knock on the door announced the arrival of my luggage, and I unpacked my outfits, almost filling the walk-in closet. I changed to a teal silk skirt and blouse and adorned myself with an elephant head pewter belt and matching necklace and black low-heeled sandals. My long blonde hair was secured with a silver clasp that held the curls I had so artfully arranged with old-fashioned rag curlers the night before. I emerged from my stateroom freshened and made another round of the deck, recognizing a few faces. I wandered to the upper deck for the sail-away party with free champagne and live music and nodded to a few familiar people from the hospitality room. I sat with the two sisters from Dallas and quietly listened as they pointed out people they recognized from previous trips, including two gays with whom they had traveled on other cruises. They told me how they had adjoining staterooms on one cruise, and that the two lovers often squabbled late at night.

The dinner hour finally arrived, and the placard in my stateroom announced my dinner table was to be number 161. As I made my way through the dining room to find the table and meet my dinner companions, the head waiter smiled and greeted me with "Good evening, Madam." I replied in kind and made my way to the third dining room. I immediately knew I was not high on the totem pole, having been assigned to the dining room at the end of the ship. As I arrived at a table for eight, I discovered only three other seats occupied. I had intentionally requested a large table so that I would have a variety of dinner companions, as most of the evening meals would be consumed in the same company. A waiter in a tuxedo elegantly pulled out my chair and repeated the "Good evening, Madam" greeting of which I would soon tire.

I met Don and Lureen and Beulah. Don and Lureen were from Florida, and Beulah was from England. Don and Lureen were retired schoolteachers, he a principal and she a reading specialist, from West Virginia. Don had a hearing aid and was a heart attack and bypass surgery survivor. Lureen was vigorous and reminded me of my Aunt Stella, always pleasant and energetic. Beulah was a widow and an avid hospital volunteer. She was dressed in vanilla colors. The other seats were vacant and remained so for the entire trip. My dinner companions were on the ship for the entire 56 days and were seasoned travelers, spending almost six months of the year at sea. They sailed this ship many times and recognized many of the passengers. Based on the fare I had paid, I wondered how retired schoolteachers could afford such luxury.

Dinner was long and laborious. The courses were not high on quantity, but rather the fare was light and delightful with lots of garnishes and fancy decorations. I ordered baked fish and grilled vegetables and passed on the dessert. Wine was complimentary with all meals, and I enjoyed a few glasses of white wine—enough to feel relaxed but not stupid. After dinner I again walked the decks, becoming familiar with the design of the ship and managing to remain awake for the show in the main lounge. I spotted the two sisters from Dallas and asked if I might join them and seated myself at their table.

Kim was the cruise director, short, blonde, dyed hair, mid-forties and chunky. She was forcedly enthusiastic, and there was singing and dancing and happiness and a prolonged series of introductions of the cast and crew and officers and the guest hosts—seven men who were there to dance every dance with all the ladies. Not one of the men stirred any emotion whatsoever as they were introduced, and I thought, "Oh, God, I'm dead after all." I wouldn't let one of them lay a hand on me, even to dance. Dancing followed the show. I watched couples performing intricate steps to ballroom music. One of the guest hosts approached our table and asked me to dance, and when I declined he danced with one of the sisters. The remaining sister asked me, "Don't you dance?"

I replied, "I only dance country and western with cowboys because they hold me real tight."

She laughed and asked if she could come and visit me in Texas, and I quickly realized that she was serious.

Honk if you married Sonja

I glibly answered, "Sure, come see me and we'll go dancing at the Lone Star Saloon in Uvalde, Texas."

I people-watched for a while and observed the guest hosts at work and knew there would be no dancing for me on this trip. From that evening on, all the widows loved me because they knew I was no competition for the dance floor and was obviously not on the make or looking for a man. I had unwittingly been instantly accepted and had made myself popular by my casual remark. I excused myself and went to bed, finding the next day's agenda on my bed with the chocolate truffle I came to expect each night.

I was awake before dawn, anxiously waiting for the 7 A.M. stretching exercises with Kelly. There were six of us. Kelly spoke with a British accent, boldly encouraging us old folks to stretch. At 8 A.M. a few more joined us for 30 minutes of low-impact aerobics. I wasn't a bit winded and returned to my cabin to dress and attend the bridge lecture given by Art and his blonde wife.

After the lecture, passengers met to sign up for bridge pairs in the game room. There were quite a few singles, and as we attempted to match, an elderly Jewish lady approached and asked if I would be her partner. She had a sparkle in her eyes, and I immediately knew we could become friends. Her name was Sophie and she was from New Jersey. I soon discovered that Sophie was a terrible bridge player but made up for her lack of skill by her charming ways. She was in her early eighties and knew everyone on the ship; in other words, she was well connected. Following the bridge lecture, I attended a lesson on the Mayans of Central America and at 11:00 a talk on handwriting analysis. Trivial Pursuit was scheduled for noon. I wandered into the lounge and joined several ladies. We formed a team of six; most were lightweights in knowledge of the game. One lady was from Wales, England, and the rest of us were Americans. I was the youngest and elected captain of the team. We came in dead last of 14 teams but were optimistic for the morrow.

We adjourned for lunch, after which I met Sophie for bridge. There were 16 tables of duplicate bridge players. We played terribly; I was too nervous to play well. My only experience playing duplicate bridge had been at a tournament at the Shamrock in Houston. At the last minute my mother needed a partner. She was a master player and assured me I would do fine. I didn't.

Sonja Klein

In spite of my fears, everyone was very good-natured and it was a pleasant afternoon. Following bridge, I went to needlepoint class to receive the kit I never had time to open, but it was free and I selected one that I thought I could sew and give to one of my children.

I returned to my room, read and took a short nap before dressing for a formal evening dinner. I chose the slinkiest dress in my closet because I was still slim; it was a long purple and silver velvet stretch gown, very flattering. The captain's reception began before dinner with free cocktails, and I emerged from my stateroom to shake hands with the captain and have my picture taken. I entered the lounge for cocktails and snacks and dancing.

After joining a group of ladies and again refusing to dance with one of the guest hosts, I watched the couples dancing to big band era music, definitely not my style. Dinner was pleasant as usual, and the evening show was Broadway, also not my style. I was happy to return to my room and hit the sack after checking the agenda for the next day and choosing which lectures and activities I would attend. The chocolate truffle was on my pillow.

Life on the ship soon surrendered to a routine: morning coffee in my room, a mile of laps around the deck and fresh fruit before dressing for the bridge lecture, followed by history, political and other lectures until noon and Trivial Pursuit. The team adjourned for lunch together or I met Sophia at her friend Frances's table in the main dining room. The buffet lunch on the upper deck was too inviting; I have a tendency to eat too much, so the lunch with the aging Jewish dowagers became my custom. The talk was intelligent and current, and I found them all to be knowledgeable and fascinating. Most of them lived in condos or apartments in Florida, California and New York. Their jewelry was breathtaking, and they always looked great and were well groomed down to their fingernails and toenails.

Fred Silverstein, a New York diamond and gemstone broker, delivered a series of lectures about diamonds, gemstones, pearls and the care and cleaning of jewelry. I emerged from the lectures loaded with new information. I learned that opals must be oiled, rubbed or watered in order to prevent them from breaking apart. From Fred I also learned that whether the jewelry is fake or real didn't matter. The important thing about jewelry was to feel adorned when wearing it. Manufactured stones and reproductions have advanced to such technology that even

Honk if you married Sonja

Fred admitted that he could not always detect the real or the artificial. Fred gave us permission to enjoy our jewelry, real or not.

Most evenings, I avoided the floor show because it was Broadway inspired, but I never missed a show with Mike, the comedian. He was the only man on the ship that appealed to me, and I lacked the courage to pursue him, not wanting to disturb the relationship with my women friends and garner their scorn for man-chasing. I did not want to become one of those widows on the ship who danced, drank and pursued the guest hosts that I judged to be dance pimps.

After several days of cruising we arrived at our first port of call, Acapulco. I had decided not to disembark but at the last minute took a half-day tour and was guided to the Flamingo Hotel, where Johnny Weismuller and his Hollywood cronies used to drink and party. We visited his house, drove by the cliffs, toured a museum and were then taken to a tourist gift shop where margaritas were dispensed to encourage spending.

Arriving back at the ship, I was greeted by a band and champagne. The sheer extravagance of the gesture was wonderful.

I had discovered the well-stocked ship's library, and I retired to my room to read for the afternoon. The lectures and activities on the ship were always suspended when in port.

Guatemala was the next stop. I had signed up for a trip to Copan, which was in Honduras. We were bused to the airport, which looked more like a military base, being guarded by boys in uniforms holding automatic weapons. Two old and dented planes sat on the grass, encircled by soldiers. The writing on the planes was Russian. I thought, "Oh boy, here we go." About 40 of us boarded the two planes.

We taxied to the runway, and the aging plane groaned into the air. We were given sandwiches and a jug of water for the short flight to what I thought was to be Honduras. We flew between the clouds and mountains lush with jungle growth and floated down in a rainstorm between forested hills to land on a grass runway in the middle of nowhere. All I could think once the plane quit rolling was how we were going to take off if it kept raining. Where the fuck were we?

Armed boy soldiers appeared from the dense jungle and escorted us to some thatched huts and bathrooms. More soldiers joined us. A few well-placed questions determined that we were still in Guatemala and that the border was just down the slope. We waited for buses to take us into Honduras and the town of Copan to visit the Mayan ruins.

I heard the buses before I saw them laboring up the slight incline across the fence from our thatched huts. We followed our leader, walked through the gate in the fence into Honduras, no checkpoint. I climbed on the first bus, which had bullet holes down the sides, missing windows and no windshield. The bus driver and his associate were smiling and wearing big pistols as they welcomed us. The bus struggled slowly down the one-lane dirt road, not daring to leave the two-foot-deep ruts. The six-kilometer trip to Copan took an hour, and I spent most of the hour looking out the window and praying for sunshine.

The town of Copan was small and well kept. We were driven to the ruins where an excellent guide conducted an informative tour. The Mayan ruins were impressive, and I didn't believe they had no knowledge of the wheel. Their chronicles were impressively engraved in the stones.

The hotel in Copan provided a delicious lunch after which we walked around the square and bought a few trinkets. I had teamed up with Ken and Shirley, a couple in their 40's; she and I enjoyed shopping together or should I say buying together.

We discovered that the other bus had broken down, busted an axle. And the other group walked four miles in the rain and mud. Their tour of the ruins was abbreviated and their lunch was late.

Shirley and I talked about how hardships bonded people and brought out their best and how in a way we envied them the adventure and experience yet were relieved we didn't have to walk in the mud through the hot, steamy jungle.

The return bus trip to the border still took an hour. The planes took off on the grass runway, and we arrived at the military airport in time to be bused back to the ship, where the band and champagne were waiting. Shirley and I were disappointed that we didn't have the opportunity to shop at the market the locals had set up next to the ship. They were shutting down as we returned, and all we could buy were some rugs and bags. The shopping was great fun, and the variety of crafts and the unbelievably low prices inspired me to Christmas shop even though it was just February.

Back to the routine of the ship, I settled into the rounds of lectures and bridge and Trivial Pursuit and enjoyed the company of my new friends. One evening my bridge partner Sophie and I had dinner in the

Honk if you married Sonja

Venice Restaurant, where the cuisine was Italian. The rack of lamb and tiramisu were outstanding.

While on board I avoided the beauty parlor and the swimming pool. I curled my hair and didn't care a shit about a tan. The morning lectures had been preparing me for Ecuador, although we had been advised that there was political unrest and the excursion was going to be flexible.

In preparation for the trip, I had bought books on all the countries and studied them. The lectures condensed what I had read and were enlightening preludes to the shore trips. We were advised how to dress and what to carry and to stay together. I felt safe and not an ugly American. We were handled first class, which is what I had paid for, and it was well worth the money. The people on the ship were just a cut above, very quiet and very classy and most of all well behaved with excellent manners. Most of them had been everywhere in the world. If they had attended all the lectures about all the countries they had visited they were better informed than I was with my minor in history from the University of Texas.

There were even computer classes and a computer lab. Of all the diversions on the ship, the computer lab and classes were the most popular. Emailing was $5 a message, but you could send the same message to five addresses. Receiving emails was free. I composed generic messages every few days. Daughter Molly at the University of Texas emailed me that she didn't get her allowance check. I mailed one from Guatemala only to be told it would take three months for the letter to arrive. I emailed her to use the credit card I had given her for emergencies.

The lectures primed me for Quito, the capital of Ecuador. The ship docked in Manta, and the small group of adventurers boarded a plane at a military airport and flew a short flight to Quito, where after landing we were told that riots were taking place and that we could not travel to the center of town. As an alternative we were provided armed guards and taken to an art gallery and museum on the outskirts of town. The view was beautiful and Quito was splendid, very European with boulevards and colonial style buildings. The capital seemed prosperous and bustling. During the course of the day we were told that the riots had been precipitated by the president wanting to declare the American dollar as the unit of currency for Ecuador and that the country had no banking regulations. Anyone could open a bank and then shut it down and take the money.

Sonja Klein

We stopped in the suburbs for lunch at a restaurant where we were entertained with Ecuadoran flute music and freshly prepared dishes, nothing fried or piled on the plate. I saw no fat or obese people either onboard ship or in any of the countries we visited. The flute music was enchanting, and I purchased a CD of the band's music. Back on the buses, we headed out to the Equator Monument to have our pictures made with one foot in each hemisphere. The shopping was great at the equator; a miniature village had been constructed composed of shops and restaurants. Unknown to us tourists, a revolution was taking place in town. Bargaining at the shops with American dollars achieved tremendous results. I had no idea except that I bought all I could carry. It was a shopper's dream come true—lots of shops and they would take almost any price offered as long as it was in American dollars.

As we began our journey back to the airport I noticed that the roads were blocked and that there were mounds of burning tires and people milling about on the streets with bottles and guns and sticks. I heard gunshots in the distance. The bus arrived at a barricaded square. Our driver rerouted the bus through an open field and back alleys until we arrived at the airport controlled by soldiers.

We were escorted into a small waiting room to rest before the arrival of our plane, which had gone on to another destination and was due back momentarily. The moments turned into hours, and we were now in danger of missing the ship's sailing. We were not allowed out of the waiting room. There were guards stationed at both doors.

The airport bustled with activity, lots of planes coming and going but mostly going. The TV blared in Spanish, and our guards watched with vigorous interest. Angry men yelled on the TV, and a general called for the resignation of the president. Members of our group were becoming apprehensive when the two escorts from the ship disappeared with the bus driver and guide. When we asked the guards where they were, we were told that they had gone to the grocery store. They returned carrying armloads of fresh roses. At first I thought the gesture to be inappropriate and then surrendered to the defining moment of luxury and elegance in the middle of a revolution.

As we witnessed many jets flying out, I jokingly remarked that one plane contained the president with his advisors, the next his family, the next was the national treasury and so forth. I had lightened the mood but had not provided the answer to where our planes were. Time was becoming of the essence when they wheeled out a Lear jet and asked for eight volunteers. I raised my hand and boarded a confiscated jet from a Drug Enforcement Administration hangar. The yellow tape indicating seizure was still on the plane. Another plane was wheeled out for more volunteers. The jets landed in Manta an hour after the ship was scheduled to sail, and we were escorted by armed guards at the airport in Manta to waiting buses. The military had seized control of the airport in Manta, and the president had fled to a U.S military installation a few miles away.

The multizillion-dollar ship had waited for us. The band and champagne and cheers that we had survived the revolution greeted us as we boarded. We were the center of attention at dinner and enjoyed celebrity status for a few days. I never felt frightened or apprehensive because we were well guarded at all times. Money bought safety, even in South America.

The ship cruised south in the Pacific Ocean towards Peru. Several days of cruising and playing bridge and attending lectures about the history of Peru, and the inhumane depredations of the Spanish had so incensed me that I wanted to go out and murder a priest, especially a Dominican, because they were the ones responsible for the rape, pillage and plunder of the Incan empire.

The ship docked in Lima, Peru. The flight to Cusco lasted less than an hour. I sat next to B.J., a redheaded widow in her early 70's who hung out with the guest hosts. She proceeded to tell me her life story, about how she was from a small town in Alabama and had been married to a building contractor. She had worked at the courthouse as a legal secretary and had an affair with the sheriff. That created a scandal in the small southern town. Both of them subsequently divorced; he retired early and they moved to California, where they then went into the Baskin Robbins ice cream franchise business, owning and operating several ice cream stores with her sons. Then the true love of her life died in his 50's of a heart attack. She continued to own and operate the stores with her sons.

At a dance class she met a man who had a drywall contracting business; he moved in with her and promptly injured his back and didn't work another day for several years until some legal matters with Baskin Robbins caused B.J. and her sons to sue Baskin Robbins. They subsequently declared bankruptcy, at which time the boyfriend moved out because the money was gone. He later married another woman whom he met at dance class. I was glad the story ended as the plane landed in Cusco, the capital of the Incan empires.

I had not been prepared for Quito and the European atmosphere of the city. I was also not prepared for Cusco. The city had the feel of native America; the smell of sage and juniper and coca leaves permeated the high mountain air. I felt as if I had stumbled upon an advanced civilization of American Indians. The town was clean, with narrow streets and tolling bells and wonderful happy people with prominent Incan noses and sloping foreheads. The altitude of Cusco was 11,000 feet, and the air was delightful, warmed by the afternoon sun. Our hotel was hidden in its own private square, blocks away from the main plaza, which was dominated by a massive cathedral as large as any I had seen in Europe.

The Hotel Montesario was absolutely the most beautiful, charming place I have ever been, and the room rates on the door were $350 a night. The hotel had been a Jesuit monastery built in the 1500's on the sight of an Incan temple. Adjacent to the lobby was a chapel smothered in gold with intricate floral carvings.

After leaving the chapel we were encouraged to drink the coca tea that would help our bodies acclimate to the high altitude. It was delicious and invigorating. Since the plant was the source of cocaine it was no wonder the people were so happy. Coca tea was legal in Peru, and I drank it at every opportunity. One 90-year-old woman also took a great liking to the tea, which tasted like green or herbal tea and had a slight musky odor.

We were given our room keys and an hour to settle before meeting in the lobby for a tour of the town and surrounding countryside.

Returning to the lobby I discovered a large silver urn of coca tea and a basket of coca leaves for either chewing or adding to the warm tea. I did both and felt great before venturing out to the plaza to board the bus. Once in the plaza I was assailed by smiling Indians with llamas for picture taking at $1 a click and vendors with blankets, jewelry, sweaters and watercolor paintings and handmade crafts. I bought necklaces and many inexpensive gifts before boarding the bus, where we were given a bottle of water and a grand tour of the Inca Park and ruins outside of Cusco as well as a tour of the city and the cathedral so covered with gold that it defied description. I have never seen so much gold, not even in the baroque cathedrals in southern Germany or the magnificent churches in Spain.

Honk if you married Sonja

We visited the Incan Palace of the Sun and were treated to more lectures of the Incan empire and the destruction in the name of God of that empire by the Spaniards and Dominican priests. How a handful of psychotic sociopath Spaniards toppled the Incan empire was never sufficiently explained except by betrayal from some of the conquered peoples of the Inca. I would never believe that they had no written language because the level of their sophistication seemed unprecedented.

We returned to the hotel for a feast and an Incan ceremonial play. The costumes, language and music were impressive, and I fell in love with the haunting flute music and drums.

The meal began with potato soup served over chunks of avocados. There was no cream of mushroom soup in the recipe, and the potatoes had a flavor unlike any I had tasted. Thirty native varieties of potatoes exist in Central and South America. Potatoes are not from Ireland but rather from the Americas. We were served squash, chicken, tamales with cheese, fresh fruit, long dark green beans and savory corn tortillas.

I refused the native alcoholic drink called pisco because I wanted all my senses to be alert for the trip to Macchu Pichu. Drinking alcohol at that altitude was an invitation for disaster. I instead drank coca tea and slept fitfully, no surprise.

The wakeup call at 5 A.M. alerted me for breakfast, where again I followed our guide's advice and drank the coca tea instead of coffee. It was barely daylight when we boarded the train for the three-hour trip across the Andes and down in altitude to Macchu Pichu. The train was modern and filled to capacity as the cars crept out of the Cusco valley and over the Andes by a series of switchbacks on which the train went forward and then backed up to achieve the climb over the Andes. We passed through lush jungles and small villages where the local Indians sold boiled corn, giant ears with white kernels the size of a large thumb.

We had been given tasty, fresh ham sandwiches, bottled water and fruit for the train trip, and while the train wound through the Andes with clouds hanging all about, I enjoyed my snack wishing for a Thermos of warm coca tea. The beauty of the Andes and the rainforest was spectacular.

The train arrived at the base of the mountains that housed Macchu Pichu. We walked in the mud to a waiting bus that would climb the mountains to the ruins perched high on the cliffs. Nothing had prepared me for the setting. I had seen pictures, but none of them had conveyed the height of the stones atop sheer cliffs overgrown with dense jungle foliage.

The bus ride lasted 30 minutes and was not for the faint-hearted. I tried to not look down, and thoughts intruded that I had to ride the bus back down. I was tempted to avail myself of the helicopter ride back to Cusco for $75. Quite a few of the passengers were unable to leave the bus once we reached the top. Several were sick and short of breath, but not the 90-year-old woman from Virginia, who was traveling with her daughter and son-in-law.

They were an interesting trio. I had sat in close proximity to them on the train, and the old lady was always demanding attention in little sly ways. She kept her daughter so busy that it was criminal. It was water or the camera or her purse or her pills. The poor daughter, about 50, never had a spare or peaceful moment in which to enjoy the journey. The son-in-law was a spin-doctor of politics and had given lectures on the ship about the workings of political campaigns. He participated in the Dole campaign, and his lectures were quite interesting in the explanation of how each campaign event was produced and orchestrated for the benefit of the public and the media.

Upon arriving at Macchu Pichu, the view was breathtaking—quite literally, but I received no spiritual flash or enlightenment. Rather, I felt that it was a quiet place of great learning, a sort of intellectual retreat for rest and renewal. The old lady picked up her cane and was off through the ruins with daughter and son-in-law trailing.

Our guide accompanied us, explaining the various theories as to the meaning of the ruins. At no time was Macchu Pichu a busy city or hub of activity; it was a place to visit, a retreat or resort. A recent theory is that aliens taught the local workers to melt the rocks in molds to achieve the exact dimensions of the massive blocks of stone. The journey there was enough in itself.

There was talk of a gondola project to facilitate the bus trip up to the ruins, but the bus drivers were against it. Many more ruins remain uncovered throughout the jungle surrounding the site, and the volume of traffic was high, providing no environmental protection. The site was not secured. People picked up rocks and stones, and there were no barriers or protective railings. Our guide played flute music, lyrical and haunting. The helicopter was fully booked with 20 people suffering miserably from the altitude, and I was left to go down the same way I came up.

Honk if you married Sonja

Since it was February, there were not too many tourists wandering about the ruins, but the group present was an odd assortment of nationalities from all over the world, including a small assortment of hippies with backpacks and lots of hair who had made the trek into Macchu Pichu that was possible for either one day or three, whichever you chose to hike.

The old lady took off with her cane and negotiated all the stairs and turns with the agility of a 16-year-old. Her daughter could not conceal her amazement, remarking out loud to anyone who would listen, "Mother complains about the 18 stair steps in her building. So far I've counted 78 steps that Mother's taken in this high altitude without a stumble or complaint."

The return bus trip was the reverse of the switchbacks and hairpin curves, and at every one was the same 10-year-old in a bright Incan dress yelling, "Goodbye" loud and clear. At the next switchback he was there again with the same goodbye, and this continued all the way down to the bottom of the mountains, where he boarded the bus with his hand out. He must have collected at least $50, and as we talked to him he said he did it once a day and worked for his family the rest of the time. He was the breadwinner of the family and made more than the average per capita income of $1,800 a year in Peru. The boys chosen to run down the mountain were all between the ages of 8 and 11, and each boy was only allowed one run a day. The careers of the boys were short-lived, but their efforts supplemented the poor living that the Indians endured in the small village at the base of the mountains.

As I returned to board the train, I walked between the booths and stalls selling handcrafted jewelry and other items. Again I purchased very cheaply, bargaining for each one. The train trip merited a nap, and I arrived back in Cusco for coca tea and was energized for more shopping. The plaza outside the hotel was full of vendors, and it was fun dealing with them. Dinner was fresh and delicious and some of us went shopping in the early evening, feeling perfectly safe walking the cobbled streets of Cusco.

Shirley and I had struck a kindred spirit of adventure and found a music store and bought CDs of Peruvian flute music. B. J. bought all sorts of junk for which she always paid too dearly and was always giving away money, but she seemed to enjoy every moment of it. I stayed close to the coca tea urn, drinking tea and munching on the leaves. Many Incan people had rotten teeth from chewing the leaves.

45

Sonja Klein

The morning fog delayed the flight to Lima, so we shopped until the fog lifted. Nina from New York was with Shirley, BJ and me, and we were a bit bedraggled from the traveling, not sporting our designer clothes and opulent jewelry. When we arrived at the Swiss Hotel in Lima a bit worse for the wear, Nina made the remark, "I can't believe I'm walking in the lobby of a five-star hotel with no jewelry, looking like this."

I laughed and said, "Nina, just put on your sunglasses, and no one will recognize you." We became friends at that point. She was my age but very tall, brunette and beautiful and elegant. She had lost her husband in his 30's to pancreatic cancer and was left with three boys, stunned by the blow that life had delivered. She married a man 15 years older. They were staying in the Penthouse Suite that cost $1,000 a day. They planned on disembarking in Valparaiso and flying to spend a week with friends who owned a private island off the coast of Chile. From there they were going to Switzerland. They were a great couple, their fondness for each other being quite evident. He had declined going on the trip to Macchu Pichu because he had already been there. He encouraged Nina to go with grace. She was a neat lady.

After checking into the hotel, we were given a tour of Lima ending with a long visit of the Gold Museum. The gold artifacts, jewelry, mummies and clothing and possessions of the Incan people as well as that of the other indigenous people of Peru made our civilization seem almost primitive. The natives of Peru were fabricating jewelry of platinum before the time of Christ, and the road system of the Incan empire exceeded that of the Romans.

After dressing for dinner I ventured into the bar for a cocktail. I was wearing a designer dress of my mother's. A very attractive man sat beside me and said, "That's a beautiful dress. Who is the designer?"

I replied, "It's a Georgio."

He bought me a glass of wine and asked my plans for the evening. I answered that I was going to dinner overlooking the ocean with my friends.

He then invited me to join him in the bar later that evening for a drink. I was flattered.

Following dinner I returned to the hotel and ventured into the bar. His back was to me. A woman older than me was sitting beside him. I heard him say, "That's a lovely dress; who is the designer?"

Honk if you married Sonja

I left before he saw me. I think that was a great pickup line, much better than one I received at a motorcycle rally. "Have you ever slept with a midget?"

Peruvian politics was an interesting subject. Our lecturer on the ship had said that Peru had the best and most stable government in South America and that Fujimori had been a great leader. Our guide and others with whom we spoke however said otherwise, that Fujimori had suspended the constitution so he could serve longer as president and that he was not sympathetic to the plight of the people of the Inca. There was no free health care. Education was free but not compulsory, and no schools existed in the rural areas. The Catholic Church ruled the country. When Fujimori came into conflict with the Church, the Church always prevailed. The people of Peru as a whole were poor, yet Peru was one of the richest countries in the world in the production of gold, silver and other precious metals. The wealth of Peru did not filter down to the Indians and was not spent on social services.

We played a quiz, and the gist of it was that if you were president of Peru what would you do first. I won because I said I would build roads. The strength of the Incan empire was in its road system and without roads you could not build schools or hospitals or explore the wealth of Peru.

We boarded the bus early the next morning and drove through the most arid desert in the world, the Alticama Desert. The rainfall of the Alticama is only one inch every 100 years.

We arrived for lunch in Tacna, Peru, a pleasant town in the middle of the severe desert. We enjoyed another delightful lunch and approached the border crossing, where we had to unload the bus, stand in line and have our passports stamped on the Peru side and then drive a few hundred yards and do it all again on the Chile side.

Before approaching the border, we were warned to have no plants or fruits and no coca tea. The 90-year-old lady and several others of our group were compelled to surrender their boxes of coca tea. We were greeted by the band and champagne as we boarded the ship in Arica, Chile.

Following the last few days of leisurely cruising along the coast of Chile, playing bridge and attending lectures, the luxury liner stopped at another port in Chile, where I had signed up for a tour of the Cerolo

Tollulla Observatory. A tour through the countryside of Chile observing the lush fields precluded the climb to the observatory high in the Andes.

The rainfall along the Pacific Coast of South America is extremely low, and it was amazing to learn that Lima, Peru, receives only several inches of rainfall a year. Their water comes from rivers originating high in the mountains filling with water in the rainy season. The roofs in Peru and Chile are ramshackle at best. Many are merely sheets of tin arranged haphazardly in layers. Why have a sturdy roof when it never rains?

The trip to the observatory took one hour, though we could see it perched high on a cliff. The journey to the top was slow and laborious with a breathtaking view at the end. The tour was perfunctory and involved a lot of stair climbing. The ride down the mountain lasted only 30 minutes, and we arrived at a small, clean village that boasted itself as the home of the famous poet, Gabriel Mistral.

Lunch was served at a charming motel built in a square around a courtyard and swimming pool. The premises were filled with Sunday locals swimming and enjoying family. A band was playing and the barbecue pits were loaded with pork, beef and chicken. Our tables were decorated with fresh flowers and herbs. The meal was outstanding, enhanced by the aromas of meat cooking in the open. Dessert was stewed papaya fruit, quite delicious. The local wine complimented the excellent meal.

The band and champagne ceremony that awaited us at the ship was becoming as silly as the headwaiter and his "Good evening, Madam." I wondered how the staff could maintain such a pleasant countenance every day for months at a time.

The ship cruised to Santiago and Valparaiso, from where I would disembark and fly home. I was packed and ready as I said my farewells and departed for a day tour of Valparaiso, after which I would be taken to the Sheraton to await transportation to the airport for my midnight flight to Dallas and then to San Antonio. The day tour was highlighted by visits to museums, cathedrals and shops and another great buffet lunch with fresh vegetables and seafood.

I was deposited at the hotel with other passengers ending their cruise in Chile. I joined Alice, the lecturing graphologist, as well as Fred, the New York diamond broker. They were lamenting the fact of a six-hour wait sitting in the hospitality room in uncomfortable convention chairs. They quickly decided that a room for the afternoon would be preferable. Alice went to the desk and asked the cost of a day room and was told it would be $250. Fred offered them $125; they politely declined. I went to the desk and found that I had a complimentary day room and invited them to share it with me.

We went up and sprawled out on the beds and gossiped about the staff and crew on the ship. We laughed the hours away, and in a jovial mood rode to the airport about midnight to find that our luggage had been sequestered and loaded on push carts to facilitate passage through customs. For that luxury I silently thanked the ship's crew.

I boarded the plane to Dallas without incident, sitting next to a doctor from Chile flying to Dallas for a seminar. He was very interesting and was responsible for bringing the 911 emergency phone call system to Valparaiso after discovering its existence on a trip to the USA. He had started with one used, donated ambulance. I connected in Dallas on time and arrived in San Antonio, jumped in my pickup, drove to the ranch, kissed the earth and thanked God for a safe trip.

10

The bicycle race

I called my son Joe in Tomball to let him know that I would be in Houston for the weekend visiting my mother so he could find time in his schedule to visit with me. This pattern was slowly emerging as my mother grew older and was losing her mobility. Every three weeks or so I would go to the suburban area known as Klein, between Houston and Tomball and spend four or five days with her and visit my son and three brothers. Joe informed me that he had entered a bicycle race in Killington, Vermont, and then asked if I would like to go with him to the race and be his crew. My immediate answer, "Why didn't you pick Alaska; it would be closer." He chuckled and I told him I would think about it and talk to him when I arrived at Mom's.

Driving is always enjoyable for me. I mentally write stories and think about many things, never turning on the radio. The silence of the road gives me time to let my thoughts wander, and as I drove I recalled Joe as a child and his love affair with the bicycle.

In fact it was my mother who enabled Joe to discover himself. I don't remember how old he was, but on one of our many trips to Colorado to visit Mother at the home she purchased above the town of Silverthorne, Joe expressed the desire to ride a bicycle from Frisco to Breckenridge, over 20 miles. My mother made it happen and that was when Joe found his heaven on the seat of a bicycle. She purchased his first serious bicycle. To this day he rides every week. I'll never forget his statement, "Mother, when I'm on a bicycle I'm totally me."

As his mother it should have been me who gave him that opportunity, but since it wasn't me, I'm glad it was my mother. She never failed to encourage anyone to stretch their horizons.

As I drove to Mother's the more I thought about a trip to Vermont, the more I liked the idea. My first impulse was to drive because I love road trips, but when I looked at the map and calculated that it would be 36 hours of driving on Labor Day weekend, I overcame my fear of flying and told Joe, "Okay, let's do it." I hadn't much relished the idea of being home that particular weekend because my neighbors from Houston would be around with lots of company. When they were in residence at their ranch over the cliff, chaos reigned supreme and drifted over the hill. I always knew.

My daughter Molly and her boyfriend were going to come to the ranch and work stock and stay the Labor Day weekend. I had a list of chores for them, but Molly had a sinus infection and was doubtful that they would be able to come. It seemed like a good time to plan a trip.

I drove to San Antonio, a three-hour drive, parked at the off-site parking lot and was shuttled to the airport, where I flew to Houston and was joined by Joe. The plane took us to Boston, where we boarded a small twin-engine Beechcraft and flew to Rutland, Vermont, arriving about 7:30 P.M. The Holiday Inn sent a shuttle.

Timmy, the shuttle driver, told us all about Rutland and the Holiday Inn. He informed us that they were 75 percent full for this evening and booked full for the weekend. He told us that most of the visitors came from Canada for radium treatments during the week and then drove the 250 miles or so back to Canada for the weekends. I didn't ask him if he meant radiation treatments or where the hospital was. After all, Rutland was a town of 30,000. It looked pristine, like a perfect New England village town that you would see in the movies. Everyone at the Holiday Inn was over 60, except for a group of rowdies in the bar having a good time. There is nothing worse than being cold sober and being around a bunch of happy souls having drinks in the lounge and being loud.

Joe and I went to bed after lugging his bicycle in a fiberglass pack, a round wheel-carrying canvas bag and a giant duffel bag, as well as my one suitcase.

I awoke before daylight and took a walk while I let Joe sleep. It was cold. We consumed the free breakfast. I indulged myself with pancakes and eggs. I ordered the pancakes because I wanted to try some of the famous Vermont maple syrup. I really wanted to see if their maple syrup was still as runny as the syrup I remembered. In Texas we use cane syrup or molasses, that dark, slow-moving stuff with a real full flavor. Here, the maple syrup was still runny.

Timmy shuttled us to the airport to pick up a rental car. We had arrived too late the previous evening to pick one up. Timmy dropped us at an unidentified hangar, and Joe and I discovered we were in the wrong spot. The people in the hangar pointed to the terminal and told us to just walk across the runway, that it was shorter. At any other airport in America, we would have probably been shot for walking across the tarmac past all the jets. We were relieved to find our rental car was a Taurus station wagon and drove back to the Holiday, loaded the equipment and navigated the miles to the Killington Ski Resort and Green Mountain Lodge to register and check in at our condo.

The condo was large and comfortable with a porch and a great view of the ski slopes and the mountains. Joe assembled his bike and took off for a warm-up ride of 10 miles up and down the mountain road to the ski resort.

The maple leaves were not yet turning. The afternoon was warm, so I reclined and read a book. Joe came in from his ride and showered, and we went to pick up his rider's packet and attend the rider's meeting. There were over 800 riders in the Killington Stage 3 Race; 118 of them were in Joe's class. There were racing teams from Mexico, Canada and all the adjoining states. It was the 13th annual race in Killington, and even the U.S. Postal Team was there but not Lance Armstrong.

Joe told me that the postal service was run for profit and that they sponsored the race team that had just won the Tour De France. Lance Armstrong, from Austin, won the tour after having beat cancer. In fact, he was the first American on an American team to win the tour, even though Greg LeMond had won the tour but raced for a French Team.

I have always loved the U.S. Postal Service and have listened to its critics with disbelief. Would you carry a letter from Texas to Minnesota for less than 50 cents? I think a stamp is the biggest bargain there is.

At the short rider's meeting, the organizers made an announcement. Under no circumstances were the riders to urinate during the first 22 miles, as the course wound through an area with camping grounds in which families with children would be present. The riders were told not to think of urinating at all for those 22 miles.

After the meeting Joe and I ate dinner at a nearby restaurant. Both of us had our tasters set for lobster since we were close to Maine and in lobster country. In the foyer of the restaurant was the inevitable lobster tank with a money slot. For $2 you could put your money in the slot and operate the tongs, and if you could catch a lobster it would be cooked for you for free. Somehow this rang like lobster abuse. We just ordered steak and lobster and enjoyed our dinner and went to bed early.

Honk if you married Sonja

I awoke before the alarm. We breakfasted on coffee, fruit and oatmeal before loading up the Taurus and driving to the start of the race. Joe's class of riders left at 8:20 A.M. from the parking lot from which the race started. I watched riders of every shape and description, not all of them speaking English. Some had dogs with them. I have never understood why people take their dogs on vacations and trips, and when I made that remark to Joe he told me that the dogs were part of the family and that you don't go on trips and vacations without the entire family.

I saw so many young bodies in revealing bicycle costumes that I entertained thoughts only befitting a dirty old woman and regretted my age many times over. It was nice to know, however, that I was not dead and still had dirty thoughts.

The officers of the race announced two minutes until the start for Joe's category, which was Cat III. They then said "one minute," then "30 seconds" and then "start," and off 118 bicycle riders rode.

I walked over to the Taurus, consulted my map and drove to the feed zone 20 miles down the road. Joe's route however was 38 miles to the feed zone—a 500-foot stretch of road where support crews could stand out beside the road with their hands held out with bottles of water or food. Joe had instructed me to give him a plastic bag with two water bottles and some nutrition bars and most of all to hold the bag high.

After waiting beside the road with other support people, the police car came by and said five minutes until the first two riders. Then came a group of 20, and Joe was there in the top 25. My heart first stopped and then went pitty pat. It was really exciting to know my child had just ridden 38 miles and was in the top 25. He snatched the bag and this old bag yelled repeatedly, "Go, Joe!" I was caught up in the emotion of the moment.

I drove 30 miles back to the ski resort and the finish line to await my son. By the end of the race, some of the classes were beginning to overlap. The riders straggled in singly; there were no energetic packs of riders coming across the line.

I waited as the winner in Joe's category came across the line and then second place a few minutes behind the winner. From then on, riders came singly or in pairs all panting and dismounting with shaky legs. I strained, looking and stretching for my son, and when I had my strongest doubts, he came across the line. I have never been so proud. I ran to him and he dismounted, legs quivering and tears flowing down his cheeks. He said, "Mom, I didn't finish within the time limit to qualify for tomorrow's race. I'm sorry I've disappointed you."

I answered, "Joe, I've never been more proud. You started the race and you finished; you rode 72 miles up and down the hills of Vermont. I am so proud of you. That's what mothers do—be proud of their children. I would be proud of you even if you didn't finish, and I would be proud of you even if you were in jail."

He walked the bike to the Taurus and lifted it into the back. I couldn't believe he could even walk, much less lift that bike. We drove back to the condo and he fixed himself some pasta. "We have two days before flying back," he said, "but if you want to change the reservations and fly back earlier it'll be okay. That way I won't miss another day of work." He took a nap and I got on the phone, made the reservation changes and when he awoke, we went tourist shopping to buy tee shirts and Vermont maple syrup. When I discovered that three ounces of maple syrup cost $3.59 I changed my mind about buying syrup for everyone. Again we feasted on lobster and steak.

On a cool and delightful morning, we arrived at the tiny airport, the only passengers. The two girls at the airport had never done a ticket change. They called their supervisor and were walked through the process on the computer. There was no metal detector or security whatsoever. We could have had bombs and machine guns in our luggage.

We flew into Boston, got on the plane and were served the same sandwiches we had eaten on the trip to Boston. In Houston, Joe's girlfriend's parents met him and I flew on to San Antonio.

Arriving in San Antonio, I noticed a tall blond aging disgracefully but well dressed in a green silk pant suit. The jacket covered a bare chemise, and she had big boobs, tanned but wrinkled skin and long blond hair done just so with a bit of curl. She looked like a 45-year-old Dallas Cowboys cheerleader who had expanded to a size 12. She was pretty but flashy. She was met by a tall blond tan Adonis in mustard slacks and a red polo shirt. He hugged and kissed her and put his hands all over her. In fact, while we were waiting for our luggage he hugged and kissed and felt her up with such passion it was almost obscene. She was dutifully enduring it all and I envied his passion, couldn't take my eyes off of them. He was so solicitous of her every move. They left the terminal just ahead of me with my scraggly pigtail, Walmart blue jeans and cowboy shirttail hanging out, wearing sandals, all alone. They walked to a shiny green pickup the exact color of her pantsuit. It was a custom match. A young man, 18 to 20, drove the truck. He was very polite, and I envied the scene as I witnessed their departure.

I walked across to await the shuttle to deliver me to my scratched white pickup with corn kernels, rusty wire and tattered rope in the bed. I was alone in my pickup for a three-hour drive to the ranch, and by the time I reached Uvalde I was angry. Why wasn't I in that picture? I stopped at the Country Junction and bought a six-pack of Budweiser and broke all my rules and drank two beers in the 38 miles between Uvalde and Camp Wood. I felt better when I remembered I had been like that for a while in my 30's—wearing size 6 designer dresses visiting glamorous places with a tall handsome husband.

Now I was an old widow woman in a size 8, wrinkled and spicy with a checkered past and it was okay. I didn't wish for any more than what I had.

By the time I reached Barksdale, 17 miles from home, I opened my third beer, put down the windows, looked at the mountains and smiled. My dog was waiting for me at the ranch. And that was enough.

11

Nicaragua

The balmy air of the late evening caressed me with a breeze as I exited the airport in Managua, Nicaragua, expecting my daughter Molly and her boyfriend David to meet me. Molly and David were not in sight. I stood outside with confidence and no fear. My contingency plan was to take a taxi to a hotel and hire a driver to take me to the village of San Juan del Sur the following morning.

Just as I had said, "No, gracias," to the umpteenth driver I looked up and saw David's brother, Allen, standing off in the dark with his arms crossed, a sly smile on his face. He grabbed my suitcase, and I followed him to an old decrepit, brightly painted school bus being loaded with people and packages.

Allen said, "I'm having trouble with my car, so we'll be taking the chicken bus."

"No problem," I replied as I rested my purse on the trunk of a car and shed my jacket in the sultry evening temperatures.

Allen then unlocked the car on which my purse rested, laughed and said that Molly had told him to make me wait and then do the chicken bus routine. I failed to see the humor of the episode.

The two-hour drive was a nightmare gauntlet dodging cows, horses, burros, bicycle riders and pedestrians. By the time we arrived at the hotel and checked into the most expensive suite in town at $65 a night and walked across the road to the bar on the beach, I had mellowed a bit. Molly and David were waiting in the bar. We drank beer and talked into the early morning. I had turned 59 two days before on January 2.

The local Nicaraguan beer sold for $1 a bottle and packed a light punch. We walked across the street to the hotel, woke up the night watchman, who unlocked the gate, and I retired to my suite. David and Molly occupied a less expensive room on the first floor, facing the courtyard. They had been sharing a room with Allen in an aunt's house and were looking forward to some privacy. After agreeing to meet in the morning we separated to our respective rooms.

Honk if you married Sonja

The sounds of music from across the street, the occasional blast of mortars and the roaring surf and truck noise "lulled" me to sleep. Those same noises awakened me the following morning. Mortars signaled the day before Epiphany, and the church bells echoed the impending celebration as I arose, dressed in shorts and a tee shirt and went down to knock on Molly's door.

Speaking through the wood, I said, "I'll meet you in the Iguana Bar across the street for breakfast."

My hangover was slight as I entered the bar perched on the white sandy beach that bordered the blue waters of the safe Pacific harbor. There was no way I could blend in as a local. I was old, blonde and had blue eyes. The Costa Rican coffee was sweeter than my taste buds were accustomed to, and the scrambled eggs and sautéed potatoes dispelled the fuzziness in my head.

Soon Allen, David and Molly appeared, and following a leisurely breakfast we took a three-mile hike along the beach before walking several blocks off the main beach road to the house that David's mother owned with one of her sisters. David and Allen were half American and half Nicaraguan. Their father had been a mining engineer from Wyoming who had met their mother in San Juan when he was working for an American mining company. He had been in his 60's with grandchildren. Their mother had been 25.

At the concrete-block house I met their Aunt Mareya and her Norwegian sailor husband. We continued up the hill that sloped down to the ocean, and I met their grandmother who was a short, thin, Indian woman aged 83. She was lively and friendly, as was his Aunt Iris, who lived with her mother. They had all survived the revolution that had lasted over a decade and had only ended in 1992. The evidence of that war was all around the small fishing village of several thousand. There were bullet holes in all the buildings.

Aunt Mareya had been a schoolteacher and had refused to teach weapons training to her young students. She had fled to Brazil for the 13-year duration of the war. Iris, another sister, had been trained as a dentist and also fled to Brazil, where she married and divorced a Brazilian. None of them had children, and according to David, they had chosen not to have children because of the hardships of the war. David remembered hiding under the bed as a child when the shooting erupted.

David's Nicaraguan grandfather had been the school principal, and of his seven children, all had married foreigners except for one son who married a Nicaraguan and lived in Managua. David had an uncle in California, one in Brazil and one in France. It was an interesting family.

We returned to the beach for lunch, eating steamed lobster covered in fresh crushed garlic with cabbage and carrot slaw, drowned with beer. We spent the rest of the evening in the beach bars, listening to music from the 70's and talking to American, Canadian and English expatriates. I met two German couples in their mid-thirties who owned two bars and a restaurant.

We met Elizabeth, a Canadian divorcee in her 60's. She had traveled Central America during the war, in the 1980's, with her sister and Pakistani brother-in-law. Their car had gone off a bridge, and the two of them had been killed. Fortunately, at the time, she was not with them. She was divorced and had a daughter who lived in Dubai. She rented a cheap room in town and spent most of her time in the bars, smoking cigarettes and drinking beer, contributing to the gossip that fueled the small town.

The next day we met at the Iguana Bar for a breakfast of fresh fruit and then began the day's project, which was to kayak, hang out on the beach and build a sand castle. David and Allen went for shovels and buckets while I rode waves onto the beach in the kayak with Molly. It was exhilarating to surf the crest of the waves in the kayak, and we squealed with delight.

The pit the men dug on the beach was 8 by 8 feet, and we kept the sand wet by carrying buckets of water from the ocean's edge. Elizabeth joined us in our efforts, and soon the beach was crowded with children surrounding the pit. The bar patrons along the beach watched us with interest. The locals and the tourists present came and commented on our endeavor.

Many beers later we had erected a castle with turrets and moats that was five feet high and at least that much in diameter. It was magnificent and everyone took pictures, noting that the incoming tide would eradicate our work. David designed the castle, and we told everyone who came by that he was an architect from Austin. I spent the day in my bathing suit with no embarrassment and felt good for 59. In the days that followed we were known as the ones who had built the sand castle.

Honk if you married Sonja

We adjourned to the bar for the sunset and became acquainted with more Canadians, Mark and Ken, from British Columbia. They looked 55 and square but in fact were older, hippies from the 60's. They had done all the drugs, listened to the music and had traveled the world. Ken had lived in an ashram. They were in San Juan del Sur to make money on the $500 million development that the government was sponsoring to promote tourism. The government was stable; the Sandanistas were coming back into power, having been converted to capitalism by the lure of big bucks, realizing that tourism brings cash quicker than long-term manufacturing development.

Thousands of acres along the Pacific coastline had been delineated in the master plan that included a golf course, an airstrip, condos, hotels and resort homes. Mark was an electrical contractor, and Ken was a paving contractor. Their associates were developers who had invested in an 84-acre tract and an 800-acre tract on the two beaches north of San Juan del Sur. The two men were pleasant company, but Molly was contemptuous of them, believing they had come to ruin the quiet fishing village and exploit the local population with no regard to environmental and cultural factors.

I did my best to convince her that change was inevitable and better executed by a bunch of old hippies who had some sensitivity to the environment, but she would not listen.

That evening in the Iguana Bar we met Paul, a retired Farmall Tractor executive. He had just completed a six-week Spanish immersion course, living with a family in San Juan and had moved into our hotel after completing his course. He planned to stay for another month. He admitted that this had been his third course; he had taken one in Mexico and one in Costa Rica. When I asked him how he did in the course, he quietly replied with no shame, "I failed."

"Well, Paul. How is your Spanish?"

"I don't speak Spanish."

When he went to the bathroom Elizabeth volunteered, "He likes young girls, and his trip is not about learning Spanish." We often saw him in the bars, sometimes with very young girls, and other times he was alone.

A 2,000-passenger cruise ship docked in the harbor, and the road along the beach was crowded with vendor's booths selling crafts from

Guatemala, Peru, Honduras and Nicaragua. Bands were playing, and the bars were full of old fat people wearing funny hats and holding hands.

Molly and I refrained from shopping too much because we had a trip planned later in the week to Masaya, where the central market was said to have good bargains. Vendors and tourists told us the cruise would end in Costa Rica the following day and then return in two days with another 2,000 tourists. The passengers on the cruise lines that had begun stopping there the previous year rated San Juan their number one favorite shopping stop. The head count of cruise ship visitors the previous year had been 45,000. This year the number was expected to double.

The full moon had enticed us into planning a trip 24 kilometers south to the beach that was the national reserve for the sea turtle hatching. Elizabeth and Achilles, David's cousin, planned to join us. We loaded the cooler with beer and empanadas, and when Achilles acted reluctant to get in the car I asked David, "Do you want me to get Achilles in the car?"

"Yeah, we need him to get in the park; he knows the caretakers."

I opened the door to the back seat, moved over and motioned for him to get in the car. He never hesitated.

Allen remarked, "He does anything a woman tells him."

Achilles was about 30 and a local fisherman.

We arrived at the reserve shortly after dark and sat quietly in the car while David and Achilles negotiated the fee down to $5 from $20. With three flashlights we traveled the path through the forest to the moonlit beach, where we deposited our blankets and cooler and settled down on the white sand with beers to wait for the baby turtles to erupt. David lit a small driftwood fire.

Molly spotted the first baby turtle coming out of the sand, and we watched with sheer amazement as the one turtle became a flower of turtles, 88 at final count. Within the hour, we were surrounded by blooming nests of baby turtles. Two of the night watchmen, carrying flashlights and a clipboard, soon joined us. They dug the turtles from the depths of the sand and put them in a pile for mutual warmth.

We spent the night digging and counting with the guards, watching the turtles make their way to the ocean. When they reached the hard sand before the ocean's edge they would hesitate, flap their flippers and wait for the wave to wash them out to the sea. Some were thrown back by the wave action. We waded and carried them to deeper water. We played with the turtles until the beer ran out and the dawn was approaching. At daylight the guards picked up the babies that had not made it to the ocean and took them to a saltwater tank to rest until darkness again fell. Leaving the babies on the beach in the daylight and heat would expose them to the birds.

The experience was one of those lifetime moments; we laughed that we had bargained our entrance fee down when people would come from all over the world and pay thousands to see what we had seen. We had even been allowed to bring our own beer and food and light a fire at the edge of the trees.

After a few hours of sleep we met at the Iguana to plan our drive to Masaya and to look forward to shopping. Elizabeth joined us. Allen gave the car keys to David and said he was going to spend the day with his grandmother. The hour-long drive along Lake Nicaragua, the 7th largest lake in the world, was picturesque. We were driving the Pan American highway through fields of sugar cane and rows of banana trees. Elizabeth talked us to death about her family, the man she had met in Costa Rica, her sister who died and her daughter in Dubai.

We turned off the highway to enter the central part of Masaya and were instantly motioned over by three young boys in uniform carrying machine guns. David left the car and went to speak with them and returned to the car for the papers in the glove compartment.

He soon returned to the car saying, "Allen didn't extend the permit for the car. It's against the law to drive during the daylight with the lights on. Do any of you have IDs?"

Not one of us including David had any form of identification. The lights of the car came on when you turned on the ignition. The soldiers wanted to put us in jail and confiscate the car.

David went back and talked to the officers again and returned, "Well, we have a choice. We can pay them $50 to let us go with the car or Sonja and Elizabeth can throw a dramatic anger episode to intimidate them because they have instructions to not upset rich elderly tourists. It's up to you."

I looked at Elizabeth. "I don't feel in the mood for an Academy Award performance. What about you?"

Elizabeth reached in her pocket and gave me a wad of bills that I supplemented and handed to David.

After disconnecting the lights we continued to the market and had a good day of shopping, not a great day because the pleasure police had been on patrol.

That evening we met a newcomer in the Iguana Bar, Arthur from North Carolina. He was in San Juan negotiating to lease a bar and restaurant on the beach. He planned on opening an art gallery, restaurant and bar. He was paying $25,000 for a 25-year lease since foreigners could not own beachfront property. Nonresidents could buy and sell property across the road from the beach but not oceanfront property.

The cruise ship was back the next morning, and we availed ourselves of the vendors and made some good purchases after the ship left and before the vendors loaded their wares. We ate yucca pancakes and cheese tortillas with the grandmother and went to bed sober.

In need of some physical exertion we took a three-hour hike up to the lighthouse at the end of the harbor. The climb was steep and strenuous, but the view was well worth the effort, and the chicken curry that we enjoyed with Aunt Mareya was one of the best meals I had eaten. That evening we returned to the beach bar for the sunset and some black conch ceviche before saying goodbyes and exchanging emails and addresses and cards.

Molly hated to be leaving. She was in love with San Juan del Sur, experiencing the enthusiasm and romance of youth. She wanted me to move there or buy a place there, an honest response to the beauty. I told her, "I have my paradise; you'll find yours."

Allen drove us to the airport in Managua. The plane was late taking off, and we all missed our connections in Houston. By the time I arrived in San Antonio and made my way to the pickup in long-term parking, it was late afternoon and January cold. I barely made it home before dark.

The first thing I did after unloading the car was bundle up and light a cedar fire outside in the fire pit. I thanked God I was home safe—scattered bits and pieces still back in Nicaragua but coming back.

I came into the house, lit another fire—this time in the fireplace—and called my mother to say that I was safely home.

The following morning at church I heard there had been a massive earthquake the day we had flown out of Managua and thousands were missing. A prayer of thanks was in order.

Honk if you married Sonja

An afternoon phone call from my brother David interrupted a nap. Always curious, he inquired about my trip and any romance. He said he had mailed me a book for my birthday about bad women in Texas and their men. I reminded him that angels always picked bad men. He advised me to pick my next man wisely. I replied, "There might be next men but there will no next man in my life."

12

The Memphis Queen

Mother and I met her two sisters, Florence and Stella, at the Houston airport, where we boarded a flight to Memphis. A representative of the steamboat line escorted us by bus to board the vessel called the Memphis Queen.

A buffet had been set up in the Grand Salon. Since we could not enter our rooms for several hours, I went to the gift shop and purchased five decks of cards for $20, and we adjourned to a lounge area where we played Hand and Foot, the Canasta-like game that the sisters favored.

Our stateroom was small. I changed into a long linen pink and red print dress as we prepared for dinner, early seating served at 5:15. The dining room was packed. Most of the passengers were elderly and overweight. I appeared to be the youngest passenger at 59 and the skinniest at size eight. Eye contact as I scanned the room rendered no connections, and I settled in for the six-days with my great mother in the company of my sweet aunts. I hoped the scenery would be worthwhile.

Our assigned table for eight was partially occupied by a couple from Indiana celebrating 40 years of marriage. The bride's mother in her late 80's, who lived in Florida, accompanied them. Marty and Bunny seemed reasonably intelligent until Bunny spoke, "Our luggage has not been brought to our room. I wonder where it is." Everyone had seen the luggage carried onto the ship; the ship was moving, therefore the luggage had to be on the ship.

When I changed the subject and asked what the annual rainfall was in their home town of Indianapolis, they all three looked blank as a rock, and when I followed with a query as to land prices for good farm land, they eyed me as if I were an alien. My last stab at social niceties entered the realm of politics. All three of them agreed that they had not been following the campaign and were not sure how they were going to vote. I wondered what they did all day. Were they on heavy medication or naturally unconscious?

Honk if you married Sonja

Dinner was a variety of common dishes but the desserts were extravagant—chocolate mousse, caramel truffle delight, raspberry eruption or carrot cake, all in very generous servings designed to tempt the heart attack candidates. Before the 6-day trip ended, the ship made three unscheduled stops for emergency health episodes.

Following dinner we adjourned to the salon and were introduced to our prime entertainment for the next few days. The band showed promise as we were introduced to the three dance pimps whose job it was to dance with the widow women on board.

We returned to the lounge for a game of cards, interrupted every few minutes by some of the following remarks and questions. "Are you playing for money? What game are you playing? Can I join you? Can my mother join you?"

Our final intruder, in her 80's, was wearing a black sequined baseball cap and displaying large diamonds on her fingers. She lingered for a while at the edge of our game, advising us, "You can get free postcards from the purser's desk rather than pay 50 cents in the gift shop." She wore a gold sequined baseball hat on formal night and a white sequined baseball cap during the daytime. The hair under the edges of her caps was gray and thick; she made a statement.

When we returned to our adjacent rooms, Florence found a bouquet of flowers and an invitation to a private captain's party. Stella and Mother were livid; Florence had never been on that cruise line but the two of them had. They agreed it must be a mistake, and Stella threatened to lock Florence in the bathroom and go to the party in her place. I volunteered to crash the party. Our efforts to make Florence feel guilty failed miserably.

While the scenery was lovely and the days passed slowly, I devoured the two books I had packed in my suitcase. Eventually Mother and Stella received invitations for a private captain's party. They attended and received the free glass of champagne and had their pictures taken with the captain. Aunt Florence purchased the picture of herself with the captain.

Our young lunch waiter launched into a story about his childhood baseball bat, saying that it had been made in Louisville. When Aunt Stella interrupted him and asked for coffee, he replied, "No one ever listens." Aunt Stella never received her coffee. The bizarre conversation only reaffirmed that I was not on the same planet as the other passengers.

Sonja Klein

The stimulating activity on the boat was people-watching. We watched a couple. She was manly, wearing muted Hawaiian-print pedal pushers with a matching short-sleeved blouse. He was paralyzed on one side, walked kind of sideways and had a funny-moving eye. He wore elastic drawstring cotton pants with elastic around the ankles and short-sleeved nondescript tee shirts. Aunt Stella pointed them out, saying, "Look at that poor couple. They must be brother and sister, and their family must have sent them on this trip."

I had a few conversations with them and found them to be the most aware passengers on the ship. Perception is a funny thing.

Every night on the Memphis Queen I dreamed about one of my four husbands. It was a strange experience because I rarely if ever dreamed about husbands one and three. Observations occupied most of my time as I noticed that only the thin passengers walked laps on the deck.

Our daily card games were located near the cookie, coffee and tea bar. Just for fun I broke some of the cookies in half. They were consumed first, less guilt for half a cookie.

One afternoon as we were playing cards Mother asked, "Florence, where is your foot?" Foot was the terminology for the second hand to be played once the first hand was played out. Both hands were dealt at the beginning of the round.

Aunt Florence replied, "I don't know; I've lost my foot."

Eyes widened at the nearby table as Aunt Florence rummaged under the table and finally exclaimed, "I found it; it was in my purse."

Immediately we understood the interest in our conversation and laughed until we cried. Aunt Florence told that story every year at our Christmas gathering. If there was a defining moment of the trip, that was it.

The evening of the captain's cocktail party was the highlight of the trip. The sisters three had all brought sequined outfits and applied their Mary Kay cosmetics with alarming detail. Formal wear had been prescribed for the occasion, but I had come to the realization that formal wear with this crowd meant polyester pant suits with rhinestone jewelry. We entered the salon and were ushered to a long line to await our handshake with the Arkansas captain and have our picture taken with him and then as a reward be handed a glass of free champagne. Snacks were served while the band played and the dance pimps performed their jobs.

Honk if you married Sonja

When I noticed how slowly the line was moving I made the remark, a bit too loudly, "I'm not waiting in line to shake hands." There was a bit of applause to my rude remark, and I went and sat down at a table, declining to have my picture taken with the captain. I did go around to the end of the line and obtain two glasses of free champagne, explaining to the servers that the ladies in my party were unable to walk that far. I then drank my champagne at leisure while I observed the snail's pace of the line.

The steamboat stopped in Shawnee Town on the Illinois side of the Ohio River. We entered buses for a trip to Henderson, Kentucky, to visit the Audubon Museum and Park. Half of the passengers on the ship crowded off the gangplank for a chance to walk in some fresh air. Most of us crowded into the gift shop at the park hoping for the opportunity to spend some money rather than tour the museum and hear a lecture about the famous naturalist, James Audubon.

On the bus ride back to the Memphis Queen I noticed that everyone in Kentucky smoked, that the price of cigarettes was $9.99 a carton whereas back home the cost was $20 a carton.

When the ship stopped in Louisville I exited for a tour of the town and Churchill Downs. Florence and Stella had been sick all night with diarrhea and vomiting, and Mother had seen the famous racetrack. I purchased some souvenirs at the gift shop, admonishing myself that if I hung anything else on the walls of my house it would most likely collapse.

We left the ship the next morning and were bused to the airport in Cincinnati for a one-hour wait before our flight. I went to the gift shop to purchase some books, and when I returned to the gate, Aunt Florence had thrown up and fainted. We pushed her in a wheelchair onto the plane early. Mother was exuding self-confidence as she boldly walked onto the plane under her own power.

The flight was smooth; we deplaned in Houston where I snagged a cart and loaded our luggage. We said our goodbyes and went out into the Houston humidity and heat to hire a taxi. The taxi moved to our pile of luggage, and when the driver got out of the taxi, Mother remarked, "My God, he's too old to be driving." I shushed her and had to help him load the luggage, thinking that we had survived the plane flights only to be killed by an over-aged taxi driver. Fortunately we arrived home safely.

Sonja Klein

The best part of the trip was the confidence that my mother exuded. She had been reluctant to go on the trip, saying she was too infirm. Sharing a room with her and watching her blossom is one of my fondest memories.

13

Bhutan

Bhutan, the land of the thunder dragon, was my destination. The itinerary promised that the flight from Los Angeles to Hong Kong would last 14 hours and 51 minutes. I had carefully programmed my psyche for that period of endurance. Unfortunately I had to reprogram some software for the journey. A voracious headwind not only delayed the arrival time but also caused an unscheduled stop in Seoul, Korea, for additional fuel, thus extending the flight for an additional five hours.

A missed connection in Hong Kong left me stranded in the transit area for six hours waiting for the next available flight for Bangkok, Thailand, where I crashed and burned after dark without dinner, leaving a wakeup call for 4 A.M. to ensure arrival at the airport in sufficient time to obtain a visa and board a 7 A.M. flight on Druk Airlines destined for Paro, Bhutan.

Airport chaos in the East has a certain rhythm, recognizable from experience. The lines are without structure, and after the check-in line comes the pay your tariff window, always in some unfamiliar currency, and then more security checks and x-rays until final arrival in the holding area.

Druk Airlines consists of four planes, two Airbuses and two smaller jets. Druk Airlines is the only airline allowed to land in Paro, the site of the one airport in Bhutan. Druk Airlines stopped in Calcutta to disgorge some Indian passengers and pick up a few more Bhutanese. The flight from Calcutta to Paro was a short 45 minutes as the pilot in perfect unaccented English advised the passengers to not be alarmed as we flew into Paro, calmly assuring us that the Himalayan Mountains would be on either side of the valley in which the plane would land. It was a bit scary flying in-between such high peaks. Mt. Everest was on my left.

I was issued my visa at the airport after confirmation that my name was on the list. Bhutan allows less than 10,000 tourists a year, and prior to the 1980's no one was allowed. To be allowed into the country the tourist must pay $200 a day in advance for the duration of his stay. That fee furnishes the tourist with a guide, a driver and vehicle, hotel rooms and meals and entertainment, whether trekking, rafting or sightseeing.

I was joining a cultural and spiritual study group of 15, most of whom I had become acquainted with on the plane from Bangkok. Our guide's name was Tashi Wangchuck, and his assistant was Dorjie; the driver's name was Jigme.

The drive from Paro to Thimphu, the capital, took a short 45 minutes—short by Bhutan travel time, as I was soon to learn. The hotel was clean, charming and lacking a phone or TV. The dinner was served buffet style. Rice and potatoes are the staples. Buckwheat is grown in the central part of Bhutan. The national dish is chili peppers with white cheese, a welcome meal for a Texan, delicious but hot.

Since Bhutan is a Buddhist monarchy, religion is a part of everyday life. The landscape is dotted with prayer flags, shrines, monasteries and forts all having unique names such as chortens, dzongs and mani walls. There are only two main roads in Bhutan, a north/south and an east/west.

After an evening in Thimphu, we traveled eight hours to cover 120 miles. The roads are one lane, twisting and winding through the Himalayas. We experienced snow in the high passes and monkeys and blooming cherry trees in the lower elevations. I spotted my first yak, a hairy cow, prized for its milk with which the Bhutanese make butter and cheese. The hot butter tea, the only thing I disliked, tasted salty and smelled similar to a billy goat.

The country is primarily agrarian; farmers raise cabbage, cauliflower, eggplant, green beans, squash and carrots. I ate fiddlehead fern for the first time, a green vegetable that grows in the mountains. It was tasty, similar to green beans but stronger in flavor. When I remarked to one of my fellow travelers, "I've never eaten or seen this served," she remarked. "It's available in many of the markets of New York City."

"Well, it looks like the ferns that grow in Louisiana. Is it the same thing?"

She assured me that it was not the same plant.

The Buddhists do not believe in killing anything, not even insects. No animals are raised for meat. Instead all meat is imported from India. When an animal dies it is buried and not eaten.

A visit to an elementary school revealed that the language of Bhutan is English. All school classes and textbooks are in English. The country speaks 19 dialects, and in order to simplify things, the king declared English the spoken language. In fact, the king of Bhutan, Jigme Wamchuck, was a suite mate of my brother David at Rice University in Houston and was a Texas college graduate.

Our travels across the countryside revealed that the people are mostly farmers. The beautifully terraced fields dot the landscape of the severely sloping Himalayan Mountains.

We spent a morning with a professor who explained many aspects of the Buddhist religion. The Buddhists believe that the mountains and lakes are sacred. No mineral exploration or fishing or swimming in the lakes is allowed. Water and timber are the country's most valuable resources, and hydroelectric power is sold to India. Timber is cut only by government permission, and a law was passed that 60 percent of the country must remain timbered. An active reforestation program is enforced. The current timbered land is 72 percent.

The professor was quite frank. Smoking in public is prohibited; plastic bags are forbidden. There is no prostitution, begging, graft or crime. The Buddhists believe in nonattachment to material possessions and that everyone is connected, that from the many incarnations a soul experiences, everyone you meet was at one time your mother, brother, sister, father. All sentient beings should be allowed to achieve happiness. The Buddhists pray for happiness to everyone.

The two weeks that I remained in Bhutan were filled with travel through the central region of the country—walks each day of two to five miles in the high elevations of the Himalayas; visits to monasteries, schools, museums, forts and shrines.

On a long day's journey we stopped in a small village for lunch. As I walked the streets in my Navajo coat of many colors, several Bhutanese pointed at my coat and smiled. Our guide remarked that they thought I had purchased the coat in Bhutan. They were amazed at the similarity of the symbols, markings and colors in the coat. And as we strolled down the streets, a shop owner approached me with a flat-billed hat that perfectly matched my coat. It was woven from yak hair. Of course I bought the hat and wore it most every day.

I attended a festival in the remote village of Ura, a masked dance festival to celebrate the planting of the crops. I hiked a mile up to a monastery and followed the procession led by a pony with a tiger skin draped across his bony back. The trip to Ura, a short 30 miles from

Bumthang, lasted three hours. There are no straight roads or 18-wheelers in Bhutan. The geography of the country prevents easy travel. Most travel is done on foot; there are few vehicles in the country.

Archery is the national sport of Bhutan. I attended the national archery finals for homemade bows and arrows. The finals were held in the capital, Thimphu. The targets, approximately the size of a coffee can, were 100 meters apart as two teams of six men competed. I was unable to see the targets from one end of the field to the other. Many of the arrows either hit the target or came close as the archers shot with no apparent ritual of taking aim. They simply walked up on their turn and shot their arrow at a target 100 meters distant. Cheerleaders chanted in circles. Colorful tents were erected as families dressed in the native fashion enjoyed the festivities.

The men wear the gho and the women wear the kera. Both are robes with wide belts and are often quite colorful. The belts are used as pockets. The king declared that all Bhutanese wear the native dress while at work. After hours they can wear jeans and tee shirts. Even the school students wear robes of the traditional dress.

I visited several homes, one a farmhouse and one a village home where the family was conducting the 49th day ritual of the dead in honor of the grandfather who had died. The ritual invited his spirit down to say hello. Food offerings were provided for his spirit as the Buddhist monks chanted, played horn and drums and prayed. The Buddhist religion is a happy religion and provides contentment.

Every site we visited was adorned with pictures of the royal family. The king is well loved by his subjects. We learned that he has four wives —all sisters—and 13 children, the oldest male being the crown prince. The king married the four sisters in one ceremony, wisely ending the controversy between the adherents of theocracy and monarchy. The fours sisters were members of a prominent political family that opposed the monarchy.

Our guide informed us that politically the country is stable and led by the king who is strongly motivated to maintain its independence from China and India, both of which border Bhutan. China absorbed Tibet and India assimilated Assam and Sikkim. Bhutan is determined to remain independent in spite of neighboring aggression.

The long hours along the narrow mountain roads provided our guide the time to relate the history and facts of this small country no larger than Switzerland. No foreign-owned businesses are allowed in Bhutan. A citizen of Bhutan must own 50 percent or more of any business, even though the road construction crews are primarily Indian. The Japanese, being fellow Buddhists, build bridges in Bhutan, but the country is basically a closed country, intent on preserving its cultural independence and natural resources while filtering the amount of western influence by limiting the amount of tourism and the quality of the tourists.

The capital of Bhutan, Thimphu, has about 40,000 residents and is the largest town in the country. The entire population of the country is about 650,000. There are no slums; schooling and medical care are provided by the government. Income over $2,400 is taxed at 5 percent. Wedding rings are not worn, and there is no formal marriage ceremony or divorce action. Men are held responsible for supporting their children. Multiple wives or husbands are allowed.

There are no mental hospitals or orphanages, and I never observed anyone drinking alcoholic beverages in public. I did sample a strong drink made of rice and a sour wine made from wheat. Both were as bad tasting as the yak butter tea. Red Panda was the name of the national beer in Bumthang. A liter bottle sold for $1. The beer was tasty.

Twenty percent of the males in Bhutan enter the monastery, some at the age of 7. Some of them continue on to become monks; others leave the monastery to continue their education in the government schools. Some leave the public schools to join the monastery. Some of the monks marry and farm as well as conduct Buddhist rituals.

The government supports the monasteries. The public gives donations for support of the monks and maintenance of the monasteries. I visited monasteries that dated from 800 A.D., most of them originating from the 1600's, when Bhutan was unified. Very few of the monasteries are open to tourists but on one occasion I discovered the definition of an Asian toilet.

We had the opportunity to use the bathroom at one of the monasteries. Several of us ladies agreed to use the facilities. One of our options on the long rides had been the bushes so we readily followed our guide. The concrete room had partial walls surrounding cubicles with holes flush to the ground. A trench carrying the raw sewage was located in the rear of the cubicle. You merely squatted over the hole, hit or miss. It was nasty.

Sonja Klein

The trip home was as long and arduous as the imagination allows. I found myself walking the deserted terminal in San Antonio near midnight. I was smiling and crying, thankful to be back in Texas and grateful for the experience of Bhutan. In the days that followed I found that I had not gathered myself back to Texas. Parts of me were left behind, pieces in Bhutan, Thailand, and even a few shards in Hong Kong. The trip had scattered my Humpty Dumpty self and strewn some bits along the way. There was no doubt that I would come together again but perhaps not in the same pattern, complete but different, the everlasting benefit of travel.

Sometime after my return home, the king of Bhutan resigned in favor of his oldest son. The government became parliamentary rather than a monarchy, and tourism was encouraged and enlarged. A cousin who recently spent time in Bhutan reassured me that serenity prevails.

14

Name Unknown

I was a merry widow, aging disgracefully up an isolated canyon in eastern west Texas. I had been on my own, living alone for six years, doing what I loved most of all, namely, writing.

In six years I managed to churn out five full-length novels, 28 short stories and two scripts, none of which had been published, but that was not my thing. I wrote because I loved to write. I was a social isolate, living in my mind and in the volumes of books I read and wrote. My only vice was ordering and reading books of all kinds—that and drinking whiskey and chasing men. Mostly, I just read, wrote and collected stuff from my travels, to the extent that my home was an eclectic collage— bright and colorful, as I imagined myself to be.

I have three brothers whom I call "the brothers Grimm." We all love each other dearly and still act as though we were children, competing with our ranches, our hobbies of growing things. We're good Germans, descended from immigrants who came to Texas before it was a state. Our roots were deep, and we had strong branches, a vast and prolific family.

My oldest brother, John, is a Texas history buff, and after my husband died he tried for two years to suck me into writing a movie script about Rip Ford. Ford was a Texas Ranger who lived in Texas from the fall of the Alamo to the years after the Civil War. I ducked John as best I could, but on one visit to the family bosom I must have been weak because I let him load me up with books on his passion and agreed to write the script. He assured me that if I wrote the script he would see it was produced into a miniseries or movie.

Marketing was not my forte and I convinced myself that if I wrote his script it would satisfy him, and I would have a market for my other work with no effort on my part. It was the old win–win philosophy.

I assured my brother John that I would have a finished script within a year and went to work reading and researching, drawing up a historical timeline for accuracy. It was a challenge. All of my other writings had come from somewhere within or without. The muse never failed me, and I knew I would never live long enough to write the books that were the gift of my fertile imagination, perhaps remembrances of lives long past. It was all there in my ecstasy, my joy of living and writing.

I delivered the script on time and waited for John to work wonders. Over the months he called me on a weekly basis. DreamWorks had the script; the script was in New York; the script was hand-delivered to Steven Spielberg. I was up and down, believing in my brother. After three rewrites and many conferences, he loved the script. All I knew was I had spent a year; and as I reworked and reread the script I had no recollection of the writing. At some point when writing, an exhilaration permeates my being and I know I am off and running, that the work has taken a life of its own. The feeling is similar to orgasm and one that I relish.

A year of ups and down passed as I finished another script, another book and continued with my writing.

I am involved in the community in which I live, and through some contacts in Uvalde with Economic Development was made aware of events and found myself on the email list of seminars, conferences and meetings held concerning economic development in rural Texas.

My mode of existence was to arise at 4:30 A.M., check my emails and write until late morning. The rest of the day was downhill—feeding stock, doing ranch chores and taking care of business.

I received the email about a seminar in Alpine in January—a slow indoor time of the year, a time for reflection, a time for regrouping, a time for planning and change. The emphasis of the seminar was on economic development in rural Texas, highlighting the film industry. In that instant was a click. Something happened. Instinctively, I had to chase the buzz. I thought immediately it was a clue, seized on the idea, sent in my $65 for the conference and planned to drive out to Alpine, visit my daughter in graduate school at Sul Ross and meet the producer of Streets of Laredo, Dead Man Walking and The Texas Rangers, who was the featured keynote speaker.

The agenda for the seminar included a reception and cocktail party in Marathon on the evening before the opening of the conference, and it was here that I planned my move. I would dress flashy, work the room and zero in on the producer, give him my spiel, charm him, deposit the script and begin the journey to fame, a good plan.

Honk if you married Sonja

The drive was uneventful, and I arrived in time for a visit with the daughter, time to dress and drive the 30 miles to Marathon. I walked into a room of about 20 people, none of whom I had ever seen before and visited with a group of women and played the "Hello and where are you from" game. I met ladies involved in economic development from Big Lake, Clebourne, Alpine, exchanged cards and moved to the next circle of people.

A glass of wine gave me some courage, and I asked one of the men in a group which ones were the filmmakers. He pointed to two men in their 40's standing by the bar. In the emotion of the moment and with the passion of my cause, it never occurred to me that they were both too young to have done the body of the work on the resumé I had read.

I sashayed over, introduced myself and told them about my script. The first one introduced himself as Tom, and I recognized the name from the program. Tom was the director of the Texas Film Institute, from Austin. I never caught the other man's name because I assumed he was Frank Q. Dobbs, the famous producer.

Emboldened by the wine I told them about the script; they asked some pertinent questions: Why would anyone want to see the movie? Where did I learn to write scripts? Did I have any other scripts? I gave great answers, having gone through all my reasons on the drive from the ranch. "Dobbs" said he would like to read my script and asked that I bring it to the seminar.

Actually, it was in my car but I did not want to appear too eager, visited some more and moved on working the room and exchanging cards, anxious to jump in my Explorer and scream "Yes!" to float away and faint with relief. My emotions were churning and the restraint I had to exercise was painful, but at long last the reception came to an end. I casually but triumphantly exited the building, climbed into my vehicle, drove off down the highway to Alpine in high elation, smiling and saying "Yes." I had done it, accomplished what I came to do.

The seminar began at 8 A.M. I entered the conference room, poured myself a cup of coffee, resisted the pastries and scanned the room. I said hello to my newfound friends from the evening before, sat at a large round table with some women from Big Lake, trying not to look for "my producer." I casually hid my manila envelope thick with my script under my conference handouts. I had decided to play hard to get, to not be anxious.

Sonja Klein

The morning progressed slowly with some lectures, panel discussions and a short break when I spotted my producer. He was looking my way, but I acted disinterested through the next talk and then he walked over and I gave him my script with a few short words. My heart was pounding as I saw him walk up to the podium, introduce himself as something— not Frank Dobbs—and began to talk about databases and computers and movie sets and the film industry.

Over lunch, the keynote speaker—the real Frank Q. Dobbs—in his 60's, spoke about the film industry in Texas. He was a great speaker and I sat there like a dummy, thinking how stupid I was, that I had probably given my script to someone who would steal it and sell it, even though I had registered the script.

It was with great humility that I approached the real Frank Dobbs after his talk and introduced myself. Before I could give him my pitch, he asked if I was the lady with the script, that he had heard there was a script floating around and that he would like to read it and he hoped I was protected. Feeling certain my script would be stolen, I assured him the script was registered.

He gave me his card and asked me to mail the script to his office. I was back up there, high again. I had been accepted as a screenwriter for whatever that meant. And then the icing on the cake: Tom, the head of the Texas Film Industry, walked over put his hand on my shoulder and said, "Good luck with your script."

I don't remember much of the five-hour drive home; my emotions fluctuated between despair, humility and excitement, but as I arrived at Vance and drove by the old cemetery it occurred to me that I still didn't know the name of the man to whom I had given the script, and I had an instant flash of the tombstone in the Vance Cemetery that read "Mexican, Name Unknown," and I chuckled, thinking Producer, Name Unknown.

15

Terlingua

We were three women from Texas. One was curvy, one was straightforward and one was cosmetically overweight. We were all over 60, had between five and ten marriages accumulated among us and had long since cared about the count. One was a blonde, one a strawberry and the other a brunette. We each had our share of life's abuses and travails, but a sort of wisdom prevailed. We were single and planned on remaining so. One had a boyfriend, comically called "Mr. New," one had given up and the other one, me, was open for anything. Marcia lived in Midland, Ira Jean in Albuquerque and I was isolated on a ranch in west Texas. We had a lot in common: there was not a gray hair on our heads, we loved to dance and we loved men.

Marcia and Ira Jean knew each other most of their lives, and I was a newcomer on the scene, having met Marcia through the common set of bizarre circumstances known as the Texas connection, whereby a person far from their comfort zone on an adventure meets someone and connects and then runs into them several times until the clue takes root and they become friends.

We met once a year at the Terlingua Chili Cookoff, camped with a bunch of men, danced, cooked, partied and said goodbyes until the following year. We kept in touch through landlines and emails, though the correspondence heightened in intensity as the cookoff date drew near. We compared lists, wardrobes and health issues as the magic date approached. Marcia kept in touch with some of the men, and the news went back and forth of who was coming, who would be absent and what had happened in the previous months to them all.

"Chuck and Bob are going on Wednesday to secure the camping area. Joe is bringing just one guy with him and a trailer load of firewood. Carl is driving in from Florida. Chris isn't coming; his wife just had a baby. Jason isn't coming until Thursday; he got a better job and doesn't have that many vacation days yet. The kayaking guide from Colorado is coming this year and bringing a friend. A new guy, Brice, is coming from east Texas; he's a great dancer. The bus is coming Wednesday night late."

The bus was a huge 40-foot border patrol bus purchased by a group of eight guys from the high plains of Texas who each pitched in $3,000 and converted it to a party bus and bunkhouse, complete with an outside shower, dynamite sound system, generator and lights. The bus pulled the chuck-wagon trailer that served as the kitchen. The downside was that it was slow and took hours to make the trip. Over the years, they had dealt with tire blowouts, an overheating engine and deficient drivers, but they had always made it. Cell phones kept those of us already in camp informed.

"The bus is in San Angelo. . . . They're buying groceries. . . . They just left Alpine." When the bus arrived, the camp was complete. The flag of Texas was painted on the side of the bus with "Hylton." The eight owners were Masons and in a group called the Jesters. The title fit them well. They were fun.

Camp always had the core group, but there were always newcomers—first-timers and those who wandered into camp the previous year and returned because they never had so much fun. The Terlingua Chili Cookoff had been going on for 40 years and was a strictly Texas event. All ages from all over the world attended on a regular basis. Once you went, you were hooked—could not imagine the first weekend in November without making the long drive to Terlingua, deep in the Big Bend area of Texas, a breathtaking area thinly populated and surrounded by rugged peaks and bordered by the Rio Grande or Rio Bravo del Norte, the home of the Indians, cattle trails and the Mexicans immigrants who also considered it theirs. Every moment in Big Bend is a marvel, night or day. The stars, the light at daybreak, the colors of the sunset, the drifting clouds, golden hues, the green shades of the cactus varieties and the light caliche earth and rocks silenced all the mind's chatter to the quiet and beauty of nature, making all else insignificant.

We all came to camp for that scenery to render our trivial day-to-day lives sterile and take us somewhere better. The booze, music, campfire food and wood smoke enhanced the experience. And then there were the women who bared their breasts for beads—fat women, ugly women, old women, pretty women. They cruised the 200-acre camping area in every sort of vehicle pulling up their scanty tops for cheap, colorful beads. Sometimes their husbands drove the four-wheeler, dune buggy or jeep. Sometimes the vehicle contained all females and sometimes it was a pickup load of men and women. The common thread was music, alcohol and laughter.

Our camp was on top of a hill in the back of the camping ground, an area called Crazy Flats. To get there, we had to drive down Pervert Row, the only caliche trail to the back of the site. Pervert Row was lined with campers, mostly men of every age, who came supplied with beads to exchange for tit views.

Being creatures of habit, most campers returned to the same campsite every year. We were neighbored by two schoolteachers from the Permian Basis who walked around every day bare-breasted and wearing only a thong, weather permitting. The prettiest one we called Barbie, and the men spent hours sitting around the campfire commenting on what Barbie was doing and how many beads she had collected. Her husband we named Ken. He smiled the whole time his wife flaunted her unnatural firm breasts.

Our men were all married and ranged in age from 28 to 78. There were county commissioners on the eve of uncontested elections, probation officers, a small-town sheriff, a water well driller, a schoolteacher, construction workers, a jewelry designer, an old fart, some young farts, world travelers and three Texas women. We were privileged to be the only women allowed in camp. They treated us like queens, setting up our tent, feeding us and treating us with kindness and respect, as well as delivering some bawdy jokes and suggestions.

The laughs were all-consuming from naming the bus, Brokeback Bus, to a comment from one of the guys when a jeep drove into camp with the word sheriff painted on the side. The jewelry designer walked up to the jeep and said, "Which one of you girls is named Sher efe?" They took it well and did not jump out and pistol-whip him into the dirt.

Every year a new story was added and retold. "Remember the year the guy from Sweden got drunk and woke up with a big hickey on his neck."

"Yeah, he was afraid to fly back and meet his wife, asked for advice."

"I told him to miss the plane."

"Me too."

"He kept ice on it all the way to the airport and by the time he arrived in Sweden, it was gone."

"He was lucky."

"Remember the time that guy came out of his tent in the morning and asked how ugly she was?"

"She was ugly, but we all told him she wasn't that bad."

"Remember that band where the lead singer drank Everclear and lit his breath on fire. Wonder how his lungs are now."

"Wasn't much fun watching him destroy himself."

The men left their women and families behind, as well as their problems. We came to dance. The dancing was heaven for us dancing fools. Most of them danced every dance and wore us down to satisfaction.

Their cooking was as good as their dancing. Every morning they cooked bacon, pan sausage, link sausage, potatoes, onions, eggs and tortillas. Afternoon snacks were grilled wild hog tenderloin, fried jalapenos, fried bread and butter pickles. Evenings were chili, beans, fried chicken, grilled fish and beef stew. We made margaritas and brought tamales.

Some of us stayed in tents, some in the Hylton bunkhouse, some in travel trailers, some in high-dollar horse trailers with sleeping quarters. A few even slept in sleeping bags on the ground. The campfire and the music went on 24 hours a day. Everyone shared and everyone got along. If someone was too drunk, we watched over them, never being judgmental. If someone was missing, we all inquired where they were. "He's taking a nap. He's cruising for tits." "Don't worry about him. He's too drunk to fight." The theme was always folks taking care of each other.

We had all had our share of bumps and bruises, had been twisted and bent but at the camp there was camaraderie pure to Texas. That's why we returned year after year.

The emails fly back and forth, "Ten months until the cookoff."

16

Rafting

The drive to Santa Fe was long and boring, though the scenery was spectacular. I was on my way to a rafting adventure in Utah after connecting with my cousin Roxanne. Actually she was triple kin, double kin on my father's side and a distant cousin on my mother's side.

The directions to her home were easy and there I met her and her husband Chuck and his best friend Chick from Nebraska. Chick was an insurance executive, married with two children. He and Chuck were childhood friends.

I could not believe the gear that was piled up in Roxanne's double garage. There were tents, paddles, a raft, coolers, dry boxes, table and even a portable shower that took the four of us two hours to assemble on a practice run.

I slept in Roxanne's son's room and when I entered the kitchen the following morning I found Chick struggling with the coffee pot, smoking a cigarette. I joined him for a cigarette and managed to get the coffee going. When Roxanne and Chuck entered the kitchen and found Chick and me smoking and drinking coffee, Roxanne remarked, "You don't smoke, Sonja."

I answered in my best morning voice, "I know it but since Chick is the only smoker I don't want him to feel ashamed."

She replied, "It's a good thing he's not a heroin addict. I'd hate to send you home a heroin addict."

The two guys spent most of the morning loading the pickup and trailer. I was dumbfounded that everything fit in an orderly fashion.

There were some last minute errands before we left at noon, right on schedule. By then we were hungry, so Chuck stopped at a roadside stand for hot dogs. I normally don't eat hot dogs, but these were so good that we ate them with a fork; they were covered in green peppers and onions and satisfied our hunger for the trip to Bluff, Utah.

Our route took us northwest out of Santa Fe through Espanola. The area had grown since I'd last visited in the 1970's. Since the road was under repair, our progress was slow. To pass the time Roxanne and I played Scrabble in the back seat. She was a good player and won the first of many matches. As the afternoon passed we played "I Spy" and the alphabet game, girls against the boys. After stopping to pee Roxanne retrieved a gallon jug of margaritas from the cooler. We finished the jug by the time we arrived in Utah.

Bluff, Utah, was a small Mormon town of about 80. Since Bluff was a rafting town, there were several motels and restaurants. Before going for dinner we attended a slide show and lecture at the motel. The information given concerned the history, geology, plant and animal life of the area as well as facts about the San Juan River on which we would be traveling for the next eight days.

The rest of our group had arrived the previous night and the plan was for all of us to meet at the launch site on the river a few miles south of the town. As we arrived at the launch site I was overwhelmed at the trucks, trailers and gear to be unloaded. There were four large rafts to be inflated as well as two rubber duckies (yellow canoes). There were coolers, dry boxes, tents, umbrellas, chairs and dry bags sitting ready to be loaded once the rafts were inflated.

No one seemed concerned about the volume of stuff; everyone acted as if they knew what they were doing. There was no shade on the riverbank and the temperature climbed steadily to 100 degrees. I put on my hat, a light tan canvas hat with a cord to secure it around my neck to prevent it from blowing off in the wind that I hoped would cool down the river canyon. I slathered my wrinkling skin with high-powered sunscreen and did as I was told.

There on the riverbank I was introduced to Big Al and Lenya, a married couple who had lived in the communes around Taos in the 1970's. Al made false teeth and Lena was a private nurse practitioner—lean, bronze and looked strong as an ox. Al and Lenya had been married for quite a few years and had children from other spouses. They lived in a full household. Al joked, "We must have done something wrong because none of our children have ever left home." With them was a woman in her early 50's, Victoria, who was the mother of either Al or Lenya's son's girlfriend.

Mario and his new girlfriend Ferris were the next to be introduced. Mario was in his late 40's, nice looking, Italian and worked as a waiter in a Santa Fe restaurant. Mario lived to raft the rivers and had just returned from a 30-day rafting trip through the Grand Canyon. His girlfriend was a massage therapist in her 30's. Ferris was the quiet type and Mario was obviously courting her seriously.

Tomas was a stonemason in his 50's and was accompanied by his girlfriend Jemma, who was in her 40's and did clerical work. With them was Tomas' grandson, Amarante, called Ami, who was 7. There were evident misgivings about a 7-year-old but Tomas assured us that Ami would be no problem. Tomas had been taking him to swimming lessons for the past two months in preparation for the rafting trip and had purchased a small pontoon kayak to tow behind his raft so that Ami could learn to paddle the river.

I was impatient to be on the river and underway and watched while they meticulously packed all the gear, inflated the rafts and rubber duckies and shuttled the vehicles and trailers back to the Recapture Lodge.

Arrangements had been made through the rafting shop in Bluff to shuttle our vehicles to the point in the river where we would re-enter civilization after eight days of rafting in the wilderness.

Chick broke his Rayban sunglasses in the course of unloading and on one of the shuttle trips had purchased a pair of mustard-colored Ferrari sunglasses that made him look like a rock star. We all had a lot of fun kidding him about those glasses.

The painstaking process of loading and inflating was finally finished early in the afternoon and we floated down the river, away from civilization.

We all opened our first beer of the day as we floated down the San Juan, Roxanne and I sitting in the front of the boat with Chuck steering from the middle of the boat and Chick floating in the rubber duckie alongside the raft. The temperature had climbed to over a 100, and when the beer pressured our bladders we jumped overboard and peed in the river holding on to one of the ropes that dangled around the raft. Climbing back onto the raft was awkward and accomplished with grunts and groans as well as laughter.

All functions of elimination were regulated by the park service. Pissing had to be done in the river so as not to pollute the sandy campsites along the riverbank. All shitting had to be done in the groover. Mario was in charge of the groover and carried it on his raft for the entire trip. The shitter was called a groover because in the past a metal ammunition box was used. Sitting on it caused grooves on the butt, but now the group of friends had purchased a commode seat over a vacuum-sealed bucket in which the shit of 12 people for eight days would be carried.

After five days our shitter was full and we used the second one. Under no circumstances were we allowed to pee in the shitter. The women all agreed that whoever had made that rule was a man because it was difficult for a woman to shit without peeing. When the urge came we had to go to the river to pee and then go to the shitter to shit. Practice made it less difficult.

We mostly stayed in sight of each other through the hot afternoon; Roxanne and I were grateful for the large umbrella on our raft that afforded shade. We were late docking at our campsite and hungry as the gear was unloaded. Meal duties had been pre-assigned and it was our raft's duty to provide the first evening meal.

Roxanne had planned carefully. She whipped out a gallon of margaritas and put out some cheese, crackers, salmon pate and fresh sliced pineapple. We then set up the two long tables that were our kitchen counter along with a large aluminum dry box that became a cabinet when the legs were attached. This box held most of the dishes, utensils and pots with which we would prepare the meals on the trip. Whole Foods in Santa Fe had prepared the dinner—barbecue brisket, beans, tabouli, humus and cole slaw. Chocolate cake fresh-baked by Roxanne was our dessert. Chick and I helped prepare the meal and then washed the dishes. We carried all garbage with us.

The wash system consisted of three buckets of river water. The first bucket was boiling hot with soap and a capful of Clorox, using the propane burner called the blaster. The second bucket contained hot water with a capful of Clorox and the third bucket was a cold-water rinse. The clean dishes were then dropped into a mesh bag attached to one of the tables like an apron and left to dry overnight and be used in the morning for breakfast.

We selected tent sites by throwing a life preserver or gear bag on the white sand. I fumbled erecting my tent and Tomas and Roxanne out of pity helped me. I was the first to crawl in my tent and left the rest of them sitting and drinking.

Honk if you married Sonja

I was joined at daylight by Chick and Ami and as I waded out in the river to pee, Chick observed, "Looks like your lady-like ways have gone down the river."

"I'm doing what I have to do."

Chick and I managed to get the coffee going and enjoyed a first cup being observed by a sleepy 7-year-old. Chuck and Roxanne joined us, scrambling eggs with onions and diced chiles. Honeydew melon and sliced pineapple completed the meal. After eating I took down my tent, packed my gear and deposited it on the riverbank close to the raft and then joined Chick to wash the dishes, pack the kitchen boxes, tie up the trash and take down the tables while everyone else packed their tents.

By the time we were again back on the river it was 10 A.M. As we floated peacefully down the river enclosed in a high-walled canyon, we observed the layers of stone and sediment, Anasazi ruins and pictographs. The river was ours and ours alone.

I spent most of the morning wondering what the hell I was doing, thinking that rafting was a lot of work and effort, that my creek and the Nueces River was cleaner and clearer and that my cliffs were just as pretty though not as high. I resisted enjoying myself most of the day, resenting all the loading and unloading.

We took a break for lunch, eating cold cuts. Some of the group hiked up a canyon to see some ruins. I told Roxanne, "I have no desire to go hiking in the rocks in this heat; I came to raft. I can hike rocks at home."

Chick went on the hike. Roxanne and Chuck and I floated on down the river to a sandbar, where we stopped, drank a bottle of wine and reclined in the shallow water along the bank under one of our umbrellas planted in the sand. That's when I began to understand what the trip was all about.

Making camp that evening was easier; my tent went up without difficulty and not having kitchen duty was a delight. Jemma played her violin while we drank wine. Big Al, Victoria and Jemma served enchiladas, fruit, beans and guacamole for dinner. My resistance was fading. I was becoming one with the river.

Chick was lost without his wife; he was one of those men who were always losing his glasses, bandana, camera or the beer holder that had been assigned to him for the trip. He quickly appointed me his caretaker. Friendships formed fast on the river.

Sonja Klein

Again I was the first to bed and the first to arise. I used the groover for the first time. It was always placed in a secluded spot; a flotation cushion marked the approach. The procedure was to take the cushion with you to the groover to let others know that the groover was occupied. Next to the groover was a garbage bag with toilet paper and several tabloid newspapers. As the days progressed we discussed the subjects of the tabloids with great humor.

The dress code was nylon quick-drying shorts, tank tops or tee shirts and Teva sandals. Roxanne set up the shower every evening and showered on a daily basis. I bathed in the river that seemed fairly clean but was cloudy with silt and sand.

We stopped at Medicine Hat to replenish our ice, dump garbage and refill the water jugs. The Navajo Trading Post was located on top of the steep cliff. The arduous climb in the intense heat was not for the faint-hearted. I made the trip three times, carrying ice and water. Everyone worked and we had a lunch of cold cuts before we floated off down the river. "I would have paid anyone $20 to fetch and carry up that steep climb," Roxanne observed. "It would be a good way for some college kids to earn money in the summer."

Back on the river we enjoyed a cold beer. I joined Chick in the duckie for a new, lower perspective of the river. Chick and I solved the world's problems and had a nice ride before the evening ritual of unloading, setting up camp and preparing a meal. Roxanne furnished vegetable lasagna and garlic bread washed down with wine and vodka and tonic. After washing the dishes, Chick and I joined the circle for music.

Our last responsibility for a meal was French toast the following morning. Roxanne prepared the French toast, Chuck cooked the sausage and sliced the fruit and Chick and I washed dishes and packed up the kitchen. A routine had evolved; I rounded up the beer holders, folded the chairs and gathered my tent and gear while Chuck and Roxanne took down the shower. The four of us had become a team and were by far the most efficient of the group except for Mario and Ferris.

On the 4th of July a short day of rafting was planned so that we could party and celebrate. After setting up camp on a sandy stretch of beach we planted our umbrella in the sand and sat in the river and drank wine while Tomas and Jemma cooked hamburgers and gave us all a bottle of bubble water to blow bubbles. Tomas had announced that it was costume day and I went into my dry pack and put on a purple spangled Mardi Gras tee shirt before replanting myself back in the river with a glass of wine.

Just as Roxanne, Chuck, Chick and I had settled in the river under the umbrella, Tomas emerged from the bushes wearing an American flag. Jemma was wearing a pillbox hat and net and wearing a little old lady dress.

Most of the afternoon was spent lying in the water under an overhang, drinking wine. Returning to our shaded spot with two glasses of wine, I walked in the river to avoid the hot sand, stepping off into a hole and being caught by the current. Not wearing a life preserver I knew I was going to drown. Just as I went under I yelled, "I'm in trouble." I held both hands each with a full glass of wine above my head as I sank under the river. The next thing I knew Chuck had grabbed me and lifted me out of the water. Not a drop of wine was spilled and everyone had a good laugh about my sinking under with the wine glasses held high. I was glad to be alive.

The hamburgers were gritty but good, and dessert was watermelon and strawberry shortcake washed down with beer, scotch or wine. It was a great 4th of July.

After pancakes the next morning, Chick and I floated down the river in the rubber duckie so that Chuck and Jeanette could have some river sex. We opened our first beer soon after breakfast. The river took advantage of our altered state and we took a wrong turn and went aground. Chick gave the orders, "Jump out and push."

"I'm not getting out in that slime. You're in charge, you get out." After some pushing and pulling we made our way out of the dead end, determined to tell no one.

As we re-entered the river, a park ranger came around the bend in a kayak. As the ranger positioned his boat, he asked Chick, "Where is your life preserver?"

Mine was on but Chick's was lying in the bottom of the rubber duckie under a shitload of beer cans. When the ranger asked what group we were with, Chick pointed to the rafts coming down the river. Once our group saw the ranger, there was a mad scramble to put on life vests. The ranger admonished us to stay in sight of our group at all times and then gave us a safety speech while we humbly listened.

At lunch break I stepped out of the duckie into quicksand, rapidly sinking to my waist and paralyzed with fear. I was terrified. Chuck quickly moved the raft that threatened to go over my head. I began to panic but everyone grouped around me and talked, telling me to be calm, wiggle my toes and move out slowly, which I did. I calmed down and eased out of the quicksand with the group's approval. No one panicked and another funny incident on the river had occurred.

Al, Lenya and Victoria prepared grilled chicken that evening. I was too tired to put up my tent and slept on the ground. At breakfast the following morning I heard the latest—that two women of a larger group camping nearby had asked Al to turn off his jam box, that the music was interfering with their wilderness experience.

Roxanne and Chuck commandeered the rubber duckie the next morning and left Chick and me in charge of the large raft. "I'm not very good at rowing," he admitted.

I replied, "That's not very reassuring." We drank beer and looked for the group all day, making a lot of mistakes. We had an anxious day, responsible for the raft and being out of sight from the group.

We were relieved when we found the group docked and stopped for lunch. I lay down under a rock ledge in the shade with my life preserver as a pillow. Then a scorpion dropped down onto my stomach. Before I could freak, Roxanne flicked it off.

As we made early camp in the hot afternoon sun, Chuck convinced everyone to hike up a canyon to a waterfall, saying, "Trust me; it's only a 15-minute hike and the reward is worth it."

We all trudged behind Chuck. An hour and a half later we arrived at some stagnant, smelly pools. After sitting under a ledge, crowded in the shade, we made the hike back to camp. When we finally settled back at camp I told Chuck, "Thanks for the hike in the hottest part of the day to a pool of smelly water. I know what the hike was really about. You were testing our loyalty and we proved it. You are our captain." We implanted our umbrella in the sand and this time stuck a cocktail table in the sand to hold our wine glasses.

Chick joined us saying, "You look decadent."

Roxanne answered, "So what?"

Mario and Ferris cooked Thai noodles with peanut butter and coconut milk. We sat in the dark talking with our headlamps on. Roxanne asked big Al what it was like living in the communes in the 70's. Al told us about the Hog Farm, a commune near Taos, saying that every few days when money was becoming scarce, some Texas trust-fund hippie would come walking up with money for food and drugs and that it had been fun. Tomas and Lenya had also lived in a commune. Roxanne and I had commented earlier that they thought differently than us capitalist Kleins. We always looked for a way to make money just like we had the inspiration for college kids to make money at Medicine Hat ferrying supplies down to the river for rafters. Again I slept on the ground.

The ranger appeared at breakfast the next morning, saying, "If you clean up this campground I'll forget the safety citation." There was very little trash, but we willingly picked it up and included it with the rest of our trash.

A long day of rafting was ahead—including the dangerous negotiating of Government Rapids. As we approached the rapids, I could hear the roaring of water even though I could not yet see the rocks and boulders we would have to avoid. The rafts pulled over and docked, and the captains of each walked around the corner to survey the scene. I chose not to go because I did not want to be fearful before it was necessary.

Chick scouted the rapids and returned saying, "I figured out the line we'll take." After drinking a beer we set off for the most dangerous part of the trip in a rubber duckie.

The rapids did not sink or eject us and we docked to watch the rafts. Al and Lenya got hung up on the rapids, but the other rafts threw them a line and pulled them off the rocks with no damage. Chuck told us that our swirl through the rapids was not pretty but that any day when you managed to stay onboard was a successful day on the river. The rapids had been both frightening and exhilarating.

The San Juan became sluggish and shallow as we stopped for lunch. We noticed three brightly colored kayaks coming down the river. Chuck, Chick and Al walked out into the middle of the river. Not one of them was under six feet. Roxanne said, "Watch this."

As the kayaks approached, Al's voice boomed, "Have you boys seen the movie *Deliverance?*" Terror was replaced with humor and we all enjoyed the laughter.

The last miles were agonizing as we looked for Clay Bank Park, where we would take the rafts out of the river, knowing it would soon be over. We arrived late in the afternoon, in the heat of the day. Our vehicles and trailers were all there; coolers of cold beer were waiting.

Sonja Klein

The group of women rafters was sitting in the shade on their gear, saying nothing, watching us enjoy the first cold beer in two days.

As we finished deflating the rafts and loading our stuff, one of them approached and asked if she could have a ride to Mexican Hat, that their shuttle service had not delivered their vehicles. Roxanne answered for all of us, "How does it feel to eat crow and ask for help from the people you scorned and were rude to on the river?"

"Not good at all."

"The first lesson of the river is that you never insult anyone because you might need them for help."

We gave three of them a ride in the back of the pickup on top of our gear. The trip took two hours and the temperature was well over a hundred. Paybacks were hell.

My first shower in over a week and the luxury of a bed were not that exciting. I remarked to Roxanne, "I could have done another 30 days." The thin veneer of civilization had worn off quickly. I had become one with the river and the environment. I had peed in the river, floated in the river, sat on its edge, been sucked away by the current and had become mired in the quicksand of its shores. I had never been a water person, reluctant to immerse in water that was not clear. I had conquered my fears and submerged myself in the river.

After a steak dinner in Bluff, I found that sleep in a bed did not come easily and at daylight joined Chick for morning coffee. We had become friends on the river, spending time laughing at our foibles and misadventures. We had conversed about the deep canyon in which we were confined, remarking that it was magnificent. I told him I felt that I was in the vagina of Mother Earth and missed the open skies of Texas. Every day we had only a narrow glimpse of the sky above the river canyon. We saw mule deer, herons, crows, hawks, otters and big horn sheep and were busted by a park ranger. One day Chick had asked, "Do you know where my bandana is?"

I answered, "I'm not responsible for you and I'm not glued to you. Will you get me a beer?" He did so willingly.

We all laughed about Mario, who every morning encouraged us to load up and get on the river before the death star came over the canyon rim. The death star was the unrelenting sun.

That morning Chuck, Roxanne, Chick and I decided to go home via Monument Valley, a three-hour side trip. None of us had ever visited the valley and it seemed a shame to be so close and not view the famous area where many movies and westerns had been filmed. I suspected we were also reluctant for the adventure to end.

We stopped in Mexican Hat for breakfast burritos, encouraging the manager to purchase some shopping carts or hire strong boys to assist rafters. Capitalism was never far from our thoughts. The river below seemed so distant and far away.

The drive through Arizona was pleasant and after paying to drive the rutted roads of the reservation, we solved the Indian problem by agreeing that assimilation was the only answer. Get the Native Americans off the reservation and into society; culture was preserved by the family unit, not by isolation.

By the time we arrived in Farmington we were starved. We found a pub in the downtown area and drank beer and ate sandwiches before continuing on our trip, playing Scrabble and the alphabet game.

We returned to Santa Fe in time to watch the stars emerge. I left the next morning, finding it nice to be behind the wheel again, on the open road. I reflected on the trip for the first five hours. The next four hours were not so much fun.

I thought about Mario and the death star, about our raft that we called The Mother Ship. I pictured Mario's girlfriend, Ferris, sitting in the shade reading poetry. I saw Big Al sitting and patiently cutting up 10 avocados and some onions and tomatoes to make the best guacamole I had ever eaten. A few nights later he had cut up cabbage and fresh veggies for slaw to feed 12. I remembered his jam box and the blues he had played, echoing through the canyon. I envisioned Lenya high-centered on the rocks of Government Rapids, strong, calm and defiant as she worked the raft off the rocks to safety. I remembered Victoria, good-natured and kind.

I smiled when I remembered Tomas cooking in the American flag and his courage to bring a 7-year-old on a rafting trip. I thought of Jemma having the added responsibility of Ami, and her grace and good manners. She never complained or had a dour expression. And there was Ami, who behaved, was quiet, cutting paper or coloring in the shade of a rock ledge while Lenya and I played a game of hearts with Roxanne and Chuck. I laughed out loud when I remembered floating in the river to muffle the farts from eating beans.

And then I took a good look at myself and the rafting voyage of self-discovery. I realized that I could do anything to which I set my mind. I had learned to put up my tent, condense my gear into two dry compression bags in a few minutes, paddle a duckie all day without being sore, manage to stay alive in the wilderness, haul gear up and down sand banks without tiring. I had been the oldest one on the trip and had the most energy. I was surprised to find that I was in excellent shape. When I finally surrendered to the river, I learned about myself. I was the good German who tried to be the best at whatever I attempted and could take that aspect of myself and translate it into any action or inaction, but the most important lesson I learned was from my body.

In the past I had thought of my body as an ugly shell that I had to carry around and of my spirit as strong and beautiful, not confined to the ugly shell—thus my affinity with turtles. On the river I lost the awareness of my body maybe because the only mirrors were the eyes of my fellow rafters. I did not care about the cottage cheese on my upper arms, the varicose veins on my upper legs or the wrinkles over my upper lip; instead I wore them with honor. My body was a well-functioning machine that had served me well on the river.

I had never felt so much myself as on that drive to Alpine. The wide Texas skies made my heart soar like an eagle, and the lightning storms on the plains were full of energy and power. Between Van Horn and Alpine I witnessed lightning strike and a circle of fire emerge in the pouring rain and then a rainbow.

When I stopped at the post office in Barksdale to pick up the mail that had accumulated in my absence, my friend Judy remarked, "You seem energized from the trip." She was intuitive.

17

The Trans-Siberian railroad

As I stepped off the Aeroflot airplane after flying 25 hours, my first thoughts were, "What have I done to myself? I'll never see Texas again." I was in Vladivostok, Russia, on the far eastern border looking out over the Pacific Ocean, a scant few hours from North Korea, China and Japan. The weather was cool and pleasant, and the adrenalin of the moment banished my fatigue. A bus ferried the passengers from the tarmac to the small terminal, and a perfunctory stamp on my passport sped me through customs.

The drive into the town of Vladivostok was along a boulevard dotted with flowers and trees. Beside the road were flower vendors selling gladioli and roses. Beyond the road were small wooden houses with lush gardens. The land was hilly, sloping down to the sea.

The hotel was modern with all the amenities including Internet service. A casino was located off the lobby. Most of the tourists were Chinese, Korean and Japanese. The city of 600,000 was located on rolling hills. The parks and plazas were dotted with petunias, marigolds and salvia, all in full bloom. Most of the cars on the streets were Japanese. Japan, China and Korea were all accessible by ferry from the port of Vladisvostok, which is kept open in the winter by an ice-breaking vessel.

In 1860 the Russian Empire annexed an important piece of land from China on the Pacific Ocean. The place was named Vladivostok, meaning, "Rule the East." Over the years, Vladivostok grew from a naval outpost to a thriving city. Due to its importance as a border zone city and being the base of the Russian Pacific Naval Fleet, the city was declared off limits to foreigners and most Russians following World War II. In 1992 the city was declared officially open and began to welcome tourists.

The traffic was helter-skelter with few stoplights. The room at the Hyundai Hotel was $250 per night. The morning fog bathed the harbor. Two of the main industries other than the naval base were the shipment of timber and the import of cars from Japan. Six feet of snow falls annually on the city, and there was much evidence of construction due to the Asian-Pacific Conference scheduled for the coming year.

An evening meal at the Versailles Hotel was quite elegant in a room with gold gilt, chandeliers and heavy velvet window coverings. The food was a gourmet's delight—halibut, pork tenderloin, grilled eggplant, cabbage and carrot salad and of course vodka and wine.

A tour of the town the following morning included monuments to soldiers, a 1938 Russian submarine and a museum honoring the indigenous settlers as well as the Mongolians and Chinese who inhabited the area before being conquered by Russia. The symbol of Vladivostok is the tiger. The symbol of Russia is the bear—bumbling, dumb, good-natured, but ferocious if provoked.

A room in the museum was devoted to Yul Brynner, a native of the city whose family were wealthy jewelers and performers. The border patrol was honored in yet another part of the museum, dedicated to those who patrolled and protected the border with China, a short distance to the south. The tour guide in the museum expounded on the border problem with China along the Amur River, "You can't trust the Chinese; they're sneaky." I found it quite humorous that the Russians did not adhere to politically correct statements.

As I strolled along the waterfront by the plaza decorated with a monument to fallen soldiers, I noticed a wedding party. The bride was in a beautiful traditional wedding dress with a hoop skirt. The groom wore a vanilla-colored suit and vest and pale patent loafers. A photographer, parent figures and friends accompanied them. The best man was wearing a pink sash like a beauty pageant contestant, and the maid of honor had on the same. The best man carried a bottle of champagne and glasses. The wedding party paused at the monument for a sensuous kiss, photograph and toast and then moved on to an arch, where they repeated the behavior. Everyone was smiling, laughing and happy. Their car parked nearby was decorated with ribbons and fresh flowers.

When I inquired as to the significance I was told that marriages are only finalized in the civil office, not in church. After the civil signing, the couple and close friends drive around town drinking champagne and taking pictures at all the important monuments. At the end of the day they retire to a party with more friends and family and feast and dance all night. In the coming days I was to observe this ritual throughout Russia—young brides and grooms driving about with flowers and champagne.

Honk if you married Sonja

After a day of touring the city, I boarded the famous Trans-Siberian Railroad from the picturesque train station built in 1912 and decorated with Socialist-Realist artwork.

My train trip on the Trans-Siberian Railroad would be a journey of 10,000 kilometers (about 6,214 miles) on the longest railroad in the world. It took 25 years to build and was completed in 1913 and in the 13 days that I was on that train it was never one minute late.

As I boarded the train I heard comments. "Are you nuts? Do you expect me to spend 13 days with a stranger in that cubicle? What do you mean the bathroom is down at the end of the car? What if it's busy? How many cars down is the shower car? What toilet is closed when the train is stopped? You must be kidding. How far down is the bar car? I can't believe this. How much did I pay for this? Whatever it was, it was too much."

My assigned car was number six, and my compartment was number five, located in the middle of a 17-car train—a chartered tourist train with scheduled stops across Siberia and Mongolia—destination Moscow. The compartment, which I immediately named "cell cinco," was 7' X 10'.

There was no apparent storage in the cubicle. There were some hooks on the wall by the sliding doors, a fold down café table under the window and two plywood slabs covered by thin foam mattresses called sofas by day and beds by night. With great effort the slabs could be raised to discover storage below but only after the table had been lifted and secured.

My roommate, Eugenie, was a Russian woman in her late 60's from Connecticut. She was born in the U.S. from Russian emigrants and was retracing her father's footsteps across Russia. She spoke Russian fluently but snored voraciously, her language skills an asset and her snoring a liability.

Eugenie was nice and friendly and thankfully an orderly person. We soon had our suitcases stashed under our slab beds with the help of our car's attendant, Alexandrov. Our railroad car had two attendants, Alexandrov and Tatiana, each working 12-hour shifts. After locking ourselves in our cell three times we discovered a call button that would summon one of them. The third time we paid attention to the instructions concerning our door.

Sonja Klein

Tea or coffee was served 24 hours a day in silver holders with clear glass inserts on a tray with a damask napkin and cookies, biscuits or chocolate. We did not abuse it.

Once the acceptance of the situation became apparent, the inhabitants of the train descended into friendliness, arrogance or outright hostility. Essentially we were all dorm mates for 13 days, and the choice was to make the best of it or complain. I chose to have some fun.

Our first meal on the train that evening was caviar, warm champagne, vodka and food that I barely remember except that it was delicious. Sleep did not come easily. From the creaking, rocking and brakes squealing, the snoring from my roommate, who was 18 inches away and the noises from the adjoining compartments, I awoke feeling sleep deprived. I did not even think about the days and hours lost on the flight from Houston to Vladivostok. The train moved on through the night across eastern Siberia.

That first night on the Tran-Siberian Railroad was the first of many sleepless evenings, alleviated only by the delight of morning coffee and sweet treats. The hearty breakfast was an eye-opener enhanced by the beauty of vast far eastern Russia. The scenery from the window was one of large forests, lush wide rivers and small villages with the ever-present gardens and greenhouses. Options in the dining car included yogurt, sausage, cheese, oatmeal, fresh bananas or apples, eggs, bacon that was more like ham, and wonderful hearty bread or crepes accompanied by butter and sugary jams.

Midmorning the train halted in Khabarovsk, the second largest city in the Russian Far East after Vladivostok. A guided tour of the city provided information and photo opportunities. Khabarovsk was founded in 1858 by the Cossacks as a military observation post and later became an important industrial center for the region. In 1894 a department of the Russian Geographical Society was formed in Khabarovsk and began initiating a foundation of libraries, theaters and museums in the city. Since then, cultural life has flourished.

The city has a long and pleasant waterfront, as Khabarovsk is built on three hills overlooking the mighty Amur River, just beyond its confluence with the Ussuri River. The Khabarovsk area is 52 percent forested, and the city boasts a population of 600,000 in a territory of 800,000 square kilometers. The distance from China is only 80 kilometers, approximately 60 miles. The forests are populated with pine and fir trees. The climate in summer is humid, with conifers growing beside liana and heat-loving plants. Lenin Square, one of the largest squares in Russia, dominates this city of many technological universities.

Khabarovsk is a modern city of parks and abundant flowers. The annual rainfall is 74 inches, and from December through May the Amur River is frozen to the extent that people can walk across to their dachas on the other side. The last defining battle of the Russian civil war was fought in 1922, 40 miles west of Khabarovsk. Monuments to fallen soldiers dominated the city squares, the most notable being the one to the fallen soldiers of World War II, in which the Russians had three times more casualties than the U.S. did.

We spent the next few days on board the train traversing the great wilderness of Siberia through towns named Chita, Obluchye, Arkhara, Magdagachi, Skovorodino, Yerofey Pavlovich, Amazar, Mogocha, Chernishevsk and Petrovski.

Lunch was the main meal served on the train. The first course was usually a cabbage or carrot slaw with fresh minced dill with oil and vinegar dressing. Salad was followed by soup with cabbage and beets, sometimes with noodles and always with fresh dill and parsley. The main course was pan-fried fish, sliced pork or beef stroganoff with potatoes and often cucumbers. Ice cream, sherbet or a strudel pastry with apples completed the meal. The meals were hearty, fresh and tasty. The evening meal was lighter—fish, salad and potatoes.

A series of lectures was offered during those days, the first being one on the Russian language, which was not that difficult once one mastered the Cyrillic alphabet. I returned from the lecture with the basics of "please, thank you and you are welcome." The rest of my Russian vocabulary was delivered with hand gestures and simple body language.

I enjoyed the lectures and additional information. The terrain of the Russian Federation consists of broad plains with low hills west of the Urals and vast coniferous forests and tundra in Siberia. The climate ranges from warm steppes in the south through humid continental in much of European Russia. The Ural Mountains divide Asia from Europe. The climate is subarctic in Siberia to tundra in the polar north, and winters vary from cool along the Black Sea coast to frigid in Siberia.

The Russian Federation covers almost twice the area of the United States of America. It occupies much of Eastern Europe and all of northern Asia, extending for 5,000 miles from the Baltic Sea in the west to the Pacific Ocean in the east and for 1,500 to 2,500 miles from the Arctic Ocean in the north to the Black Sea, the Caucasus, the Altai and Sayan Mountains and the Amur and Ussuri rivers in the south. The Urals form the conventional geographic boundary between the European and Siberian parts of Russia. The country is bordered by Norway and Finland in the northwest, by Estonia, Latvia, Belarus and Ukraine in the west, by Georgia and Azerbaijan in the southwest and by Kazakhstan, Mongolia and China along the southern land border.

Although the Russian Federation is the largest country in land area, it is unfavorably located in relation to the major sea-lanes of the world. Much of the country lacks the proper soils and climates (either too cold or too dry) for agriculture. It does, however, have enormous resources of oil and gas as well as precious metals.

Our female guides were well informed as to the facts of their country and their lectures continued to keep me entertained. The population of Russia is over 141,000,000. The ethnic composition is 80 percent Russian, 4 percent Tatar, and many other minorities. The primary language is Russian, with other languages such as Turkic and Uralic. Education is compulsory for nine years and the literacy rate is 99.6 percent. Russian Orthodox leads the religions with 18 percent, followed by Muslims at 15 percent. Most Russians are nonpracticing believers due to 70 years of Soviet rule. There is no Sunday observance and all stores are open seven days a week.

The days on the train had given me the semblance of familiarity as I asked the Russians onboard why they smiled rarely. I received two answers: "We don't have anything to smile about after 70 years of Communism." "Russia is about pain and suffering."

While the lectures were informative, my co-travelers interesting and the food and drink consuming, I still craved the countryside and was looking forward to Mongolia. After a brief stop in Ulan Ude, the train turned south to Ulaan Baatar (Red Hero). We reached the border crossing between Russia and Mongolia at 10:00 P.M. in whatever time zone. Having lost 15 hours to time zones, I was now regaining them. Some nights the newsletter instructed us to turn the clocks back one hour. Other nights I set my clock back two hours. The 25- and 26-hour days became quite normal. As we approached the Mongolian border the train personnel instructed all passengers to surrender all papers at 10:00

Honk if you married Sonja

P.M. Four hours later, the papers were returned and the train traveled a few miles into Mongolia, where we went through the same procedure only with Mongolian officials, finally clearing Mongolian customs at 6:00 in the morning in some unknown time zone. In all, I crossed eight time zones before reaching Moscow. I finally gave up and just surrendered to being in the twilight zone.

Mongolia looked like New Mexico. I observed mostly dairy cattle and horses as well as herds of sheep, camels with two humps and goats herded by solitary Mongolians. I overheard a comment on the train, "They look just like the Mongolians on the History Channel." There were few trees and the terrain was rolling with modest grasslands. The temperature was in the 80's. The annual rainfall is 15 inches per year.

More lectures kept us in touch with our surroundings. Mongolia was under Soviet rule until 1991, when it became an independent democratic country. The total population of Mongolia is 2,600,000 and the capital of Ulaan Baatar has 800,000 inhabitants and lies 4,000 feet above sea level. The unit of currency is called the Tugrik. One U.S. dollar equals 1,100 Turgiks. The religion of Mongolia is Buddhist. There were only three monasteries left after Stalin, but more have been constructed. I toured one monastery, beautifully nestled on a hill above Ulaan Baatar.

Pork, lamb and eggplant were served for lunch in a local hotel before driving two hours to Gorkhi Terelj National Park and a traditional Nomadic ger camp. Gers or yurts are the round homes of the nomadic Mongolians. At one time, 90 percent of native Mongolians followed a nomadic lifestyle. Now over 30 percent of the population lives in the city of Ulaan Baatar, which spreads from east to west along a large wide fertile valley. The Bogd Khan, Bayanzurkh, Chingeltei and Songino Khairkhan Mountains surround the city. The Tuul River runs from east to west in the south of the city. I gave up trying to pronounce the names.

Gorkhi Terelj National Park boasts some of the loveliest scenery in the country and lies on the edge of the Khenti Mountains, where Genghis Khan was born. After visiting a traditional ger, I had a dinner of barbecued sheep, mare's milk yogurt and fermented mare's milk. The yogurt was salty and the fermented mare's milk tasted yeasty, not something I would ever order in a restaurant. Mongolian herdsmen approached the campground. One had a golden eagle on his arm; another held a falcon. The birds with their bright eyes were magnificently perched on the arms of their trainers.

The return drive to Ulaan Baatar was emphasized by grinding gears, potholes, honking trucks and prayers from this passenger. While the roads were minimal, the city was not lacking. Department stores selling Gucci and Versace were busy with Oriental customers and the market was a sensory bonanza. Mongolia appeared to be a thriving country and the inhabitants are apparently prospering.

The train beckoned once again. The eight-hour border crossing was repeated in reverse and the Trans-Siberian Express clicked, clacked and groaned through the night, our next destination Ulan Ude, capital of the autonomous republic of Buryat, located in the middle of Siberia.

More lectures punctuated the long days spent on the train—Siberia: Melting Pot of Cultures and Spiritual Beliefs, Collapse of the Soviet Union and Its Effect on Ordinary People and Let's Talk About Russian Music. Animism is still a part of the Russian culture. The people are very superstitious. Flowers on graves are placed in even numbers and given to lovers for happiness in odd numbers. They don't like banks. They talk late at night on their cell phones, spilling their problems. But they do not talk about sex or use seat belts. The Ouija board is alive and well in Russia.

There is a culturally strong and large indigenous population. The collapse of the Soviet Union left many people without jobs or pensions, but laws were enacted allowing them to own their own flats and to buy a share of the country's industry. The people seem to be adjusting and thriving. One notable sign was seeing cars with only one passenger. There is now one car for every three people and many of the cars are not Russian.

The evening lecture on Russian music featured classical as well as folk music. The vodka and high spirits contributed to everyone's night of pleasure.

Morning found the train stopped in Ulan Ude, which means red river, the capital of the autonomous Republic of Buryatia, located in the middle of Siberia. The best interpretation I received about Buryatia was that it was similar to an Indian reservation. Ulan Ude is home to the largest ethnic group in Siberia, the Buryats, who were originally nomadic herders, and have cultural and language similarities to the Mongolians and religious similarities to the Tibetan Buddhists.

In 1649 the Cossacks founded the city as a winter encampment on the Selenga River. The city later prospered as a major trading post along the tea route between China and Irkutsk. The Cossacks erected a fort and traded for furs, primarily sable, and fortified the border from China and Mongolia. Ulan Ude is also called, "The Gate to the East."

Imagine disembarking from a train and hearing the tune, "We Wish You a Merry Christmas" followed by an announcement in a foreign language. The computer music without words preceded every announcement, and after the miles and time zones I didn't know where or who I was, just smiled and kept on walking through the train station. At that point nothing disturbed me. I had been captured by Mother Russia.

It was a welcome relief to be off the train as I toured the town. Ulan Ude is a large city of over a million. New construction is in evidence. The national circus is housed in a large amphitheater. One of the main industries is the manufacture of train parts, which employs over 7,000 workers. Fourteen colleges dot the city. Buryatia had been a separate republic before becoming part of Mongolia and then was later absorbed into Russia. Seventeen nationalities exist, 25 percent of them Buryats. The republic is as large as Germany.

Fifty kilometers from Ulan Ude is a unique village inhabited by the Old Believers, a dissident group from the Baltic area and Poland. In 1653 the Russian Orthodox Church changed procedures involving the crossing of the chest from two fingers to three fingers or vice versa. I wasn't entirely clear. These people refused to change and were exiled to Siberia. The walk took over one year, and there are currently 4,000 of them in Buryatia. They have retained their own customs and language and have toured all over the world giving performances of their culture.

Because there are limited numbers of the Old Believers, marriage involves going back nine generations before approval in order to establish no close genetic kinship.

They entertained with a show of dancing and singing and delicious food—squash rings with potato salad, carrot and cabbage slaw, cucumber sweet pickles, sliced ham, sweet rice pudding and of course warm champagne and vodka.

One comment came from an English-speaking Old Believer matron, "Our people walked for a year and received no monuments like your American Indians."

A fantastic day evolved as the train wound through tunnels and around cliffs along the shoreline of Lake Baikal, traveling on the Circumbaikal Railway, the original line used by the Trans-Siberian before the present-day route was completed.

Sonja Klein

Lake Baikal was one of the largest obstacles in the building of the Trans-Siberian Railway. The lake is the oldest (25–30 million years), deepest and largest by volume freshwater lake on Earth. Baikal has as much water as all of the Great Lakes combined—20 percent of the fresh water on the planet.

In the early 1900's, the line ended on each side of the lake, and a special icebreaker ferryboat was purchased from England to connect the railway. In the winter, sleighs were used to move passengers and cargo from one side of the lake to the other until the completion of the Lake Baikal spur along the southern edge of the lake.

The train stopped at the mouth of the Ungara River, and I took a ferry across the river to the village of Litsvyanka, a charming little lakeside town. I visited the Limnological Museum, which highlighted the complex ecosystem of the lake and where I saw the nerpa, Lake Baikal's unique freshwater seal. Of the 336 rivers that flow into Lake Baikal, only the Ungara River flows out and eventually into the Arctic Ocean. Over 100,000 seals inhabit the lake and the water is clear down to 40 meters. Sturgeon and omul are found in the lake. The forests are abundant with larch, pine, cedar and birch. Moose, bear, lumber wolves, lynx, raccoons, weasels and sable inhabit the land.

I visited the open-air Wooden Architecture Museum, a replica wooden village from the 1800's and enjoyed a picnic lunch of grilled whole fish, pork, pickled vegetables and roasted potatoes on the shore of the Ungara River. The day was delightful and pleasantly cool. Without my Navajo coat of many colors I would have been uncomfortable and again I was accused many times of purchasing my coat in those cold climates. The coat had become my talisman for my adventurous travels. I returned to a warm welcoming train, and we moved through western Siberia.

The lectures were enchanting. Beginning in 1581, the Cossacks crossed the Urals and captured the land of the Sib Er, which means Sleeping Land. The Irkutsk region borders the lake and has a population of about two million. In 1900 the city of Irkutsk earned the title, "The Paris of Siberia." The current population is over 600,000. Alexander II began the Trans-Siberian Railroad in 1891 and the first train reached this capital of eastern Siberia in 1898.

The Cossacks founded Irkutsk in 1661 on the crossroad of the famous trade routes. The region is rich in metals and minerals.

Honk if you married Sonja

I visited the house of Count Vronsky, who was one of the Decembrists, the group of noble dissidents who rebelled against Tsar Nicholas I in the 1800's. As a result he and others were exiled to Irkutsk in Siberia, where they lived for 20 years before being allowed to return to St. Petersburg. Irkutsk became the major center of intellectual and social life for exiled Russian artists, officers and nobles. Much of the city's cultural heritage comes from them. Many of their wooden houses, adorned with ornate hand-carved decorations, survive today in stark contrast to the standard Soviet apartment blocks that surround them.

Count Vronsky's home has been restored, and there in his home I attended a classical concert of music by Chopin and Schubert and poetry readings of Pushkin, Russia's favorite poet. A wonderful meal was served after the concert—lamb, fish filet, soup, cabbage and baked Alaska.

The train rolled on through the vast Siberian taiga, the immense forests of pine, larch, spruce and fir, as we passed through towns named Tayshet, Yurty, Ilanskaya, Krasnoyavarsk (the geographic center of Russia), Mariinsk and Novosibirsk.

We spent a day touring Novosibirsk. The town did not exist before the Trans-Siberian Railway was built. It was founded in 1893 as the future site of the rail line's Ob River crossing and is now the largest city in Siberia. Novosibirsk boasts opera and ballet companies, the largest in the country. During World War II, most of the treasures of Russia were stored in the Opera House. I visited the railroad museum and the mineral museum on the outskirts of town close to an area of universities.

In the 1950's many scientists moved to Novosibirsk, where scientific research was conducted. The city also contained a large flour mill and was modern and busy.

It was Saturday evening and the main square in the center of town was hosting live music and dancing. The tunes varied from rhumba and samba to waltz and polka. Middle-aged couples dressed in the styles of the 50's were dancing and drinking champagne. Women danced with women and the couples moved their feet in classic ballroom steps.

Still journeying in Asia, the train stopped in Ekaterinburg, also called Sverdlovsk. Imperial Russia ended here in 1918 with the execution of the last tsar, Nicholas II, and the imperial family—three daughters, a son and his wife. Today the Cathedral-on-the-Blood has been constructed on the site of the executions. The city is also known as the birthplace of

Boris Yeltsin. Ekaterinberg was named after St. Catherine, patron saint of mines. The area is rich in minerals—gold, copper and iron. Over 800 minerals have been discovered in the Urals. Peter the Great founded the city after fighting Sweden for control of the Baltic.

Since the beginning of the 19th century the city has been an important administrative, mining and Ural-wide machine-building center and is the historical and economic center of the Urals. The city has been open to foreigners only since 1990, due to the many defense plants. A drive outside the city took me to a marker designating the line between Asia and Europe, where I stood with one foot in Asia and one foot in Europe. Champagne and chocolates were passed around and everyone took advantage of a Kodak moment.

The train clattered through Europe and the Urals to Kazan, the capital of the Republic of Tatarstan. Kazan is an old city founded in 1723 with a fascinating multiethnic history on the Volga River. The city is large and bustling, with a Hyatt hotel being built for the Shanghai Conference, which was to be held in 2009. There is a big mall with an Ikea; and Volvo, Toyota and Mercedes auto dealerships flank the roadways. Young people rollerblade along the river speaking on cell phones and listening to music.

Kazan has well over a million in population. The Tatars, who make up a majority of the population, are actually Turkic Muslims. Over 50 percent of the population speaks Turkic, and the predominant religion is Islam. There are 106 nationalities in Russia, difficult for an American to understand. It is hard to imagine governing a country almost twice as big as the U.S. with all those languages and ethnicities.

The architecture of Kazan is European, with a stunning opera house. Nureyev, the famous ballet dancer, was born in Tatarstan. The Kremlin or fortress in Kazan dates from the 1700's and contains an elegant mosque within its ancient walls.

Women were selling fresh cut flowers along the river. In broken Russian I tried to purchase a bouquet of flowers but had no rubles. A kind Russian woman with many smiles and gestures gave me a handful of fresh, long-stemmed colorful gladioli. She refused my dollars and accepted a hug instead. The flowers remained in cell cinco for the remainder of the trip.

A boat cruise on the wide Volga ended the evening with dancing and singing. The last leg of the trip was ahead—Moscow.

Honk if you married Sonja

Moscow is the capital of the expansive Russian Federation and the largest city, with over 10 million in population. Moscow is pronounced with a long O. There is no cow in Moscow.

Our female guides continued to lecture. Russia is a federal republic with a bicameral legislative body. The president is head of state and the prime minister is head of government. Reforms have been implemented in the areas of tax, banking, labor and land codes. Growth is steady and inflation is below 10 percent. Oil, natural gas, metals and timber account for more that 80 percent of exports and 32 percent of government revenues. The manufacturing basis is dilapidated and must be modernized. Russia has made little progress in building the rule of law—the bedrock of a modern market economy. The middle class is growing, and the country is optimistic and is very supportive of Putin, who was In charge at the time of my trip.

Moscow was founded in 1147 and rose to prominence during Mongol domination. After 200 years of Mongol domination, the Principality of Muscovy was able to conquer and absorb surrounding principalities. In the early 17th century, a new Romanov Dynasty continued this expansion across Siberia to the Pacific. Under Peter I, who ruled from 1682 to 1725, hegemony was extended to the Baltic Sea, and the country was renamed the Russian Empire. More territorial acquisitions were made in the 19th century. The imperial household was overthrown in 1917, and the Communists under Lenin seized power and formed the USSR. The USSR in 1991 splintered into Russia and 14 other independent republics.

My farewell to the Trans-Siberian Railroad was short and sweet as I exited one of the nine train stations in Moscow. That faithful train had carried me 10,000 kilometers across Russia and into Mongolia, still on time. I cannot say I was sad to leave, but I can say I have a lot of respect for the Russian train system.

Driving to the city's center, I passed the Bolshoi Theater, which at the time was under renovation, and the infamous Lubyanka prison, as well as the KGB headquarters, now government offices.

A Russian joke: "From the top of the KGB building you can see Siberia." Siberia was the home of dissidents, free thinkers and independents, somewhat similar to our West. If you didn't fit in you, were sent to Siberia. While Siberia may have only two seasons, winter and summer, it is a fertile and beautiful region with room for everyone.

I spent the afternoon in Red Square, perhaps the most recognizable symbol of Russia. St. Basil's Cathedral dominates the square. It is one of the most colorful and vibrant cathedrals I have ever seen. The square was surrounded by expensive department stores and the crowds were intense.

The Moscow Kremlin or fort reflects Russia's medieval past. The Kremlin walls extend for 1.5 miles. Inside the fortress of the Kremlin resided the tsars and their families. Within the Kremlin are palaces, government buildings, cathedrals and the Armory Museum.

I spent the afternoon in the Armory Museum, viewing such treasures as religious icons, Fabergé eggs, bejeweled chalices, scepters, magnificent crowns and Catherine the Great's ballgowns and shoes. She was corseted to a 17-inch waist. No wonder she often fainted! The tiring day ended with a light dinner of chicken kabobs and vegetable crepes.

After a wonderful buffet Russian breakfast, I visited the Tretyakov Gallery, founded by a 19th century Russian merchant who spent 40 years collecting and preserving Russian art. The pieces date from the 11th century to the present and include mosaics, icons, paintings and sculptures—over 35,000 items.

I found Moscow to be a traffic-congested, busy but beautiful city and departed in the late afternoon for one more train ride—the express to St. Petersburg.

Business class on the express train was quite different—roomy, comfortable seats, a smooth ride and complimentary meal and drink service. The restored palace hotel in St. Petersburg was a welcome relief after a long day. The Helvetia Hotel was yellow, European in style and surrounded a courtyard off the busy streets of St. Petersburg. A room, a bed and privacy were sheer luxury.

St. Petersburg was founded in 1703 near the Gulf of Finland on the Neva River. In 1712 it became the capital of Russia. St. Petersburg is built in European style and is often called, "The Venice of the North." Forty-one islands make up the city. There are over 60 canals with 150 miles of waterways. Today the population is 4.7 million, and it is the second largest city in the Russian Federation. I found it to be the most beautiful city I have ever visited.

Old buildings and palaces dominate St. Petersburg, but the most beautiful feature is the Winter Palace, the home of the tsars and royalty of Russia. The Winter Palace has 1,000 rooms, and nothing had prepared me for its grandeur and delight. Hours were spent walking through much of the restored palace and the adjacent Hermitage Museum. The guidebook said that the walk was 14 miles if done completely. While I don't believe I walked 14 miles, it seemed as though I had done at least three or four miles. Nearby I viewed the Stroganoff Palace. Count Stroganoff had only one hand and instructed his chef to prepare a dish he could eat with one hand—beef stroganoff.

I visited the Peter and Paul Fortress, named for the saints. It was one of the first structures built in the city. The guns were never fired and it was never used as a fortress. The 26 wars fought between Russia and Sweden came to an end before the fortress was completed. Instead it was used as a prison for dissidents. All of the tsars and tsarinas are buried in the cathedral. In 1998 the remains of the last tsar, Nicholas II, and his family were discovered and entombed in a small chapel within the cathedral.

I visited the Church of Spilled Blood, where Tsar Alexander II was assassinated. Next on the day's tour was St. Isaac's Cathedral located near the river. It took 40 years to build. It was designed by a French architect and was rebuilt after Napoleon destroyed the city.

The foundation is 21 feet thick, the walls 15 feet thick. The oak doors engraved with bronze reliefs weigh 10 tons. Three domes of different sizes dominate the interior. The mosaics inside the cathedral are splendid and intricately detailed. The Russians used mosaics rather than oil paintings in some of their cathedrals because the smoke from the candles destroyed the paintings.

After a light evening meal, I enjoyed a canal boat cruise along the waters of St. Petersburg. The canal was clean. The miles of palaces and restored European-style buildings made a memory of beauty I will hold forever.

The following morning I boarded a hydrofoil for a ride up the Neva River to the site where Peter the Great built his estate named Peterhof on a ridge by the Gulf of Finland, 19 miles outside St. Petersburg. I was not prepared for the splendor of Peterhof.

After disembarking from the hydrofoil and standing on the dock, I saw the palace in front, at the head of a canal. The view took my breath away. The imperial residence is surrounded with extensive parks and gardens intended to rival Versailles, complete with an array of gilded statues, magnificent palaces and gravity-fed fountains. Peter the Great accomplished his purpose. Peterhof outshines Versailles.

Peter the Great wanted Russia to become more like Europe. He required the Russian nobility to shave and taxed those who would not part with their long beards.

Peter the Great had a sense of humor. Among the fountains and courtyards in the hundreds of acres are joke fountains. Certain rocks when stepped on squirt. Children dominated the joke fountains, and it was pleasant to hear the laughter and shouts of children sprayed by cool water in any language.

Inside the palace's 54 rooms that are open to the public, shoe covers are required to protect the delicately inlaid parquet floors. The palace rooms are ornate, gilded in gold and were beautifully restored after the Nazi occupation during World War II. Many palaces of the imperial family grace the parks and grounds surrounding Peterhof and are in a state of restoration. A fascinating book to read is the biography of Peter the Great, entitled of course, *Peter the Great*. He was a visionary and interesting man.

The Nazis came within miles of St. Petersburg, besieged it for almost two years and retreated in defeat. One remark overheard, "I know why the Nazis didn't enter St. Petersburg. They had it too good in the palaces outside the city."

A bus took me on the journey from Peterhof to Catherine's palace. The trip led through the suburbs of St. Petersburg, past new developments and large two-story suburban homes. I stopped for lunch in Pushkin, the site of the royal residence, Catherine's Palace, originally built in 1717 by Catherine I.

Putin celebrated his 50th birthday at this restaurant, which was made of logs. Caviar, cheese, cabbage, cucumbers, fish, pork and potato soup were served with champagne and vodka to typical Russian music.

Again I was not prepared for the grandeur of Catherine's Palace. Elizabeth, the daughter of Catherine, expanded the palace and named it in honor of her mother. The palace is painted pale blue with white trim. The entrance and stables are beyond imagination. The palace tour again requires shoe covers to protect the inlaid floors. The gold-gilded rooms and furnishings are magnificent. The fully restored Amber Room was a highlight of the tour—a room decorated entirely with carved amber panels in gold, green and ivory.

Honk if you married Sonja

The restoration from Nazi destruction began in 1979, with the U.S. furnishing $21 million and the Germans $7 million. The restoration continues.

My final dinner in Russia was in Tchaikovsky's home—chicken Kiev, cabbage and baked apples, toasted with champagne. I left parts of me in Mother Russia, parts that needed to be left, and brought back some of Russia to Texas.

The immense wealth and size of Russia and the generosity and kindness of the people will remain with me forever. I must admit I did not expect the ornate palaces, the magnificent cathedrals, the natural beauty of Siberia and the modernity of Mongolia. As always, traveling dispels myths. The rocks and dirt of Real County welcomed me home, and I once again kissed the ground of Texas.

18

The dedication

For months, I had been dreading having to speak at the dedication of a church in Hockley, Texas. I can talk forever in a group of friends or even strangers. In front of children I am an awesome speaker, but to stand at a podium in a church and give a speech causes gallons of perspiration to pour out of my armpits.

It all started with my mother's failing health at the age of 80. She had gotten to the point that she needed someone with her at all times, and the family friend that had cleaned my mother's home for some 30 years gave up her other jobs and went to work at Mother's full time, five days a week. Helen's skin was black, but her heart and soul were the same as mine. We were the same age, and I felt as though she were my sister even if her lifestyle and mine were not the same, and our backgrounds were just as diverse.

Helen was deeply religious. Her husband of over 30 years worked as a welder for the county and was a minister on the weekends. He had a dream and a vision of a church on a corner lot that Helen had inherited from her family. The corner lot was next to a lot on which their neat brick home across the railroad tracks stood in the tiny town of Hockley.

In an effort to accumulate the money with which to build the church, Helen collected newspapers and aluminum cans and sold candy and drinks to the children in her community. She and Milam held services in their home on Wednesdays and Sundays and had a small gathering that included some of her five children and their spouses, as well as part of her and Milam's extended family.

Helen shared her dreams with my mother, and at some point Mother decided to build the church for Helen and Milam. Mother's health had more or less kept her housebound. For someone as energetic and full as life as my mother, it was similar to a prison sentence. The four of us children were all over 50 and stable and off her worry list. Mother had sold her home in Colorado that she loved and had a chunk of change, having made a substantial profit off the Colorado ski resort market.

Honk if you married Sonja

Together Mother and Helen designed the church and had plans drawn; and Mother engaged her cousin Ozzie, a solid German builder who had built my parents' home at the farm when my father retired. I was given progress reports as the structure became reality. Though her body was failing as she was gradually losing her mobility, Mother had a project and a mission to keep her mind active.

At some point in the construction she asked if I would speak on her behalf at the dedication, and I immediately answered that I would. I was in the habit of going for the weekend every month to stay with her and giving my brother Allan and his wife Alma a break. Allan and Alma had moved in with Mother, and my other two brothers lived less than five minutes away. It was a long drive from the Nueces Canyon ranch where I lived, some six or seven hours, depending whether I stopped in Austin for a visit with my daughter Molly, who was a student at the University of Texas. The visits always left me emotionally drained and a few pounds heavier, as I usually sat around and ate the entire time I was there. That's just what you do when you go to Mother's house.

I had put my peace of mind in jeopardy from the minute I agreed to speak until that moment of truth when I would give my speech. Over the Christmas holidays I learned that the date of the dedication had been set—January 21. I had written a few notes toward a speech but was not in love with the effort. Nothing I wrote seemed sufficient, and that was unusual for me.

I had committed myself to picking up Aunt Beverly in Kerrville on the way to Mother's for the dedication. I was looking forward to the company on the long familiar drive to the area north of Houston, where my family had settled back in the 1840's. Aunt Beverly was pleasant company, and we talked long and hard and shared our grief for our losses. She had lost her husband and only child within 13 months. The trip was short and I cannot say that I remember much of it except that it passed remarkably fast.

Mother was not feeling well when we arrived on Friday afternoon. She was just beginning a prescription for antibiotics that the doctor had sent her to combat the flu. The prognosis for her attending the dedication was not good and was compounded by a fall on Saturday morning that appeared to have done no damage but would be assessed during a round of CAT scans and an MRI scheduled for the following week.

The dedication was set for 2 P.M. on a Sunday afternoon. When it became quite clear that Mother would be unable to attend, we gave her the option of choosing who would stay with her while her children represented the family for the dedication. She decided that brother John would keep her company and designated Allan and David and me to attend. I had known all along that I would be going to the dedication. My months of dreaded anticipation would not go unrewarded. I was going to stand up and speak. I had carefully chosen a red velour dress that would hide my damp underarms and was resigned yet looking forward to attending the joyous event.

Dreams come true, and Helen and Milam's dreams were coming true before my eyes. I was grateful that I was going to witness the event. Aunt Stella and her grandson Roger and his fiancée were also attending, so there would be a goodly number of us whose skins were different. Helen had warned us that the service would last over two hours, and I was as ready as I could possibly be for the occasion.

We drove up to the white wood traditional church of about 3,500 square feet, complete with steeple. The parking lot was full. Outside, the weather was cold and drizzling, but inside was a church full of warmth and love and shouting and singing. We were ushered to front row seats. Brother David and wife Mary and their four-year-old twins, as well as Roger and Lisa and Aunt Stella were already seated. Allan and Alma and I joined them. The sounds of joy and praise resounded in the full church to the accompaniment of a piano, drums and tambourines. Someone would shout a phrase and the rest of us sang choruses like "I'm saved by grace" or "Jesus is the greatest." Arms were extended and bodies swayed. The presence of the Holy Spirit was felt and emotions were high.

We sang a while and we sat while people stood up and testified what the Lord had done for them. Each testimony was followed with singing, and I had a chance to look around. The front stage was filled with men in suits and there was a row behind them of women and men in the choir. Every man in the church had on a good-looking, well-tailored, well-fitting suit, and the women were dressed in cocktail dresses and suits and hats of every color and description. We were well but modestly dressed, but the others in that church named Prince of Peace Church of God in Christ were dressed in splendor. Helen was up front in a burgundy suit with beadwork and a black fur-trimmed hat. Her daughter Rose, who led the choir, wore a beautiful gold-beaded dress.

Honk if you married Sonja

The history of the church was read, and Helen was referred to as the first lady of the church and Milam as Elder Milam Allen. There were visiting preachers from the community and two visiting choirs from Tomball, an adult choir and a children's choir dressed in blue robes. The program gave us a vague idea, but it was a full 30 minutes before I had time to pause and glance at it. The service was dynamic and after every session of talking there was singing. The singing was a form of chanting with one calling out the lines and the rest of us chanting. It was not like the Gregorian chants that were popular a few years back. The chanting was from deeper within, from an emotion that most of us try to deny. It was so easy to become one with the music. The piano player had no music in front of her and played fast jazz rhythms that had no harmony with the singing and chanting, but somehow it all blended. We all sang with joy.

At some point Helen introduced our family, and we all stood and I said a short speech and thought I was through until I glanced at the program and saw that we all had a place on the program.

The scripture was read, as was the lesson for the day, and we said an affirmation of faith that was printed in the program, all interspersed with singing. There was no script or words for the music; it was totally spontaneous. The men on the podium would be introduced and speak the perfect words for the occasion. Every few sentences they would ask for an "amen" and the congregation would respond with a loud "amen," not the mumbled "amens" that we say under our breath at our home churches. Then they would say, "Give me a thank you, Jesus" and the crowd would respond with a loud answer. The Holy Spirit was alive and well in the Prince of Peace Church of God in Christ and everyone in that building was totally there and one with God, unlike other churches in which you feel that half of the people are present but not there.

You could visibly see and feel the love, kindness and joy in that church from everyone present and I was awestruck at that strong outpouring. I felt at one with God and everyone. It was pure joy.

The moment of truth had come. My brother Allan went first and said great words to the extent that "amens" and "praise Jesus" followed his sentences. David went next and even rose to higher emotions and again the affirmations were loud and clear. My turn came and I expressed the sentiment that I could not say anything better than what my brothers had said and that I was touched and knew that my mother would be touched by their prayers for her health.

The sermon, based on the psalm that said, "Let us go with joy into the house of the Lord" was given by the superintendent of the loose confederation of Churches of God in Christ. He shouted and he ran, stomped and sang, and it was 45 minutes of pure evangelizing. The collection was taken in salad bowls, and they were emptied upon a table up front as they were filled and counted and marked on a paper.

At the end of the service, some three hours after we had entered, it was announced that $3,129 had been collected in the offering, and Elder Milam Allen stood and said that in case anyone thought he had control of the money he wanted to say that he could not sign on the church account. He also said that when he retired from his county job, he would spend much time on his knees in order to be one with the spirit and that it was hard to work in the world and to be one in the spirit.

I was amazed that everyone in that church knew what being one with the spirit was; I had been wrestling with the notion for months and had come to the conclusion that I preferred being in the spirit more than anything else in my life and preferred my solitary life in order to facilitate that desire. Here I was in a church with people of like minds in Hockley, Texas, for which my mother had provided the funds.

It was with sheer gratefulness for my parents and their emphasis on giving that had permeated my life that I drove home with Aunt Beverly, deeply reflective of what I had shared in Hockley. My mother had made one of the best gifts anyone could offer, and as Helen said, "Thank you is not enough."

19

The 100th meridian

The 100th meridian is an imaginary line that bisects the United States going through the middle of Texas. Walter Prescott Webb, a noted historian, wrote that the 100th meridian divided the West from the East.

My ranch lies a few miles west of this invisible line, thereby automatically classifying my ranch as being in the West.

All sorts of stories have been concocted concerning this magical line that in reality does not exist.

The 100th meridian is the migration trail for the butterflies, hummingbirds and all sorts of other creatures above. The Indians migrated north and south along the meridian according to the seasons. The four-footed game traveled that same line, most likely making it a busy highway as the seasons changed.

How can an invisible line convey such profound meaning to the creatures of nature? Is there an innate mathematical calculator programmed in everything that tells living things where the line is? Is it part of the genetic code imbedded deep within our cell structure?

As the world was mapped mathematically, why was this line delineated as the 100th meridian? Would it still have significant qualities if it were 30 or 40? Is the universe just a mathematical formula and are we just robots responding to numbers?

The mystery and magic of the 100th meridian is just another of those questions for which there are no answers. As a searcher and learner I have lots of queries for which I have never received adequate answers.

Love is another one of those questions. What is love but an intensity of passion, similar to a roller coaster ride or being a passenger on a runaway train? Once on the ride of love, the only recourse is to hold on until the bitter end. Wouldn't it be better to stop the ride, come to a screeching halt and disembark? A lot of pain and distress would be avoided if that were possible.

Sonja Klein

In our desire to possess everything, we prevail with our grasp until our strength is depleted and we emerge from the ride wounded and scarred, staggering from the loss of energy asking the questions, "What happened? What went wrong? Where did I fuck up?" And why are human beings possessed of such stupidity that they pursue the ones that hurt them the most?

20

Perception

When I look in the mirror I see an image of myself that I perceive as me. Some mirrors are better than others. A photograph on the other hand is usually viewed as not being me, not the person I see when I look in the mirror. The camera, using the laws of physics or science, reproduces an image but is that image the same as the one I see? Someone else looks at the photograph and sees someone entirely different than the person I view.

Which is the correct image? Is the scientific image the correct one and where does our perception overtake science? If our perception can alter the physical photograph what else does perception alter? Is the world as we see it different from the scientific reality? Do I see the world just like anyone else? Is beauty perception and is perception a figment of our imagination?

Memory is not the same for everyone. My children have differing recollections of events from their childhood and their conceptions are estranged from mine. Where is the truth or is there no truth? We are all clouded, subject to our perceptions. How easy is it to change perceptions? Can you just order them changed and thus it is so?

What if governments or powers could change the perceptions of their subjects, or can they? Isn't that what marketing is all about, programming, television, music, books? The ability to change perception is the tool used to market the products of industry. Why not use that power to change emotions, to make everyone love each other, to quit fighting and give up centuries of feuding?

The mysteries of life can be overwhelming but the crux of living is about people, relationships. The only rule or command to follow is to love the God to whom you pray, vis-à-vis love ourselves and love our fellow man, see the same amount of God in him that we view in ourselves, and what we give to others we give to ourselves. If we are full of the spirit of our personal God then we see that same fullness of spirit in others and treat them accordingly. After all, every religion seeks the same thing, to end up in a heaven of some description.

Love is the most important thing we experience; there is no disembarking or stopping the roller coaster of love. The more we stay on the ride, the smoother it becomes so that we are no longer frightened by the intensity but instead enjoy the trip.

21

Dream on

The fascination with the dream world has always occupied man's thoughts. The ancients were obsessed with the dream world, the night lands. Books have been written on the subject, and psychiatrists have always encouraged their patients to write down dreams. Dreams reveal the innermost thoughts and adventures of the subconscious. Is the subconscious actually the conscious and the conscious the subconscious? Which is real, or which is more real?

I am convinced that the world of dreams is as factual as the sphere of our waking moments. Often I have spent a night of physical exploits in my dreams only to awaken tired and exhausted from a night of action. I have journeyed over to the other side and visited family and friends who have crossed over.

Some of my dreams are of a recurring nature—ones that involve going back to school and losing my class schedule or having to return for additional classes. Books I have read explain that theme as a reluctance to shoulder responsibility and a desire to embrace the freedom of youth, not a reckless wish.

A recent theme occurring in my dreams has been one of losing my purse, a frightful thought. My life is in my purse, and while the first scenarios of the loss were disturbing, the following episodes were less so. In my dream I somehow became aware that it was a dream and did not embrace the drama. I found that I could stop the action in the middle of the dream and insist it wasn't so.

My trips to the other side have always been enlightening. After my husband died I traveled to the other side looking for him. I waited in line outside a terminal building only to be told he was being processed. I sensed his disquiet and impatience in being on the other side. Later I walked the streets of the other side looking for him, and as I walked I noticed people looking at me, noticing that I had a white cord going upward from my head. On the other side the people were happy and at a large building I was told without the use of words that he was in orientation.

Months later I read a book that said visits to the other side were characterized by a white cord identifying and attaching the visitor to the other side, our current dimension. The minute I read those lines I thought, "Wow." At that reading I became serious, realizing that my dreams were real, instinctively having known it for a long time. At some point in my dream adventures I realized that everyone on the other side was the same age, about 35, and when I read the same in a book I was awestruck and knew for certain that when I slept I left my body and journeyed to other dimensions.

A repeating dream manifests itself on a regular basis. I receive a phone call or visit a small town and find my husband not sick with cancer, living a normal life and I am angry that he has not contacted me. He is about 35, handsome, and reluctant to see me, he sends me away. I awaken and realize that I have visited him on the other side and cannot remain there. Sometimes we are affectionate, not sexual, and I depart his company content. Other times I am forced to leave and recalcitrant to exit his world. I have seen where he lives, embraced him and touched his essence.

Recently I had an affectionate visit with John and awoke the following morning with whisker burn on my right chin with no explanation. None of my bed covers are sufficiently coarse to cause chafing. From past experiences I was not alarmed and could find no explanation for my reddened, peeling chin.

I dreamed of walking the paths in a Buddhist country, burning incense in a swinging brazier as I strolled the mountain paths. I awoke with the lingering smell of eastern incense and irritated eyes from the fragrant smoke.

My children relate stories of attempting to awaken me, my lifeless body not responding to their insistent touch and my having no recollection of the experience. They tell me I was not in my body.

At times I yearn for the peace of the other side, prefer my dreams to my waking moments and lose days contemplating reality and perception. The journey of life is not to be made following the path, but rather to blaze one's unique trail on the path of discovery.

The dream world is a path of discovery I rather enjoy.

22

Hats

I met Marcia in west Texas at Lajitas Resort, deep in the rugged Big Bend Country along the Rio Grande. Even though it was October, the relentless sun baked the dry caliche, and the occasional breeze only stirred the white powder. There was no humidity, and it was obvious why the women of the West were bronzed and wrinkled, like the Indians they dispossessed.

Marcia walked into the small café where I was waiting tables. There was a crooked smile on her face; she was cosmetically a few pounds overweight, battling her early sixties and losing. Her "Hi, there" echoed a west Texas drawl, and I immediately pegged her from the high plains, maybe Midland or Lubbock.

There were two young good-looking men with her, obvious professionals, uneasy in their surroundings and first-timers to Big Bend. They selected a table for four and sat on the small uncomfortable metal ice cream chairs, savoring the aromas from the grill. Before I gave them their menus and took their drink orders, I gave them time to look around on the walls at the old farm and ranch implements artfully arranged on hooks.

The men ordered hamburgers, and Marcia ordered a club sandwich. My friend who owned the café had seen them come across the wide unpaved street. She remarked that they had come from the hospitality room for the far west Texas county judges and commissioners. The conference was a yearly event and was the occasion for my being there waiting tables, washing dishes and cooking.

My friend was a widow woman, a retired school administrator, who owned a ranch, all sorts of residential and commercial property and the small, modest café that kept her occupied six days a week. I was cast in the same mold, a widow at odds with age, present and working due to my friendship with her sister, who lived in Vance near my ranch. We worked long hard hours for no pay; the laughs and dances compensated us generously.

Most of the men were married and respectful. The best part was that they were good dancers. I loved to two-step and waltz. It didn't matter that they were missing teeth or youthful bodies. The only thing that mattered was the dance.

I saw Marcia on and off for the next few days. I learned that she was the west Texas coordinator for the law firm that collected delinquent property taxes for the many counties in the west Texas district. Marcia knew everyone; she always was kind and friendly and felt like a sister in the sorority of widows.

The dance was held the last night of the convention, and I immediately noticed that Marcia sat at a table of men and danced most every dance. She was a natural dancer. When the conventioneers left the resort the next day, I told her goodbye. Instinctively, I knew I would see her again. Texas was not that big.

The next month I saw Marcia dancing at the Chili Cookoff in Terlingua. Again, she was surrounded by men who were good dancers. I spoke with her, lingered in her presence and danced with her men friends. She readily included me and made me feel welcome.

The next year I was again waiting tables in October, and Marcia was hosting the hospitality room. By then we were long-lost friends. The following month we shared a tent at the Chili Cookoff, and in the ensuing months, attended a Willie Nelson party that was a fundraiser for Kinky Friedman. Kinky was running for governor on the independent ticket. We paid handsomely to his campaign election funds for the privilege of spending an afternoon with Willie, Kinky, Jerry Jeff Walker, Jesse Ventura and Billy Jo Shaver at Willie's ranch outside Austin. His ranch was in Luck, Texas because if you were at his ranch you were in Luck and if you weren't at his ranch you were out of Luck.

What to wear became the priority. I told Marcia to dress flashy western and wear a hat. She didn't much like the idea. "I don't wear hats."

"Now you do. If you want to be noticed, wear a neat hat. A hat, big earrings, and long hair take off 20 years. Besides, a hat shadows the wrinkles. You can find one at the western store in Midland."

"I have some western hats. Don't have to buy one."

My closet was full of hats, mostly western that my mother had given me from her horse racing days. I loved wearing hats, supposed it was from my mother. My father always bought my mother hats and she had worn some neat ones over the years.

Marcia and I met in Austin. I drove in from the ranch and picked her up at the airport. We shared a hotel room and attended the party dressed western chic and sporting hats. The reporters and photographers had fun with us. We were the only women wearing hats in a crowd of about 100. Marcia was on the front page of the San Antonio paper. The following week she emailed the pictures to family and friends. Marcia had become a hat believer.

Our friendship blossomed. We telephoned every Sunday, met for the west Texas conference, camped at Terlingua for the Chili Cookoff and danced every chance we could. As the years flew by, Marcia spoke of retiring. I encouraged her to.

"I'd die if I retired. There's nothing I want to do, nowhere I want to go. I don't like traveling because I travel so much with my job. I don't like to sew or play cards, and I'm too old to do anything physical. I can't retire."

"Oh, Marcia. There must be something you would like to do if you didn't have to work."

"No, I just like coming home from work, eating a bowl of beans and putting on my pajamas. That's all."

"Well, think about it."

The following Sunday she called. "I want to go to the Kentucky Derby and wear a big hat."

"I'll make the arrangements. How many days do you want to be there?"

"Three is enough for me."

"Okay, Marcia, but you'll have to buy two hats, big flowery ones, and figure out how to carry them on the plane."

She found a lady in Midland who made hats. While visiting family in Houston, I made a trip to a big department store in Houston and found my hats. We met in Louisville, attended two days of races, sat in clubhouse seats, won a few bets and lost only a few others. As we parted at the airport, I asked her, "What's next?"

"I haven't decided yet, but whatever it is, I'm wearing a hat."

23

Watch your step

The first time I stepped on a scorpion in the privacy of my own home was a disaster. In spite of immediate attention with baking soda and toothpaste, my foot swelled up to resemble the Pillsbury Doughboy. Only ice and constant application of baking soda brought relief sufficient to sleep.

Reluctant to kill living things, I excluded scorpions from the sentient being list and killed them with vigor every time one appeared in the bathtub, shower or kitchen sink. Hornets, crickets, flies, grasshoppers, bees and wasps I usually shooed out the door if possible.

The second scorpion was smaller than the first, but his venom was stronger. The pain was almost intolerable. The skin on my tender foot turned bright rosy red and the swelling moved up to my ankle. A week went by before I could even think about going dancing.

I began to think seriously about foot pain. Beating the soles of prisoners' feet soon became obvious as torture. Foot reflexology revealed a deeper meaning. Obviously the extremities of the human body contained numerous nerve endings too sensitive to ignore.

Over time, the pain of a stubbed toe or an invasive cactus thorn intruded upon my sense of well being, and I developed an elaborate sense of survival to protect my feet and fingers, taking care to wear gloves, thick shoes and socks when working outside on my nature-hostile ranch. Horror stories of brown-recluse spider bites abounded. Lost fingers and cavities in flesh resulted from the bite of the tiny arachnid rumored to be a recluse.

One day when I was not paying attention, I sat down on the front porch bench to remove my shoes and socks after a day of ranch work, weed eating and cleaning flowerbeds. My pants legs were covered with grass burrs, bits of grass and debris from the day's chores. That morning I carefully dusted my clothing with powdered sulfur to discourage chiggers and ticks from taking up residence on my tender skin. Having survived the day's work without incidence, I removed my socks and used them to wipe off the bits and pieces clinging to my clothing.

As I arose to go into the house and shower, I stepped on fire in the form of a four-inch centipede. Gratefully, it was under the high arch of my right foot because I cannot comprehend worse pain. I probably would have died had I stepped on it flat-footed. Baking soda and toothpaste and ice alleviated the worst of the fire on my instep. For three weeks my body fought the poison.

Once the swelling went down, the itching drove me so near crazy that I wanted to scratch the skin off my foot and not just the site of the bite but my entire foot. After 10 days the evidence was startling. My instep looked like someone had made an incision. There was a line down the middle with crossties and blisters on the ends of the crossties. I applied Neosporin. The blisters popped and the itching returned. I forgot about dancing.

My main concern was how to keep the critters from entering my house across the thresholds. I always went barefoot in my house, except for winter, when I wore socks. I would not compromise my comfort for fear of those horrible insects. I would not let fear drive me away from my routine. Then I found out that scorpions, millipedes and centipedes were not insects but closely related to lobsters, shrimp and crawfish. How ridiculous that they could be related to something that tasted so good. Mother Nature does have a funny way of patterning her creations.

Once I realized that I could see daylight between the bottom of my door and the thresholds, I ascertained that my house was not secure. I debated having a carpenter install new thresholds, and then I noticed the sack of sulfur in the utility room. I would pour sulfur heavily on the outside of the thresholds. After all, if it worked to deter chiggers and ticks, it should annoy the poisonous critters.

Yellow dust outside the doors was not all that attractive, but it did install a modicum of security. And I relaxed, confident that the sulfur would work and maybe alleviate the bad karma received from killing these lower sentient beings. I had read that there were six classes of sentient beings with God on the top and creepy crawlies near the bottom.

And then one morning I picked up the dishrag to wipe up some coffee I had spilled on the counter. A scorpion and a small brown suspicious-looking spider dropped into the sink. I was right back where I had started—living in west Texas on Ambush Hill in the middle of nowhere. What else could I expect?

24

The long ride

Being a goat- and sheep-ranching widow presents problems. The first year after my husband died, I was faced with working the small amount of stock remaining after John sold most of them, while the cancer moved swiftly through his robust body. I watched him disintegrate before my eyes. After his death, I was faced with the responsibility of tending to the animals.

The first time I had to pen the sheep for their biannual shearing was a disaster. The ram charged me from behind and knocked me face down on the rocks—not once but several times—before I summoned the courage to get up and hit him with a rock, stunning him momentarily and allowing me time to get up and run like hell. The first thing I did when I recovered my senses was to look around and see if anyone had seen me make a fool of myself. There was no one for miles around, but still I looked.

Then anger set in and I managed to sneak around, throw some corn in the pen, circle and close the gate, vowing to send the ram on the long ride, the 60-mile drive to the auction barn in Uvalde. By the time the shearer arrived, I had selected several others for a trailer trip to the auction. The ram was first on the list as the shearer helped me hook the stock trailer to my pickup, back it up to the pens and load the selected animals for the long ride.

Confident that I had solved the sheep problem, I next took notice of the goat herd that continued to increase. Some of the nannies were quite tame, and I prized my lead goat, Stella, named after one of my hardy aunts. Penning them was easy since Stella willingly lead them into the pens for the kernels of corn they enjoyed like candy.

Selecting the older and wilder ones, some with broken or sagging bags, was not difficult, and I managed to keep the herd at a constant number, periodically hauling goats on the long ride to the auction. Over the years, I obtained help to butcher the kids and lambs and kept my freezer full, as well as supplied neighbors with meat as additional payment for repairing the bump gate, fences and water gaps and changing the occasional flat tire.

As long as I paid attention to my animals, they were easy to control. I kept mineral and salt blocks out and at least once a week would call them and feed them corn, pellets or an occasional chunk of alfalfa hay. They thrived and reproduced on the rocky, cedar infested ranch named Ambush Hill.

Being easily distracted, I gradually became less attentive to my animals and my fences. The goat herd became quite adept at jumping fences or crawling through where hogs had made incursions. I found them on the Girl Scout camp that joined me on the western border; they went east to feast on my neighbor's flowers and north on the hill above to disturb yet another neighbor. A bucket of corn always led them home for a short sojourn before they left on another excursion. As long as my neighbors didn't complain too loudly, I was comfortable with the goats' adventures, confident that they would come home to kid, sometimes even bringing stray billy goats and scraggly nannies that I penned and took on the long ride. One year they brought three ibex, wild Asian goats, which a helpful neighbor promptly shot. The youngest of them ended up in my freezer.

Times changed and new neighbors replaced older, savvy ones. These were city people, ignorant of goats and canyon ways and intent on contouring the rugged canyons to suit their city egos. They spent thousands of dollars poisoning cactus, cutting cedar and rearranging rocks. The yearly floods kept them discouraged, but they persisted in spending their dollars rearranging the stones in the creek bed.

I had met my new neighbor to the north on the roadside as he entered his ranch through the new solar-powered gate. We exchanged pleasantries, names and phone numbers and spoke of getting together. The next contact came by telephone. "Do you have a stock trailer?"

"Yes, I do."

"Well, your goats are on my place, and my wife is upset because they are dropping their little pellets on our sidewalk. Can you hook up your stock trailer and come get them? Can you do it by yourself?"

My thoughts: 'Of course, you fool. I can do that.'

I had seen my goats, counted 19 new kids, just a few days before and knew they would come home if left alone.

Honk if you married Sonja

Recalling the layout of his house and pens, I asked, "Isn't there a fence around your house?"

"Yes, but why should I have to close the gate every time I leave the yard? I don't think you're being a very good neighbor."

I knew my goats would not fit in my trailer, that they would never load in a strange place and that his old sheep shed had no chute.

"Do you have a chute?"

"I know a lot about goats and I've fixed that shed, repaired the holes and will help you load them."

Knowing it was a stupid exercise, that it would not work and that the goats would come home, I nonetheless tried to be a good neighbor and drove to his ranch, dragging my stock trailer, resigned to playing the fool.

The scene played just as I had imagined. I drove to the shed with no chute and observed the gaps remaining in the tin panels that served as walls. He was waiting. "Let me back up the trailer." I surrendered the truck to him while he backed to the gate. After watching him inadequately block the spaces beside the trailer I spoke.

" I had 19 babies a few days ago; where are the babies?"

"Oh, I guess they are in the brush up the hill."

"How long have you had my goats penned?"

"About 30 minutes."

Alarms went off. How could they drop pellets on his sidewalk and become a nuisance in 30 minutes? I knew I was in trouble. He was lying and my goats would never jump in that trailer. Yet, I had to go through the motions like a dummy and let my goats make a total fool of me for the sake of being a good neighbor.

I led the goats into the shed shaking my battered bucket of corn. They followed warily, saw the trailer, and scattered through the rusty gaping panels. My neighbor came out of hiding, perfunctorily propped up some of the tin panels and instructed, "Try again." Once again my goats made an idiot of me, acting even wilder, finding new holes.

"Okay, if you'll take your bucket of corn and lead them out through the pasture, there's a gate in the corner. Just open it and put them back on your place."

The referenced corner was a long distance, and my emotions, while under control on the surface, were pouring rivulets under my arms. The temperature on that hot August afternoon was in the triple digits. The herd followed me dutifully as I walked across the treeless pasture. Fifty feet from the gate, the entire herd veered to the left, jumped the fence and went up the rocky hill back onto my ranch.

I carried the bucket back to the truck, said pleasant goodbyes, laced with abject apologies and drove home. The goats were grazing on my cliff that evening, and I never saw any of my babies. I considered sending him a bill for 19 kids at $50 each; instead I adhered to the good neighbor policy.

As the goat herd became increasingly wild and larger, my focus faded, and I remained confident that Stella would always bring them home to kid and eat corn. My good neighbor waved when I saw him on the road and there were no more phone calls.

On another hot August day I received a phone call from some other neighbors, more city dwellers who had purchased a section of land, 640 acres, a mile beyond my boundaries. The neighbor introduced himself and asked, "Are you missing some goats?"

Answering truthfully I replied, "Yes, my goats have been gone for a few weeks and I've been looking for them."

"Well, they're here on my place under my deer feeder, eating my corn."

Knowing they would be home to kid in a few weeks and aware that it was useless to explain, I drove down the dirt road, opened and closed four gates and pretended to care about my goats. The same act: I had to take a bucket of corn, scramble over rocks and up the hill while my goats made a fool of me. That is exactly what occurred. The temperature was again over 100 degrees. The goats were up on the hill munching his corn under his feeder. They looked at me with my bucket of corn as if to say, "What are you doing here?"

I shook the bucket; they followed me reluctantly down the steep hill and stopped short of the gate to his pens. Several went inside. Then a minor noise scattered them back up the hill and I stumbled over the rocks and went through the same actions with the same results.

The neighbor and his wife were in the house watching me play the idiot. When I felt that I had satisfied them with my good neighbor behavior, I knocked on the door, was invited in for sweet iced tea and had a nice visit, interspersed with abject apologies, promising to return and try once again, offering to pay for the corn.

Honk if you married Sonja

Several days later, on a first-name basis, he called to say the goats were back up on his hill. Not being able to tell him that the goats would eventually come home and that Real County had open stock laws—if you didn't want your neighbor's stock on your property it was your responsibility to fence them out—I gave up, sick of the goat herd.

"I can't come and get those goats. You can have them. Shoot them all if you want; or if you can trap them and haul them to the auction, all the money is yours."

"Oh, we can't do that."

"Well, I can't come and lure them home. They won't come. Just shoot them. They're yours."

"I understand." I believed him.

After more profound apologies, I hung up the phone, resolved that if they ever came home, every last one of them would take the long ride, even if I had to make two trips.

Within a week the entire herd was home, pregnant and happy. Stella led them into the pens for some corn. When I shut the gate on the last one, I had a great moment of satisfaction, punctuated by a few unrepeatable remarks. The entire herd took the long ride, Stella included. Before loading them, I took some pictures, noticeable for the fact that two of them were standing on top of the four-foot high feeder in the pens, proof positive that you can't keep goats penned in this rough rocky country. I felt good that I had won. Then I realized that there were no winners.

25

The Middle East

After my last adventure, which took me to the Far East, I was intrigued by the Middle East. The media portrayed America's involvement in the fractious countries on a daily basis, and I wanted to see for myself the countries that dominated the news.

I purchased two cardboard boxes full of information about the countries from a used bookstore in Dallas and began my studies and research. Six months later I felt better informed on the history, culture and religion of the countries I planned on visiting.

The roulette wheel of traveling overseas with multiple connections was favorable. As I sat in the airport in Amsterdam waiting for the last connection that would deliver me to Dubai, I looked around the waiting area. My fellow travelers were mostly men, Americans, and they were flying to the Middle East for technical support, engineering and construction jobs. There were a few veiled women and a small assortment of seasoned ones like myself. We gravitated to each other.

I met a woman from New Hampshire on a journey to Afghanistan to educate women in midwifery and set up rural clinics in remote areas of the country. She was a retired nurse, energetic and dedicated, hitching a ride on the United Nations plane leaving after midnight from Dubai to Kabul.

An older couple from Georgia was on their way to Pakistan to assist the earthquake victims, disappointed that their visas were granted for only 30 days. The ensuing conversations left me with guilt for going on a luxury cruise trip for my own enjoyment. These people were going to danger zones to help others. I had an impulse to cancel the trip and join the Peace Corps. The impulse swiftly disappeared when I remembered there was no refund.

The flight from Amsterdam to Dubai lasted six hours and I slept most of the way, arriving about midnight. I arrived in Dubai, on the continent of Asia, in the ancient lands where civilization was spawned.

Honk if you married Sonja

A young woman from Yemen who worked for the Grand Hyatt Hotel met me outside customs, escorted me through the lines and led me through the airport. I could not neglect noticing the beauty of the ornate airport. There were towering three-story living palm trees, room-sized chandeliers, fresh flowers and living plants everywhere. The ethnicity of the people in the airport was a cornucopia of colors, races and attire.

There were tall Africans in long flowing robes with turbans and tattoos, Arab-speaking men dressed in Armani suits speaking on cell phones and men in white robes with the familiar Palestinian red and white checked headgear. Also present were blue jean- and tee shirt-clad oilfield workers as well as European businessmen in stylish suits. My first impulse was to just stand and absorb the smells and scenes of the multitude of races.

The streets of Dubai were busy but not congested. There was not one piece of plastic or trash on the smooth roads flanked by blooming, colorful flowerbeds absent of weeds. The lights along the avenues were fancy. I saw no burned out bulbs. Every vehicle was shiny, most of them were white and of recent vintage. There were no old rusty junkers moving in Dubai.

The Grand Hyatt had lush gardens, luxurious foliage and water fountains. As I reached over to thank my escort, I touched her. She instantly recoiled as if I had shot her when I too late remembered my months of research. Touching is prohibited unless family. My apologies were profuse, but the mistake had been made.

The hotel room was large, fancy and decorated in dark green marble. The furniture was massive pieces of burl. The bathroom resembled a large garden. I soon discovered that the room card key activated the light system. None of the lights in the room remained illuminated unless the card/key was in the slot beside the door. It was refreshing to observe that in spite of the obvious wealth of Dubai, the citizens and government of the United Arab Emirates were also energy conscious.

The following morning I dressed conservatively and made my way through the atrium, shuttered boutiques and lobby to a lovely sunken garden area with café tables and immaculately dressed waiters. I received a newspaper with my first cup of coffee. Surprisingly the paper was glossy, leaving no black residue on my fingers, as I read the world's news.

In the dining area was an assortment of mostly men, some in robes, some in suits and a few women in robes, some veiled, some attired in tailored suits.

The breakfast buffet seemed to go on forever—miniature papayas, fresh figs, dates from big and brown to small and golden, grapes, eggs, herring in every imaginable sauce, pastries to tempt the steadfast, cooked cereals, yogurt, hummus, hot pepper mash and marinated olives of every variety. The selection was enormous. After a light breakfast I found the hospitality desk and visited with a young Arab woman, dressed in a navy blue pantsuit. I remembered not to touch her. She was quite helpful and spoke perfect English, and efficiently called for a guide and driver for the day.

In less than an hour, Sahira, a middle-aged Arab woman from Oman —a coastal country on the Indian Ocean—met me. A middle-aged man from Pakistan drove the shiny white Toyota sedan. As we exited the landscape of the Grand Hyatt, Sahira inquired, "What would you like to do and see?" Her English was impeccable, with a slight trace of British accent.

"I would like to tour the city, visit the market and do some shopping."

There were no slums and no plastic debris, and the river that coursed through the city was a beautiful, clear blue. Sahira related a short history of the country. Dubai was one of the seven countries or sheikhdoms that comprised the United Arab Emirates; Qatar was another one. In earlier times the area was called the Trucial States because they were a loose confederation of sheikhdoms bound by truces. The visionary Sheikh of Dubai formed the United Arab Emirates in the 1970's. Then oil was discovered in Qatar and the newfound wealth was shared in a series of loans to the other emirates. Not all of the sheikhdoms joined the coalition, and when they later saw the advantages, it was too late.

The United Arab Emirates became a shining example of using money to help their citizens. Dubai is no third world country; everything is new and first class. The buildings are diverse in their stunning designs. The reigning sheikh, who was the son of the old visionary, is much loved by his subjects and is known for wanting the best for his country. Dubai is currently the home of the world's most luxurious hotel. It looks like a ship at sail. Each suite is two stories, and the cheapest room is $1,750 per night.

Honk if you married Sonja

As we drove down the six-lane boulevard in the early morning, Sahira pointed to the famous hotel in the distance, perched as if in full sail on the shores of the Persian Gulf or Arabian Gulf, depending on the visitor's ethnicity or knowledge of history.

Sahira was a fountain of information. Foreigners are not allowed to own land, and all businesses have to be 51 percent or more owned by natives. The currently loved sheikh, who is an absolute ruler, has four wives and is intent on building the biggest and best in the world. A tall building under construction will be the world's tallest building. The architect is an American. The world's only indoor ski slope is in Dubai. The largest man-made island was under construction in the distance.

Dubai is reportedly the world's largest container port in the world. The port was formed by dredging out the river that entered the Persian Gulf. Dubai was originally a small fishing village known worldwide for its pearls. When the Japanese perfected cultured pearls, the pearl industry in Dubai crashed.

Sahira revealed that she was a diver and that the water in the port was clear to a depth of 20 feet and constituted a healthy environment. She had been part of a team of divers that evaluated the port waters. Observing the port, I could not doubt her words. She answered my questions without hesitation. Eighty per cent of the population of Dubai are expatriates, and 70 percent of the expatriates are from India, Pakistan, Sri Lanka and Bangladesh. Rent is super expensive, and most employers furnish housing and transportation for the workers. She said cars were cheap.

According to some world organizations, Dubai is the safest country in the world. I saw no beggars, panhandlers or poor people, not even in the crowded bazaar or market. The country exuded prosperity, cleanliness and modernity. There are 667 mosques in Dubai, lovely from the outside, none of which I was allowed to enter. Sahira told me the insides are very plain—no altars, niches, statues or gold leaf—just large areas with rugs.

I saw very few Americans during the day's tour. Sahira informed me that, due to the severe penalties, there is no drug problem in Dubai. AIDS is also not a problem because all the expatriates are given a yearly blood test in order to renew their visas. The sick ones are deported.

According to my guide, the worst problems in Dubai are traffic, alcoholism and homosexuality.

Sonja Klein

Alcoholism is a problem because the Arab culture and Muslim religion forbids the drinking of alcoholic spirits. When the Arab-speaking people, primarily men, drink, they fall under the nomadic custom of consuming it all before it spoils. There is no constraint or social experience with the consumption of alcohol. They drink until it is all gone.

Homosexuality is another problem. Women's roles are well defined. Virginity is expected at marriage. The sexual revolution does not exist in Arab-speaking countries. Women are protected, sheltered and treasured. In the Middle East, women are safe. Having no outlet for their sexual desires, the men find release in each other, especially the young men and teenagers.

Sahira took me to the summer home of the old sheikh who had led Dubai into the modern world. The home was close to the beach on the outskirts of town and had become a museum of sorts. The grounds surrounding the modest structure displayed an irrigation system and native plants.

The house is modest, with the main rooms on the second story. Porches surround the house. The upper level has two rooms—a living room with rugs and cushions, and a small alcove for preparing snacks and tea. Supposedly the old sheikh came to this home to enjoy the sea breeze and beauty of the gardens.

The day's tour included the oldest section of Dubai, where the fishermen and pearl divers had lived. The area has been restored into art galleries, restaurants and shops. We walked to the banks of the river and took the free open-air water taxi to the other side of the river.

The bazaar or souk across the river contains blocks of shops selling gold, spices, food, exotic fruits, tea and any other imaginable products from the East. Gold jewelry is sold by the ounce in the market. The fragrance of the spices was so enticing that I purchased saffron quite cheaply, cardamom, paprika and several curry powders. The stall burning incense beckoned and I added myrrh, frankincense, amber and cloves to my heavy bag.

The day had passed swiftly as I returned to the hotel, checked out and boarded a shuttle to the small luxury ship ready to sail to Muscat, Oman.

Muscat, Oman, is a beautiful port city on the Arabian Sea located on the southeast side of the Arabian Peninsula. The city is modern and clean, accented with blooming flowers and clear, blue port waters.

138

Honk if you married Sonja

Unfamiliar sensuous and exotic smells permeated the soukh, just a few blocks from the port. I walked freely through the market, enjoying the variety of goods offered at exotic stalls—spices, gold, leather, brass, cotton from India and Pakistan, artifacts made from camel bone and cashmere shawls from the East. The famous Omani Khanjars, or daggers, were on display in many shops.

Most of the women were veiled with only their heavily made-up eyes in evidence. They walked in groups, laughing and chattering, and I could only imagine their jewelry and designer dresses under the flowing robes. The men, too, were in groups, smiling and strolling through the market in long white robes and wearing checkered headgear.

As I looked ahead in the soukh, I saw a tall familiar figure. It was Nina, with whom I had traveled in Peru. Our eyes met at the same moment. I called, "Nina."

She returned with, "Sonja." We embraced and found to our delight that she and her husband had boarded the ship in Oman. We would be traveling together for the next few weeks and spend many fun days together. As we strolled through the market we discovered the many perfume shops, designed to create one's individual perfume. Being totally ignorant, we watched as men developed their own scent. We were told that men drape their clothing over a tepee-like structure with the scent in the core to permeate their clothing.

Later in the day I engaged a guide, a young university student whose English was flawless. His comprehension, on the other hand, was flawed. The canned speeches and information he delivered were easily understood, but any question baffled him completely.

We drove to the Grand Mosque, passing through an area of exclusive residences, elegant villas, embassies and shiny car dealerships.

Not allowed inside the mosque, I admired the beautiful exterior of the edifice ordered by His Majesty, Sultan Qaboos bin Said, whose purpose was to create a central, major place of worship in the Sultanate, as well as to propagate Islamic religion and culture.

The official residence of the Sultan Qaboos is the Al Alam Palace, an architectural blend of oriental and occidental styles in rich hues of blue and gold. The palace is positioned between the two medieval fortresses of Jalali and Mirani overlooking the port of Muscat. The Sultan's yacht was anchored in the harbor.

My guide had a canned speech. Oman has a population of 2.3 million; 600,000 of them are expatriates, mainly Pakistani and Indian. The country has been independent since 1971; prior to then it was under Portuguese control. The main exports are oil, gas and fish. Tourism has become an important industry, though I didn't see many tourists. The few I did see were Australian and European.

The guide continued with additional information. The aging, unmarried Sultan rules Oman absolutely, and his successor will be chosen from his family. I encountered no hostility, only friendly faces. It was a nice place to visit.

From Oman, the ship rounded the Arabian peninsula and entered the Red Sea, which was not red but rather blue. To the south is Africa, and to the north is the vast Arabian Desert.

The ship stopped in the port of Safaga, Egypt, where I disembarked, destined for Luxor, Egypt, and the Valley of the Kings.

Safaga is an important port from which bauxite is shipped to the aluminum factories in Luxor. Wheat from Australia enters Egypt from Safaga. Sugar also passes through the port. Safaga continues to be a gathering place for pilgrims from Africa on their way to pilgrimage in Mecca.

A military convoy joined the coach on which I traveled and escorted us from a checkpoint on the outskirts of Safaga. The military convoy consisted of a group of Toyotas carrying soldiers with automatic weapons. The three-hour journey was interrupted by several checkpoints as I traveled across the harsh desert. In the distance I spotted camels, sheep and goats grazing on what seemed to be sand. Tents of the nomads that followed the animals dotted the landscape.

The guide informed us that the Egyptian government estimates there are two million nomads in the country, who they are trying to settle, educate and integrate into the general population. The nomads resist, preferring to migrate with the seasons and pasturage. Skin disease is common among the nomads due to the lack of vitamin C and vegetables in their diet.

Education in Egypt is compulsory from the ages of 6 to 16. According to the abilities of the students, they can attend technical school or college free.

Sugar cane is grown in the south, while cotton and grains are grown in the north. The climate is so mild that three crops a year can be harvested in the fertile valley of the Nile.

As I approached the Nile Valley, the landscape turned from brown to green. The Aswan Dam on the Nile created the world's largest artificial lake—550 square kilometers. Irrigation canals, pumps and many ditches flanked the highway.

Men, women and children worked in the fields. Small tractors, donkeys, camels and water buffalo worked them as well. Many people wearing all colors and styles of clothing walked the sides of the road.

The atmosphere was African, far different than Dubai and Oman on the continent of Asia. Egypt is the only country in the world that is on two continents, Africa and Asia. The atmosphere of the Middle East was one of survival, whereas Egypt felt more metaphysical with spiritual leisure due to the lush, fertile land.

My first stop in Luxor was the magnificent Karnak temple complex that was built, enlarged and decorated over many years. The ancient Egyptians worshipped the sun, and Karnak was the most important sanctuary and the heart of sun god worship. The entrance and main axis of the complex is the avenue of ram-headed sphinxes that leads into the Great Court, the largest single area of the Karnak complex, containing many massive stone columns.

The hotel that was to be home for the next two nights was located on the eastern bank of the Nile. From the dining area and rooms, the visitors are treated to a stunning view of the wide, slow-moving Nile. Across the river on the west bank are the mountains and the Valley of the Kings, where the pharaohs are buried. The east bank contains the living, and the west is home of the dead.

Grazing across the river were water buffalo, horses and camels. In the foreground felugas, dramatic sailboats, moved upriver into the interior of Africa. The prevailing winds from Europe coming off the Mediterranean allow boats to sail upriver as well as downriver.

The buffet lunch was an international delight—lamb, fish, veal and chicken seasoned with curry and other eastern spices. When I asked for water, the waiter replied in English, "Mineral or still?" Dishes with grains and beans were plentiful—tabouli, hummus and barley. The vegetables were numerous—eggplant, Brussels sprouts, carrots, beets and squash served at room temperature and marinated with olives and peppers in olive oil.

After lunch I walked to the temple of Luxor, a massive complex on the banks of the Nile in the center of the city. The temple is in a great state of preservation. The first temple was built over an older sanctuary that dates back several thousand years before Christ. Over the centuries, various rulers including Ramses II added statues of themselves as well as obelisks. Later the Christians worshipped in the temple that Alexander the Great used several hundred years before the birth of Christ.

The sun worshippers believed that when you died you lost your name, shadow and voice. They believed that the soul returned to the body, so they preserved the body and created statues in the likeness of the deceased and wrote the name in the tomb so that the soul would recognize the body. The soul was called Ka.

When death occurred, a boat conveyed the soul to the west, to the underworld, where a series of obstacles had to be overcome every 12 hours. The heart was weighed on a balance scale with a feather. If the heart weighed more than the feather, then the soul was condemned to suffer in the underworld. The ideal was to have been such a good person of light heart that the feather outweighed the soul.

Luxor was known in ancient times as Thebes. Over centuries, the people of Thebes fought wars against the Hittites and the Nubians and later the Greeks, Romans and Turks. Luxor was a city of workers, nobles and kings.

I learned that the Nile is over 6,000 kilometers long and is the lifeblood of Africa, civilization thriving along its banks. The stark contrast between the cultivated lands along the Nile and the gravelly, rocky mountains beyond is severe. Rain falls two days a year. The roofs are thatched because rain is scarce.

The following morning I crossed the Nile into a barren area to reach the Valley of the Kings. The road wound up from the fertile valley into desolation containing no shrubs, grass or landmarks. The land was uniformly gray.

Here in this isolated area, the great pharaohs and their families were laid to rest, cleverly concealed in tombs dug into the barren cliffs. I visited the tombs of several of the Ramses and King Tut and then noticed a current dig, a tent and a man obviously American standing within a roped area.

He introduced himself as Dr. Ertman from the University of Memphis. He was in charge of the discovery of KV 63, a new tomb. The excavation had progressed to the first antechamber. He explained that 18 feet down they had found broken pottery and were currently excavating the next chamber. He added that funding was short and encouraged me to visit their website.

Dr. Ertman added that the team could only excavate until June, at which time the government required them to re-cover the excavation with the same dirt until the weather became more tolerable. It was in the middle of winter, and the temperature was in the 80's—hard to imagine what the summers were like.

I found it amazing that any tombs had ever been found in the barren surroundings. The tops of the steep crests were dotted with armed guards. There were few tourists present. Most of them were African, European or Asian.

While walking through one of the tombs, a Japanese tourist took a flash picture. A guard quickly led him away. No pictures are allowed in the tombs because the flash damages the paintings in the narrow passageways chiseled from solid rock. The colorful paintings represent the afterlife and the obstacles to be overcome. There are niches carved into the wall that held artifacts and many side chambers that contained treasures.

On the return to the east bank I visited the temple of Queen Hatshepsut, a magnificent restored monument on the west bank. Queen Hatshepsut seized the throne of Egypt after the death of her husband by proclaiming she was not a woman but half god with the attributes of a man and a woman. The intrigues of the court and her subsequent departure from the throne caused her successor to obliterate her name and statues from the landscape.

Still on the west bank, I visited another splendid temple complex that was built by Ramses II. It was a weekend palace. Ramses II warred with the Hittites and Nubians, offering a bounty for their heads. He soon realized that heads were not proof positive and changed the bounty to penises because the Egyptians were circumcised and their enemies were not.

I arose the next morning before dawn to observe the famous morning light over the Nile. The light was gold and rose-hued, much like that at home, and I watched women herding goats throwing rocks to control them, much like my daughter and I do at our ranch. People are much the same anywhere in the world.

The bus and armed convoy delivered me back to Safaga, where I joined the ship, my next destination Aqaba, Jordan.

Aqaba, Jordan, is a mid-sized city located on the Gulf of Aqaba. A taxi invited me for a ride to the Israeli border, a few miles distant. I declined and instead boarded a bus for the two- to three-hour ride on the modern desert highway to visit the most famous of Jordan's attractions —the rose-red city of Petra.

Once off the highway the bus took us through a series of small villages, where the long walk through the siq would begin. The site is reached via a narrow, half-mile walk between rock walls that rise over 650 feet on both sides. This served as a defense as well as a path to deliver the incredible water system for the city of Petra.

When I emerged from the narrow path I was standing in front of Khazneh, the Treasury, the impressive, red-colored façade, pictured in the final scenes of *Indiana Jones and The Last Crusade*.

As I approached the steps to the Treasury, I noticed a tall, handsome Jordanian in robes with ammunition belts crisscrossed on his chest. After permission from him I asked a tourist to take our picture. He asked, "Where are you from?"

"From Texas."

"Do you have horses?"

"No, I have sheep and goats. Do you have camels?"

"Yes, I have over 90 of them. Do you have guns?"

"Yes."

"Good."

"I like your coat. Where did you buy it?

"In America, from the Navajo Indians."

"It's very nice, very colorful."

"Thank you."

With a handshake and smile we parted only for his next Kodak moment.

I sneaked up to a group of tourists and listened to their guide. More than 2,000 years ago the Nabateans occupied Petra. They created their fortress city from the caves and rock outcrops. Moses journeyed through Petra on his way to the Promised Land flowing with milk and honey. Supposedly Aaron, the brother of Moses, is buried at Petra.

Beyond the Treasury are hundreds of structures, most of them carved out of the stony terrain. They include soaring temples, elaborate royal tombs and a theater with seating for hundreds of spectators. The city of Petra encompasses a vast area.

I spent the cold windy afternoon exploring the site. It was easy to feel the age and isolation of the site but hard to separate it from the movie, *Indiana Jones and the Last Crusade*.

The following morning I departed Aqaba for a visit to Wadi Rum, the desert oasis frequented by Lawrence of Arabia, who is revered in Jordan for helping to free them from Turkish domination.

A one-hour drive on the desert highway took me to the Queen Alia Foundation, where I boarded a four-wheel drive vehicle before proceeding into the desert. The beauty was astounding. Black hills stood like sentinels upon pale sands, interspersed by dramatic rock formations. We stopped at the Wadi Rum Rest House for tea. In the distance I saw a Bedouin community residing in the traditional black tents surrounded by small herds of camels.

The trip into the desert provided awesome and ever-changing vistas of limestone cliffs that faded into the expanse of sand. Parts of Wadi Rum's moon-like landscape are aptly called the "Valley of the Moon." Here the legend of Lawrence of Arabia was born. I had read his book, *The Seven Pillars of Wisdom*, before the trip. He was a fascinating historical figure.

I returned to the ship as we departed Aqaba, continuing in the Red Sea to Sharm-El-Sheikh. Sharm-El-Sheikh is a relatively new city, built and developed by the Israelis when they captured the whole of the Sinai in 1967 and controlled the Suez Canal.

The city is a beautiful resort with hotels, palaces and casinos. All of the structures are elaborate and new. The streets are lined with blooming flowers. Sharm-El-Sheikh means City of Peace and is a popular destination for presidents and prime ministers—Bill Clinton and Tony Blair, for example.

The Sinai, the Suez Canal and Sharm-El-Sheikh were returned to the Egyptians in 1982 as a result of the Camp David negotiations. I cannot imagine what Jimmy Carter promised the Israelis in order for them to return such lucrative property.

The resort is restricted; all buildings must be white and cannot exceed four stories so that the view of the sea is not obscured.

I joined a small coach tour of a dozen fellow adventurers for the 225-kilometer trip to St. Catherine's Monastery. There were no other Americans on the coach. The guide, Mara, a middle-aged Egyptian woman, had flown from Cairo to escort the tour.

Mara informed us that the monastery was closed to the public on Sundays, but that the monks had agreed to open it in exchange for the four cases of wine that were secreted in the back of the coach. We followed the familiar Toyota truck with soldiers in the back. This was considered to be our military escort through the Sinai Desert, stopping at checkpoints manned by young Egyptian soldiers with automatic weapons. Our guide casually informed us that the guns had no ammunition and the display of force was merely part of the international peacekeeping agreement in the Sinai.

I learned that the Sinai is divided into four sectors or quarters. Each sector is guarded by a different national force with no-fly zones. The French and Italians are among the peacekeeping forces. Mara added that military duty in the Sinai was the worst possible deployment until the development of Sharm-El-Sheikh made it a desirable posting because of the casinos and elaborate resort.

The population of the resort is 35,000. Land is priced at $25,000 per square meter. Even more shocking to hear was that cruise ships pay approximately $130,000 to transit the 100-mile Suez Canal. Tankers and cargo ships pay even more. Egypt receives approximately $12 million a day in transit fees. It again caused me to wonder why the Israelis gave it back to Egypt and for what concessions.

The drive across the rich copper and turquoise deposits of the Sinai was punctuated by peaks as high as 2,865 meters. The nomad camps with their herds were noticeable along the way. The Sinai also produces alabaster, iron, manganese and bauxite. Sinai means moon, and the Bedouins depend on the moon for navigational guidance.

The trade routes through the Sinai were historically important, linking the East to the West. The Crusaders built fortresses in the Sinai in the 12th century, when they attempted to reclaim the Holy Land. Pilgrims from Africa traveled through the Sinai on their way to Mecca, dressing their camels in jeweled cloths to signify that they were pilgrims on a holy mission.

Mara told us that 50,000 Bedouins live in the Sinai, consisting mostly of 10 tribes. Each tribe has their own territory, carefully delineated by rock piles. The Egyptian government builds houses for them, but they reject stone walls, insisting they belong to the land, and instead house their animals in the shelters.

To protect birds and the environment, the government has designated reserves. They are attempting to encourage ecotourism in Egypt. Herons, storks, osprey, red fox, gazelle and turtles abound in Egypt, and the mangrove swamps and coral reefs of the Red Sea are also protected. Over 120 species of plants grow in the Sinai.

The history of the Sinai came alive as we drove through the desert. Moses spent 40 years cleansing his soul in the Sinai until the Lord revealed Himself at the burning bush, supposedly within the walls of St. Catherine's Monastery. Here Moses enlisted his brother Aaron's help. At the monastery's well he met Jethro, his future father-in-law.

The Egyptians especially revere St. Mark because he established Christianity in Alexandria in 54 A.D. Christians who lived in Luxor escaped into the Sinai during times of persecution, beginning the practice of monasticism.

In 284 A.D. Christians settled the Oasis of Feran, where the monastery lies. The Roman emperor Diocletian persecuted the Christians and killed them by the thousands until 325 A.D., when Christianity became the official religion of Egypt.

In 394 A.D. the empress Helen, mother of Constantine, visited the site of the burning bush and ordered a chapel built on the site. When invading Turkish tribes threatened the Christians in 525 A.D., the emperor Justinian ordered the site and chapel protected.

The chapel and monastery remained in use and was named St. Catherine's Monastery in the seventh century. The story of its naming is quite interesting. An Egyptian girl named Dorothea from Alexandria was persecuted, tortured and decapitated for her Christian beliefs. One of the monks on Mount Sinai supposedly found her body intact. It had miraculously been transported. The body was in a state of oozing fragrance on the mountain. The monk remained with the body for six months, brought it to the monastery and renamed Dorothea and the monastery St. Catherine.

Currently there are only 15 to 20 monks residing at the site. Most of them are Greek Orthodox. They study the ancient texts housed in the library. St. Catherine's is the oldest active Christian monastery in the world.

One Bedouin tribe resides around the monastery and Mt. Sinai. When the emperor Justinian ordered that the monastery be protected, he imported 500 Bosnian slaves to serve the monks. The Bosnians intermarried with the local tribes, became their own tribe and are still there serving the monks. Many of them have blue eyes and light features. They are Muslim.

The library at St. Catherine's is regarded as the richest collection of manuscripts, second only to the library at the Vatican. Their precious icons and the oldest copy of the Bible, The Codex Sinaiticus, dating from the sixth century and written in Greek, is prominently displayed. When I viewed the Codex, it was open to the book of St. Mark because they especially revere St. Mark who brought Christianity to Egypt. A fire at St. Catherine's in 1989 uncovered even more manuscripts behind stone walls. Some were stolen by the Russians and sold to England. The Egyptians are unhappy that many of their artifacts and documents are in the hands of other countries and are still attempting to regain possession.

During the reign of an Egyptian ruler, a mosque was built inside the walls of the monastery. Recently, leaders of Egypt came to Mt. Sinai to pray, fast and experience Ramadan, the Muslim Holy Period. Even the prophet Mohammed gave his protection to the monastery, not odd since the Muslim religion recognizes prophets of the Old Testament—Moses, Abraham and Noah. Our guide said all languages were derived from the Sinaitic writings that were found within the copper caves in the Sinai dating from 1400 B.C.

The monastery itself is a tall, imposing structure surrounded by sheer stone walls. The only previous entrance into the monastery was by a lowered basket. Now a road leads to the walls, and a small opening allows visitors into the courtyards within. Our coach was allowed access close to the gate so that the cases of wine could be easily delivered.

The monks were grumpy, rude and sullen, following us as though we planned to steal their treasures. The winter day was windy and cold, the skies gray. I imagined Moses aggravated with the complaining Israelites out in the desert and going for a walk up Mt. Sinai to distance himself.

Honk if you married Sonja

One of the Europeans asked our guide how the Bedouins existed in the desert and about the harsh reality of their life. She replied that she often wished to live the life of the Bedouin, that to be a Bedouin was to trace lineage back 20 generations. Their life was good; they were always protected by the tribe and had no worries. They made money from their camels, smuggling, tourists, goats, sheep and sheep's milk. Bedouins must marry within their tribe. They are Muslim, have large families and rarely have more than one wife. There are few divorces.

According to our guide, today the nomadic tribes settle their own legal problems. Death payments are 200 camels for a man, 300 camels for a woman and 400 camels for a child. The price of a camel ranges from $500 to $1,000. Bedouins bury their dead in cemeteries and believe that Aaron is buried at St. Catherine's rather than at Petra.

Most of the coach passengers slept for the return trip through the quiet reverence of the Sinai to the opulence of the villas, casinos and hotels of Sharm-El-Sheikh.

Leaving the resort town, the ship entered the Suez Canal with a convoy of cargo ships. Civilization was scattered on both sides of the canal, with monuments commemorating the war dead from World War II as well as the more recent Israeli war. The transit through the canal took eight hours.

Once the ship docked in Port Said, Egyptian Minister of Antiquities Dr. Zahi Hawass visited the ship and presented a slide show of him crawling into tombs and narrow passageways, digging in debris while he discussed the planned excavations of the Great Pyramid and the Sphinx with a robot designed by the Germans. Dr. Hawass has been on many Discovery and History Channel shows and was quite entertaining, admitting that his favorite guest celebrity to guide was Princess Diana.

Again we were well informed of the facts. The population of Egypt is 75 million, 25 million of which live in Cairo. Egypt has a literacy rate of 60 percent, and 55 percent of Egyptians are farmers. Military service for one year is compulsory. The Moubarak Peace Bridge, which spans the Suez Canal, connects Japan, Europe, Asia and Africa.

The drive to Cairo from Port Said was again with a military convoy. The area through which I traveled was a well-cultivated region with everything from mango trees to cotton and sugar cane. Canals fed the fields with water. Pigeon towers, tall wooden structures that harbored pigeons for consumption dotted the landscape.

Sonja Klein

Cairo is a huge city with freeways and slow-moving traffic. I spent three hours in the famous museum in the center of town. The treasures from King Tut's tomb occupy most of the second floor. There are thousands of artifacts.

I saw intricately carved alabaster artifacts over 5,000 years old. There were elaborately carved stone coffins that fit inside each other, weighing tons. They had been removed from the Valley of the Kings. King Tut had a folding camp bed with hinges of bronze for his camping excursions into the desert. The museum was crowded.

The pyramids are part of the city of Cairo, open to the public and sitting massively, stone-faced in the desert sands. Between the pyramids sits the Sphinx, guarding the souls of the past. Adjacent to the Great Pyramid of Giza is a museum housing a ship discovered in a pit next to the Great Pyramid. The ship was found in lined stone pits, disassembled. The reconstructed ship is the length of a football field, in excellent condition and prepared to carry the body of a pharaoh across the Nile to the Land of the Dead.

The Egyptians are extremely proud of their history and treasures and quick to complain that conquering countries and archaeologists have stolen many of the relics from King Tut's tomb. They often blame Lord Carnahan, whose family is still said to be in possession of many of them.

The massive size of the pyramids in the middle of the sandy barren desert struck wonder, and I could not help but imagine the manpower required to build them. Again the metaphysical atmosphere of Egypt was clearly felt, and I sensed the spirituality of the ancient civilizations that had inhabited the banks of the Nile far into the depths of Africa. Most of all I had a sense of the throbbing soul of Africa far to the south of Cairo.

Leaving the Red Sea, the ship entered the Mediterranean. I entered Lebanon at the port of Beirut. The first afternoon was spent with a local guide visiting a museum and walking through the central district. As the sun was setting we drove along the coastal highway, past the rubble that was once the American embassy.

My guide added to the knowledge I had acquired through my studies. The Ottomans, who conquered most of the Middle East, invaded the country of Lebanon in the early 1500's. The population of Beirut is about one million, and the French influence was obvious in the architecture and sidewalk cafés. There is a European feel to the city, an intercontinental atmosphere.

Honk if you married Sonja

The French ruled Lebanon from 1920 to 1943. The civil war that dominated life in Lebanon in recent times was in gruesome evidence with piled rubble, bullet holes in old buildings and construction sites on every block. The city was being rebuilt at every notice. Luxury hotels were near completion along the sea, and the town felt dynamic and optimistic. It was easy to see why Beirut had been called the Paris of the East.

I noticed armed military everywhere, and while there was peace, the atmosphere was somewhat restrained due to a political conference taking place. Due to scheduled peace talks, the central district was closed to vehicle traffic, and armed sentries overlooked the squares and boulevards of the downtown district from the rooftops.

The civil war that lasted from 1975 until 1990 was a conflict between the Christians and the Muslims. Currently, over 400,000 Palestinian refugees live in Lebanon. There are 18 religions in the country in addition to six Muslim sects. About 50 percent of the four million Lebanese are Christian and 50 percent Muslim.

My guide emphasized that there was no Arab culture, only the Arab language and that Lebanon had its own unique culture, as did Syria, Jordan and the other Arab-speaking countries—just like English-speaking countries have diverse cultures—the U.S., England, Australia and New Zealand.

I saw Roman ruins being restored in the heart of the city next to modern French-styled buildings and was told that only 1.8 percent of the national budget was reserved for culture. Most of the restoration being done is financed privately by other countries and individuals.

Beirut was founded about 300 B.C., and the country of Lebanon has been invaded many times by different cultures, among them the Hittites, Canaanites, Hyksos, Ammonites and Phoenicians. Seventeen civilizations have left their impact on Lebanon; the Syrians, Persians, Romans, Greeks and Ottomans are only a few. According to my guide the name Lebanon means belonging to the soil. I drove along the famous "green line" that had divided the city between the Christians and the Muslims. The traffic was fast and scary.

When I asked the guide how the museum had withstood the war, he showed me the ancient columns and statues too large and heavy to be moved. They had been cemented on the site to prevent looting. The smaller artifacts had been stored. An assortment of burned and melted items, damaged when the storage facility had been bombed, were displayed.

The Phoenicians settled in Lebanon along the coast, while the Canaanites lived in the hills overlooking the Mediterranean. The Phoenicians were famous for their sailing skills and settled Carthage, Tunisia and Crete as well as other cities along the coastline of the Mediterranean.

My guide told an interesting story. In recent years National Geographic initiated a study to determine from which area the Phoenicians originated. Five hundred Lebanese were randomly selected and their DNA compared to that of skeletal remains. Only two were genetically Phoenicians. My guide was tested, but he was not Phoenician.

Towering piles of gravel along the beach attracted my attention, and when I inquired, my guide said the gravel was ground-up rubble from the war. The gravel would be the basis for a park along the beach.

The following day I left Beirut through the fertile Becka Valley. We drove east on the main highway from Lebanon to Syria. Our destination was Baalbeck to see the Roman ruins of the largest unrestored temple in the world.

There is no desert in this lush country. We were traveling the route of the Silk Road, the ancient trade route through forested hills and valleys. The valleys were flanked on both sides by beautiful snow-capped mountains.

The guide provided much information on the current situation in Lebanon. The people displaced by the civil war were given a $10,000 indemnity. The country is a democratic republic with 128 members of parliament and has been ruled by the Christian majority since 1943. The president must be Christian; the prime minister must be Sunni Muslim and the speaker of the house a Shiite Muslim. The president is elected every six years.

I learned that there are three kinds of cedars in Lebanon and that one variety does not grow below 3,000 feet. In ancient times the lumber from Lebanon was shipped to Egypt since Egypt had very few trees. The country is currently very involved in reforestation. Pinon pines grow in Lebanon, and the Becka Valley, through which we were traveling, was eight miles wide and 120 miles long and produced 60 percent of the agricultural products of the country. The almond and cherry trees were in bloom, and the light pink flowers in the orchards presented another Kodak moment.

Again the guide continued. Israel was to our south, Syria to the southeast. There have been no trains or trams since the civil war. Lebanon imports all its fuel and no minerals have been discovered.

The current administration is focusing on tourism. The highest mountain in the Middle East is in Lebanon at over 9,000 feet and ski resorts dot the landscape.

I saw few veiled women. Unlike in Saudi Arabia, women have the right to vote and drive. English and French are taught in the schools. I was told that the country had suffered for 30 years from poor leadership and corruption, that free government health care was inadequate and that only the rich could afford private and expensive treatment. The price of gasoline in Lebanon was $2.80 per gallon, land sold for $1,000 a square meter and most jobs paid $600 to $700 a month.

We drove through Christian villages with churches and cathedrals and through Muslim villages with mosques. I saw poor village settlements of Palestinian refugees selling Hamas tee shirts. There was no hostility, only smiling, worn faces.

The Becka Valley was lush with hillside vineyards and wineries. The hilltops were dotted with the ruins of Crusader castles.

The ruins at Baalbeck were 100 percent Roman. The Romans ruled the area for 400 years. Their policy was to let the locals keep their traditions while paying tribute to Caesar. Traders came from Tyre and settled the rich valley. Alexander the Great was in the valley in 400 B.C. The Armenians came after him and then in 27 B.C. the Romans appeared.

The ruins were massive, over 20 acres, adjacent to a Palestinian village. On one side of the road I saw the poverty of the Palestinians and on the other side a vast complex of Roman ruins bigger than the Acropolis.

The largest temple was dedicated to Jupiter, the second temple was in honor of Bacchus and there was a third smaller temple. Paul the apostle passed through the area in 50 A.D. on his way from Sidon to Turkey.

The emperor Theodosius declared Christianity the official religion of Lebanon in 395 A.D. The ruins are in remarkable condition, even after having been damaged in a massive earthquake in 1759. Most of the temples are constructed of limestone found in a quarry less than a mile distant. The 1,200-ton blocks of limestone were moved to the site in much the same way as the building stones of the pyramids. The marble and granite found in the temples were imported.

After a delightful lunch in a Christian town, I stopped at a winery that has been in existence since 1857. Most of the wines tasted earthy, rather like dirt, except the expensive stuff that was saved until the end of the wine tasting session. The wine did not impress me, but the cool walk through the caves where the wine was stored was refreshing.

My guide tackled the most difficult question of the day when I asked him to tell me about the civil war. He was uncomfortable with my question but forged ahead. He said the war started in 1969 when King Hussein of Jordan kicked the Palestinian refugees out of Jordan. They came with their weapons to Lebanon. Since the Christian majority ruled Lebanon, they weren't sure they wanted the Palestinians in their country.

On April 13, 1975, a soccer game between the Christians and Muslims took place. As the armed Muslim players drove through a Christian area, 25 of them were killed by Christians. Within hours 50 checkpoints were established. The Muslims manned the checkpoints. Since everyone's papers identified their religion, the Muslim soldiers killed the Christians.

In 1977 Syria became involved in the battle. Six Arab countries sent troops to control the slaughter. Months later the Arab countries withdrew. Syria refused to leave. When the Christian Lebanese finally kicked the Syrians out, everyone started fighting each other until 1989.

My guide said the war was about power and money. He placed a lot of the blame on the country of Syria, who did not protect Lebanon from Israel in the years 1977 to 1989.

I had noticed that my guide's nails were bitten and that he clicked his worry beads even though he claimed to be a Christian. The worry beads and the evil eye were cultural. Christians and Muslims alike use worry beads and hang talismans to ward off the evil eye in their vehicles and homes. I have a few hanging in my house and in my vehicles.

The scenes of the current bombings in Lebanon are disturbing. A country that was torn by civil war and is now trying to rebuild and establish democracy is again being devastated. No matter a person's politics, the destruction of a beautiful country and the danger to its civilians is tragic.

Honk if you married Sonja

Our next stop was Syria. Many on the ship declined to leave, citing the fact that Syria was dangerous. The ship entered the port of Tartous, clearing customs easily, and I hired Assam, a Syrian, as my guide. His bearing identified him as ex-military, and when I inquired about his background he replied that he was an athletic coach.

My destination was the oasis in the valley of Palmyra, a three-hour drive through the countryside of Syria and through the oasis and valley of Homs. As we left the safety of the harbor area I learned that the city was new, only 30 years old.

Assam informed me that the population of Tartous was 900,000 and that the main industry was the manufacture of cement. President Assad had recently opened the country to foreign trade.

I observed the numerous olive trees and the big public hospital as we drove the dusty streets flanked by multi-storied apartment buildings. When my guide remarked, "Syria is bordered by occupied Palestine on one side and by the United States on the other side," I felt sure I was going to be kidnapped. I was wrong.

He continued with information, telling me that almost half the land is in agricultural use. Cotton is king, followed by wheat, lemons and oranges. Half of Syria's income comes from oil. The soil in Syria is black, compared to the reddish tint of the earth in Lebanon.

There are over 30 Crusader castle sites, mostly in ruins, throughout Syria and the country always controlled the route to Jerusalem. Due to the decline in tourism, the government has no current plans to restore the sites. Bedouins inhabit the desert regions of Syria, but most of the country is fertile, hilly and well watered.

Assam was full of facts. Unemployment is 15 to 20 percent. The government is encouraging foreign investment. The average salary is $300 per month and a 900-square-foot apartment costs approximately $50,000. Assam added that with permits and regulations, most people find it easier to build illegal dwellings on vacant property. It is cheaper to go the illegal route. Women can move freely in Syria and all religions are respected. As we drove through Homs, a town that dates from 1000 B.C., I saw the Crusader's Castle de Chevalier perched high on the hill overlooking the green valley.

Syria has hosted many civilizations. The French ruled Syria from 1920 to 1946. According to Assam, there are 18 million people living in Syria and 86 percent of them are Muslim. Most of the land is owned privately.

Sonja Klein

Education is free through high school. There is no income tax, just a car tax.

He was proud of the history of Syria and added that five Roman emperors were Syrian. As we continued through the Homs Valley, the almond trees were in bloom and the pale pink blossoms and fragrant aroma lasted for miles.

Most of the women I observed were covered, but Syrian women can drive and vote. Thirty of the 250 parliament members are women. Two government ministers are also women. Women have the freedom to go to court and ask for divorce. He said adultery was uncommon. Most Syrian men would rather take an additional wife than commit adultery.

As we approached our destination, the desert oasis of Palmyra, I noticed that the tents of the nomads were larger, their herds of sheep and goats more numerous. Shiny four-wheel drive vehicles and satellite dishes were obvious outside their black hair tents.

When I shared my observations with Assam, he replied that the Bedouins in Syria were wealthy because of the smuggling, that there were over a million Iraqi refugees in Syria and that we were traveling along the main smuggling route from Iraq. Not once in the three-hour drive from Tartous did I see a checkpoint or observe a military presence.

Palmyra, the city of palm trees, once had a population of 50,000. Traders journeyed through the oasis before the time of Christ. Some of the Hammarabians still speak Aramaic, which is a Semitic language. These people were cousins of the Nabateans in Jordan. Alexander conquered Syria; later the Romans came and then the Persians.

The ruins of the Greek, later Roman, city stood out magnificently in the valley amid the palm trees. A Crusader castle overlooked the valley. The town was quiet. For less than a dollar I purchased a kilo of fresh dates. They were golden and delicious. The local museum was small but well arranged.

I spent most of the day wandering among the spectacular ruins spread throughout the valley. The main thoroughfare in the middle of the ruins sparked my imagination, and I could easily visualize the caravans entering the valley, their camels laden with spices, salt and goods from the east or west. The camels I observed in Palmyra were the healthiest and most well bred that I had seen. Some were almost white.

The ruins contained baths, water conduits, a marketplace, towering columns and temples. Palmyra was widely visited by traders. St. Paul mentions visiting Palmyra in the New Testament.

The trip back to Tartous was uneventful, and I left Syria with a pleasant memory.

The ship moved on through the Mediterranean to Rhodes, Greece, the next destination. Rhodes is the largest of the Dodecanese Islands, located 225 miles east of Athens and only 12 miles from Turkey. It lies among three continents with the rough Aegean Sea on one side and the calm Mediterranean on the other side.

Tourism is the main industry, obviously because of the beauty of Rhodes. The current population is about 100,000, and the island has been inhabited since 600 B.C. Rhodes was a popular stopping place for the Crusaders. Their castles dot the mountainous cliffs guarding the ports.

The terrain is rocky, the climate semi-arid. I saw lots of goats, sheep and olive trees. Rhodes reminded me of my county when I observed all the deer. They were imported to the island hundreds of years before Christ in order to kill the numerous snakes. Today the symbol of the deer is an important part of the island's culture.

The mountains of Rhodes go all the way to the sea. I noticed pinon pines and lemon and orange trees. The Crusaders were in Rhodes in the 1400's and the Knights of the Order of St. John lived in Rhodes for over 200 years.

Three ancient sites are found on Rhodes. I walked through a medieval village to reach the site of Lindos, which dates from 600 B.C. and is older than the Acropolis in Athens.

The King of Lindos was one of the seven wise rulers of ancient Greece. My destination was the temple to Athena.

The trail to the temple took me through narrow cobblestone streets between homes and shops selling everything from olive oil to beautifully embroidered linens. A small Greek Orthodox Church was nestled along the alleyway. The hundreds of carved steps up the mountain made progress slow but afforded the opportunity to enjoy the view of the blue Mediterranean, the white ships in the harbor and the villages far below.

As I passed a terrace, there was a rocked water well and a 50-foot-long carving into the solid rock of a sailing vessel. The fluid lines of the ship reminded me of a carving in the Louvre. I was not surprised to hear that the artist was the same who carved "Winged Victory" in the Louvre.

The next series of steps was precipitous and steep with no handrails. Toward the top was a Crusader castle and tombs built over the ancient ruins. At the very top were the Roman ruins with the magnificent temple to Athena. The sanctity, view and scenery took away what little breath I had left. The crumbling stones were crowded with centuries of history.

The walk down was far less strenuous. I enjoyed a Mediterranean lunch overlooking the harbor and joined a group of Greek dancers, who whirled me into the dance. In the course of the afternoon I learned that four kilos of olives produce one kilo of olive oil.

Napvilion was the second stop in Greece. The city is on the mainland and has been conquered many times. The Turks occupied the city for over 400 years.

Napvilion is a city of about 11,000 and is also known as Mycennae. The Mycenaean empire existed in 1500 B.C. and had a population of half a million.

Napvilion was the city of Agamemnon, the brother of Menelaus, the famous participant in the Helen of Troy story. Mycennae was the first capital of Greece and the first area to be liberated in the Greek War of Independence in 1842. Greece has never had a Greek king. All of the reigning kings came from elsewhere.

I learned that there are 54 provinces in Greece and the fertile valleys of this province produce 40 percent of the oranges. Though the temperature was cold and it was windy, I saw vegetable fields as well as olive, orange and lemon trees. Tobacco and artichokes are also grown in the area.

The history lesson continued. In 1828 the Greeks defeated the Turks, and in 1831 Otto and Amalia became the King and Queen of Greece. Since 1974 Greece has been a republic with a parliament that elects the president. There are 300 members of parliament, and 97 percent of Greece's population is Greek Orthodox Christian.

Following an excellent Greek lunch, I visited the Fortress of Palamadus. He was the king of Napvilion in 1200 B.C. and fought in the war with Troy. Palamadus was a doctor, astronomer and the inventor of the game of backgammon. The fort, perched high on a rocky cliff overlooking the port, was Venetian in design. Succeeding generations and cultures altered and used the fort.

I was fast approaching sensory overload from my month-long journey. Turkey was my final destination.

I entered Turkey through the port of Kudasi, a beautiful coastal town on the Sea of Marmara. The harbor was full of large elaborate yachts, more than I had ever seen in one place. The terraced rocky hillsides, dotted with olive trees and many varieties of pines, slanted down to the sea. Next to Kudasi, across the harbor was Ephesus, a fertile delta area famous for its wine and soap.

The mulberry trees were in full bloom, and I learned that one cocoon produced a mile of silk thread. As I traveled across the swampy estuary, I viewed wheat fields, tangerine and peach orchards and cotton fields as well as a water park and modern condos. Kudasi is located only an hour from Smyrna and was inhabited by the Seljuk Turks, who preceded the Ottomans in 900 B.C.

Again a guide complemented my information. Turkey contains over 20,000 archaeological sites, and Ephesus is one of the most significant. The ancient city of Ephesus was large, over four square miles and once hosted a population of 250,000. I entered the ruins from the crest of the hill and strolled down a mile-long paved road through central Ephesus. I walked where traders, travelers, and John, Paul and other apostles had walked.

Ephesus was a central trading port, and the ruins of the magnificent library dominated the central part of the ruins. The library was a beautiful Greek structure reported to be second in manuscripts only to the library in Alexandria. There was even a tunnel leading from the library to the brothel. The stones were carved with arrows pointing the way to various areas of Ephesus. The public toilets were carved from solid stone with flowing water for waste disposal as well as for cleansing the hands.

Alexander the Great left General Marcus in Ephesus around 300 B.C. with the orders to build a great city.

When Alexander conquered the area, he asked, "Where is the temple to Artemis?" He was told it had been destroyed by earthquake and fire. He then asked, "Where was the goddess Artemis when this was happening?"

The natives wisely answered, "She was assisting your mother at your birth."

Restoration of the city was underway with many participating countries excavating sites, courtesy of the Turkish government. As I approached the amphitheater where Paul spoke I was amazed at the size and seating capacity of the stadium. The acoustics were remarkable.

My guide entertained with stories of Greek mythology. He said, "When lust and desire found the psyche or soul, then love was created."

From Ephesus I walked down the hill to the Basilica of St. John. The word basilica means courtyard. St. John, the most beloved disciple, lived here until he died. As I walked through the ruins I saw the chapel, baptismal font, courtyard and living quarters.

According to legend, Mary, the mother of Jesus, was cared for by the disciple John, who brought her to Ephesus. I traveled up a winding road to a rugged tree-covered hilltop, where a small chapel had supposedly been built upon the site of the house where Mary lived.

I spent the remainder of the day in the silk rug market watching the technique of hand weaving silk rugs. I drank Turkish coffee and visited the market, buying some talismans to ward off the evil eye that had thus far ignored me.

My last evening was spent dancing with a native of Zanzibar, an island off the coast of Tanzania, Africa—a fitting end to a journey that had taken me to three continents.

26

The power of the press

My friend Linda called from Uvalde, "Sonja, have you ever been to the Kerrville Folk Festival?"

"No, but I've been to the Terlingua Chili Cookoff and Willie's Fourth of July Concert. Kerrville is on my list to go to before I die. Have you been?"

"Yes, I've been and it's a blast. My husband went once and doesn't like festivals and concerts. My girlfriend from Dallas, the one you call 'Linda minor,' will be 50 that week. Why don't I call her and let's all go?"

"I'm in. Great idea. When is it?"

"Memorial Day weekend. I'll get us press passes and reserve a room at the YO Resort."

Packing was easy, comfortable shoes and clothes that would tolerate Texas weather before summer settled down to serious heat. I picked up Linda in Uvalde in my cowboy Cadillac—a Dodge diesel four-wheel drive with the long bed, dents, scratches and caliche icing. Everything from wine and champagne to a decent-sized coffee pot and gourmet ground coffee occupied the back seat.

The Linda from Dallas, a recent widow, planned on flying into San Antonio and renting a white convertible for the three of us. After all, it was her birthday.

After a fortifying Mexican lunch, we checked into the resort, unloaded the truck and opened a bottle of chilled white wine. Then we reclined on the queen-sized beds and anticipated an evening of music and men. I was a long-term widow, older by a decade than the other two. At close glance, we could all pass for a few years younger.

My friend Linda from Uvalde was blonde and buxom, a songwriter, guitar player and dental hygienist married to a dentist. Her friend Linda from Dallas was blonde, pretty, an executive assistant and still in the man market. I was petite, blonde, a veteran of four marriages and a widow who was no longer looking for marriage, having graduated to the category of being a nurse or a purse for elderly disintegrating gentlemen or non-gentlemen.

Since Linda, the birthday girl, was not scheduled to arrive until late Friday evening, Linda and I drove out to the ranch that was the scene of the festival.

As we entered the gate and alerted the attendant that we were press, Linda inquired where to pick up our passes. I remained in the truck, doing the old-woman thing and blocked the road, ignoring the comments, "You can't park there. You have to move your truck." I stayed in place until Linda returned with our passes. I drove back into Kerrville, where we met some friends of Linda's for pizza.

Arriving too early at the pizza parlor in downtown Kerrville, I parked and we walked the block to a bar for a $7 glass of wine served by a surly bartender. The object of sitting at the bar is primarily to be entertained by the bartender, but those days seem to live only in memory. I was reminded of the scene in Lonesome Dove when Gus bloodied the bartender for rude behavior. I longed for a pistol to slam him across the face, a mere widow's aggression.

As we walked back to the pizza parlor, we encountered a younger man sitting on a bench eating peanut butter out of a jar and drinking a non-alcoholic drink. Having sought affable male company and failed, we stopped to visit with him. He was a homeless Desert Storm vet, a medic. After telling him how much we appreciated his service, we left him with $40, feeling better for not having tipped the bartender.

By the time we arrived at the pizza parlor, Linda's friends were on their second pitcher of beer and had ordered pizza. We joined the rowdy group and contributed our share, and by the time darkness descended upon the Hill Country, I knew I was unable to drive without risk. Linda drove the pickup to the resort, and our friends delivered us to the gates of the festival after I assured them I could find us a ride back with no problem. I had reached the omniscient stage of overconfidence, still having the assurance of being a world traveler, able to extricate myself and others from risky situations.

The festival was dark; cedar trees and native growth crowded the rocky hill. The light reflected from the dusty road was our only guide— that and the sound of the music. The crowd was mixed—all ages, sizes and predilections. Linda was enthusiastic and bubbly; she had been to Kerrville twice before. I was the virgin and reluctant to engage.

Honk if you married Sonja

The music was folksy; the entertainers appeared to be Austin artists. One pounded on his guitar more than strummed. I didn't like the music, the feeling of the crowd and the darkness. Linda led me backstage, hoping to find a party. There was nothing happening. We returned to the uncomfortable rickety benches. Linda enjoyed a glass of wine. I drank a bottle of water. The music continued. The entertainer beat on his guitar as if it were a drum.

Midnight sobering at a festival, I glanced over at Linda. She was the musician and songwriter. She was asleep, nodding on the bench. I nudged her, "Linda, if you can find the gate, I'll get us a ride back to the resort."

"I'll call a taxi." She used her cell phone to contact the local taxi service, and when she was informed that it would be $30, replied, "Isn't that a little high?"

"Then walk." The dispatcher hung up on her.

We found the entrance, where the gate was well manned by volunteers. With the charm of a teenager, I inquired, "Our ride left us and we need a ride to the YO Resort. Could you help us?"

Noticing my press pass, the young attendant offered, "No problem; I'll call the VIP van. Just wait right here."

A young man arrived in a shiny new white Suburban, opened the door courteously and drove us safely to our home away from home. On the trip, I ascertained that he was from the same town where Linda was born and that he knew mutual friends of mine from Alpine—a clear indicator of the "six degree" theory that states if six people are together, there will always be a connection.

When we arrived, Linda from Dallas was at the desk in the lobby. Our timing was perfect. We were hungry, made a quick trip to Sonic and indulged in cheeseburgers. I slept like a baby.

IHOP was their choice for breakfast. As we entered the restaurant, Linda from Dallas looked around. "I like Kerrville. Everyone here is old and I really look young. I could live here."

I replied. "I couldn't. I find it depressing."

Linda from Uvalde answered, "I think the competition would be rough."

The birthday girl bragged. "Not at my age."

"True."

After a hearty breakfast, we found our way to the Arts and Crafts Festival near Schreiner College. Acres of booths and tents were before us—a shopper's dream. The three of us methodically set out to cover the entire arena of art. We browsed jewelry, pictures, sculptures, ceramics, woodcrafts, leather goods, body products, hand-hewn furniture, glassware and ingenuous miscellaneous items. Linda from Dallas purchased some Christmas presents; I purchased a few small plaques; Linda from Uvalde bought an airplane kit for her young son.

The afternoon heat discouraged more shopping, so we returned to the parking lot and the white convertible. The top would not go down all the way, just partially. We stood in the baking parking lot for what seemed like hours trying to figure out why the top was hanging up before it disappeared into the trunk. Finally we abandoned hope and we set out to satisfy our hunger. Our destination of choice was a small Italian restaurant near the old hospital. The sign on the door indicated that they closed at 3:00. There were ten minutes left. As we entered, Linda from Uvalde inquired, "Is it too late for us to have lunch?"

The savvy waiter noticed three women with PRESS PASS plastered on their shoulders. "Come on in. Of course it's not too late."

Forgetting about the press passes on our shoulders, we thought he was merely being nice. Before we had a chance to look at the menus, he offered. "Let me bring you some fresh fish tacos; they're our specialty."

We dined well.

Returning to the motel, we opted for a dip in the pool and shower before the next segment of our adventure.

We entered the festival site in the convertible that refused to convert. Our press passes allowed entrée to the VIP parking lot, even though the distance was not to our liking. We had dressed casually and comfortably. As we approached the music pavilion and stage, guitar music drifted through the cedars. As we cruised the many vendors, the aroma of cooking tickled our hunger. We settled on lamb gyros, hoping it was really lamb. As we settled at a picnic table slanted down the hill, we observed the crowd. This was definitely no Woodstock.

Seeking thrills and excitement, the two Lindas trekked backstage, instructing me to wait at the table. I enjoyed my glass of cheap wine, valiantly trying to remain on the bench that slanted downhill and required a bit of muscle tension to remain seated. Several 40ish men occupied the upper end of the bench and I valiantly attempted to engage them in conversation.

"Nice evening. Thank heavens it's not too hot."

"Not bad for the end of May in Texas."

"Yeah."

"Where are y'all from?"

"Austin."

"What about you?"

"West of here, from Barksdale. Those two are from Dallas and Uvalde."

As the Lindas rejoined me on the downhill bench, names were exchanged. Linda from Dallas connected with one of men and went off to his camp. The other three left after inviting us all to their camp back in the dark brush. They assured us that there were some great songwriters and musicians in their camp and that there would be a good story. The press passes shone like a neon sign advertising our deception.

Linda from Uvalde wandered off to check out the vendors, and I maintained my muscle tension to not roll downhill. Home base had been established, and I was the designated umpire.

A young man took the upper end of the table before I could switch sides.

I was the first to speak. "Hi, there."

"Hello. Who do you write for?"

"Um, the *Uvalde Leader News, The Canyon Broadcaster* and an Austin magazine called *Women In Bloom*. By then I had the spiel down pat. "Where are you from?"

"Pennsylvania. My name's Martin the troubadour."

"Do you write songs or play them?"

"Actually, I produce CD's and some videos."

"Really. Is this your first time here?"

"No, I've been coming every year for eight years. I used to live in Austin but moved back home when my mother became ill. I live with her and take care of her and have my studio in the basement of her house. Have you been to any of the camps?"

"Not yet. I'm with two friends. I'm keeping home base."

"When they come back, I'll take you to the camps. There're some great songwriters in the girls' camp, and then we can go to Shakespeare's camp, where Willie and Billy Joe Shaver used to hang out. You can find a good story there."

As the music emanating from the stage died down, we followed Martin the troubadour through the dark lanes to a group of women singing off key. They welcomed us profusely, moved some chairs to include us in the circle and continued their playing and singing.

One of the singers commented, "Wow, we saw y'all sing. You're great."

Martin added. "These are the Dixie Chicks."

The word spread rapidly through the darkness. "The Dixie Chicks are here."

"Where?"

Martin smiled. We followed him like chicks following an old hen—Martin the troubadour.

Through the twisted paths and tents, campers, RV's and trailers, we trotted to the far reaches of the campground. The camp was on the fringe, the end of the road where the brush met civilization. The camp was big; there was an assortment of travel trailers, small RVs and some tents, as well as a kitchen area with tables and cooking apparatus set under a large tent canopy. Off to the side was a circle of singers and guitar players. Shakespeare was the easiest to spot—long hair, mustache and the wrinkles of time. He was by far the best guitar player. They gathered chairs, enlarged the circle and sat up a bit straighter. After all, the Dixie Chicks had arrived. The other women in the camp had been worn down by harder times. They were disheveled, overweight and colorless. We must have appeared as peacocks rather than chicks.

Martin borrowed a guitar for Linda from Uvalde while the other Linda and I sat beyond the circle. Our friend was in the circle. She sang and played a song she had written. They all applauded for her as much as they applauded for themselves. Hours passed as we patiently waited for Linda's next turn. It was 3 A.M. before Linda played again. We waited a polite period, said our goodbyes and thanks and walked back through the maze of camps to the convertible that wasn't. Music drifted through the cedars and agarita bushes, the faint whisper of those who wouldn't quit.

Sunday morning found us at the IHOP, three chicks among a lot of old hens and roosters. Linda from Dallas raved about the event. I knew there were better festivals; the Terlingua Chili Cookoff for one was a good place to dance.

I had come to dance but just waddled home like an old duck.

27

Fear is irrational

Growing up in Texas I was instilled with fear. "Don't climb that tree. You'll fall down and die of a broken neck. Don't pet a strange dog. He'll have rabies, bite you and you'll die before you receive the seven painful shots in the stomach. Don't play in the ditch after a rain. You'll get typhoid and die, or a cottonmouth moccasin will bite your leg and it'll be amputated. You don't need to go to the beach with the church group. There're sharks, jellyfish and the deadly current that will suck you out into the ocean and you'll drown."

Maybe because my father was considerably older than my mother and had witnessed tragedy, he cautioned the four of us children at all times. Never can I remember him saying, "Have a good time." On the other hand, my mother's favorite words were, "Go for it." Her recklessness balanced his circumspection. As a result, perhaps the four of us children were conflicted.

Every day I hear both voices, the one of encouragement and the one that advises worry and fear. I worry all the time about going broke, dying, having a car wreck. About having visitors to the ranch that get hurt, destroy my equipment and hurt my livestock. I worry about brown recluse spiders, snakes, scorpions and cactus thorns. I worry about dying overseas or in a plane crash or being debilitated in a car accident. Cancer and health issues add to my worry list as I age ungracefully.

When my husband John was alive, he worried too. When we discovered that we were both worrying about the same things, he admonished me, "You worry about the house and money and I'll worry about the equipment and livestock." Relief flooded my perception. At last I had someone to share the burden.

I worry about a job being finished, celebrating a completion, no matter how small. Even a completed vehicle inspection warrants sublime happiness.

Recently my 18-year-old Explorer needed an oil change and inspection sticker. For the two months prior to the inspection deadline I began to worry, worry if the vehicle would make the 60-mile trip to Uvalde, worry if the air-conditioner would work in the June heat, worry if the vehicle would pass the test, worry if I would have to wait too long to have the oil changed and then worry if I might make the trip back safely. The morning of the planned expedition, I almost cancelled the trip, choosing to take my new pickup for groceries instead. Then I remembered my daughter's admonition, "Fear is irrational" and my mother's words, "Go for it." I did indeed go for it and succeeded in a completion.

28

Cheez Whiz and Peanut Butter

❝ Hi, it's Linda. What are you doing?"

"Just sitting around eating Cheez Whiz and peanut butter and getting fat," I said.

"I can't believe you have Cheez Whiz in your house. You're such a fanatic about fresh food."

"Well, I can't believe it either. I had to buy a jar of the stuff because my brother Allan came for a visit earlier this month. He's a real finicky eater and the only way he eats green vegetables is with heaping tablespoons of that yellow stuff on it."

"How much have you gained?"

"About five pounds. Of course there's always the possibility that my housekeeper messed up my scale."

"Do you really think so? Have you checked the setting?"

"I can't; it's one of those digital things."

"You can lose the weight."

"Not till I finish the jar of peanut butter."

"What's so bad about peanut butter?"

"I can just walk by a jar and gain weight. I don't usually keep it around."

"Throw it all away."

"You know that's against my principles; it's wrong to let food go to waste. The best thing is to eat it quickly and get it over with."

"That's a desert mentality. Eat it before it spoils."

"The nomads have existed for thousands of years on that philosophy and they're not extinct or overweight."

"Why did you buy the peanut butter if it makes you fat?"

"You have time for the story?"

"Okay, tell me."

Sonja Klein

"When my dog Easy got sick a few months ago, the vet prescribed 30 days of antibiotics. It was a pain to get the pills down his throat. My daughter told me to put the pill in a lump of peanut butter and he would gulp it down. It worked. I'm on my second jar, creamy no less. A lump for him and a lump for me."

"How much longer do you have to give him the pills?"

"About another 10 days, two pills a day. I'm trying to make it last so the last pill will be in the last glob, but at the rate I'm going I may have to buy a small jar to make it come out right."

"How big is the jar you're working on now?

"One of those big two-pound plus ones."

"Good grief, Sonja. Well, you can always exercise to offset the peanut butter. How much Cheez Whiz is left?"

"About half a jar. I've been putting it on flour tortillas with chopped up fresh jalapenos. I'm trying to finish the jar at the same time I finish the pack of tortillas. I think it'll come out even."

"Start walking every day. I lost 12 pounds walking three miles a day."

"I don't exercise. I do ranch work. The best exercise I get is pushing my luck, jumping to conclusions, stretching the truth and running my mouth."

"Very funny."

"I thought you might like that one."

"I plan on cleaning out my closet. I'll give you all my fat clothes just in case you don't lose the weight."

"Thanks a lot. You're a real friend."

"I read that if you wear your tightest clothes you won't be tempted to eat much. Maybe you should try that."

"Easy for you to say. I've got two jars of poison to finish."

"Do you do the same thing with a box of candy?"

"Of course."

"It's a miracle you're not as big as a house."

"I think I was a nomad in a hot climate in another life. I've always been like that and you know I really hate the cold. No, I don't hate anything, I dislike the cold."

"You just have poor circulation because you used to smoke."

"No, that's not it. I can't remember not being cold. I was born in January and I think my mother let me get cold on the way home from the hospital. That's why I'm going to be cremated so I'll be warm at last."

"My husband loves Cheez Whiz. He thinks it's better than the invention of the wheel. Heaven knows what's in it. He thinks it's pure cheese because it's yellow. I think it's too shiny to be real."

"Yeah, shiny doesn't necessarily mean good."

"Diamonds are good and they're shiny."

"Men are so transparent and dumb."

"You say that just because you're not married. I gave away all my rich leftovers after Christmas. Sent them home with my dad. He was tickled to have them and I didn't want to be tempted."

"Maybe you were a nomad too."

"I just had a thought. Maybe it's the drops you're taking for your eye inflammation. You said they were steroids and you know how steroids make you swell up like all those athletes."

"Anything's possible. I'll quit taking them and see what happens."

"If the eye turns red again, start using the drops. It's worth a try."

"The best bet would be to lay off the Cheez Whiz and peanut butter and quit looking for a quick fix."

"We can always go to the fat doctor in Piedras Negras. I'll go with you."

"Thanks, girlfriend. Love you."

"Love you too. Later."

Later that week I called Linda. "Hi, girlfriend. It's Sonja. What's up?"

"Just the usual," Linda answered. "What's new with you?"

"You were right. It was the steroid eye drops. I quit taking them and dropped three pounds in two days. Isn't that weird?"

"Not really. Did you lay off the peanut butter too?"

"But of course. I convinced myself that every time I gave the dog a lump of peanut butter, it was dog food. The jar is holding steady since I convinced myself it was dog food."

"Good move. What about the Cheez Whiz?"

"I managed to finish it off, wash the jar and put it in the recycle bin. There are some tortillas left but I plan to use them for enchiladas when I have company next week."

"Excellent decision."

"About all I have left in the refrigerator is broccoli, beets, carrots and cabbage. Can't get into trouble with that."

"Good girl. I'm proud of you."

"Thanks for your help. Don't know how I would survive without you."

"Ditto."

29

Take a nap

Stress and anxiety wreak havoc on all beings. Some internalize and others externalize. I have discovered that I am one of those who internalizes when confronted with situations in my life over which I have no control, not that we have control over anything.

As my mother aged and confronted her physical ailments, she was prone to overmedicate, causing those of us who love her to become concerned with her decreasing mobility. On one such episode, I was cajoled into sleeping with her. After three days of literally wiping her ass and becoming her shadow, I returned to my home in west Texas, thoroughly spent, emotionally drained.

Within a day of reclaiming my territory, I discovered that the complete left side of my face was sore and swollen; even my ear canal was affected. My first thought was that I had some sort of ear or sinus infection, but when a lump surfaced on my lower left gum, I came to the conclusion that it was an infected tooth. I zeroed in on a molar that had been filled more than once, a result of wearing braces.

A trip to my dentist revealed that I had a necrotic root on the molar. The dentist examined my mouth and then looked me square in the eye and asked, "Have you been under any type of stress lately?"

"Well, yes. I was taking care of my mother."

"You are grinding your teeth when you sleep and have cracked that molar, and the root has become infected."

"Great. What do I do now?"

"Get rid of the stress and meditate, and as soon as the infection clears up, that molar needs to be pulled. Since it's cracked there's no need for a root canal."

"Thanks, Doc."

I drove home amazed that stress had caused me to grind a tooth with such vehemence that I had cracked it. Determined to not have a tooth pulled, I nursed that cracked tooth for two years, sleeping with a rolled up washrag in my mouth until the infection disappeared and I quit grinding my teeth. Mother was better.

Every time I went to the dentist for a tooth cleaning, I advised the dental hygienist to leave that molar alone, not to stress it or disturb it. I was determined to keep that rotten tooth. But when I realized that the crack in the tooth was housing excess bacteria and the bad taste in my mouth was a potential source of bad breath, I made an appointment and had the tooth pulled without consequence.

The next battle with stress dealt with contemplating self-publishing a book. A printer came and stayed at my ranch for five days. I hosted a dinner party and after five days, there was another lump on my lower left jaw, adjacent to the gap created by the missing split molar. I returned to my old habit, sleeping with a washrag in my mouth, waiting for the lump to dissipate.

After my company departed, I was involved with a local fundraiser and had agreed to drive a friend out to Big Bend, pulling my flatbed trailer to haul some appliances. My plate was full, and that rolled-up washrag was the only thread keeping my sanity intact. There was no Gorilla Glue that could solve my problem.

Dreading the drive to Big Bend, I went to feed my stock, and as I stepped into the feed bin, I felt a horrible pain at my waist, like a pinched nerve or torn muscle. The pain was like a knife, but I continued on, picking my garden and doing some yard work, thinking that whatever was pinched, pulled or torn would repair itself.

By the time I ventured indoors for a shower, the pain had spread to my entire left side. I was now suffering up and down half of my body, from my jaw to my toes. As I turned on the shower I discovered that there was no water. Troubleshooting my water system involved a walk down a steep hill through cactus and brush, checking breaker boxes and turning valves on and off to ascertain whether it was a broken line, thrown breaker or dysfunctional submersible pump.

In the frenzy of my detective work, I forgot the pain or perhaps ignored it, and when a call to my well service man produced results, he discovered that ants had invaded the control panel. Water was restored the same day, but my body was not.

By the time I went to bed, I could not move without pain and had a restless night, tossing and turning in an attempt to achieve comfort with a rolled up washrag in my mouth.

Honk if you married Sonja

The next morning I carefully eased out of my high four-poster bed, called my friend and canceled the trip and spent the day on the sofa, sleeping off my stress and alleviating my pain with slumber. After two days of self-nurturing, all pain had disappeared. The remedy for stress and anxiety—Take a nap.

30

Traveling the silk road across central Asia

Getting to Kazakhstan was easier than I had imagined—a simple nonstop flight from Houston to Frankfurt, Germany, a six-hour layover and then a direct flight via Lufthansa to Almaty, Kazakhstan. The visas had not been easy, four months and $750, the reason being that the five "Stans" are independent countries, among the 13 members of the CIS (Commonwealth of Independent States) and require separate visas.

The atmosphere in the Frankfort airport was exotic and the departing gate area was crowded with travelers on their way to Addis Ababa, Ethiopia and Khartoum, Sudan. Most of them were men; I had rarely seen a rougher group and imagined them to be oilfield workers, adventurers similar to those who had settled our West. I was wrong. Visiting with one of them, a Canadian, I discovered that he was a contractor for the United Nations, flying to Khartoum to install over 200 generators. His crew had been there for four months, laying the lines. He would oversee the completion for the following six months. I asked him about the danger. He replied it was minimal as long as the workers remained in their camps. He had done the same sort of work in Afghanistan. My pleasure trip paled in comparison to his mission.

The seven-hour flight to Almaty, Kazakhstan, ended near 1 A.M. , and as I disembarked from the plane, the familiar smell of wood smoke— perfume to my senses—welcomed me to central Asia. The modest hotel was mediocre, located in the central district. The tiny room was equipped with a small, clean bathroom and a single bed.

The following morning I joined a group of 17 in the lobby of the hotel for breakfast, an inviting spread of cheeses, cold cuts, boiled eggs, and the fruit and wonderful melons I was to enjoy the entire trip. Unfortunately, the coffee was Nescafé; central Asias drink tea, either green or black.

Honk if you married Sonja

As the morning progressed I learned from our guide that Kazakhstan is the 9th largest country in the world, larger than the whole of Western Europe combined. The population is over 15 million, most of them being Kazakhs. The major religious groups include Sunni Muslims and Russian Orthodox. Official freedom of religion and religious tolerance are a result of a long history of mixed ethnic groups and cultures. The society is bilingual, speaking Kazakh and Russian.

The country has been independent since 1991, and the average annual income is about $11,000 per year. Kazakhstan has large proven oil and natural gas reserves as well as reserves of uranium, chromium, lead, zinc, manganese and copper. Foreign investment of over $40 billion has been attracted in recent years. Pipelines throughout the country deliver gas to Russia to be sold in Europe. The cost of living is higher in Kazakhstan than any of the other central Asian countries. The hotel room was $200 and meals were over $20.

The morning was spent on a city tour. Almaty is a large, modern city of two million with boulevards and lovely gardens. There was considerable traffic on the streets; most of the cars were Mercedes, BMWs and other luxury cars. The guide said that under the Russian regime there were three problems—no food, no roads and crazy people; two of the three problems still exist—no roads and crazy people. He said that under the Russians, the Kazakhs pretended to work and the Russians pretended to pay them. The city has a continental climate, similar to ours but subject to floods and earthquakes.

The Tien Shan range's snowcapped mountains ring the city. Ski slopes and resorts are located 20 miles from the city, with the tourist season lasting from October until April. The Asian winter games are held outside the city, where the world's largest outdoor ice-skating arena is located. It seats 12,000. The mountains are dotted with springs and resort spas.

The fall leaves were spectacular in their changing colors from golden to bright orange—aspen, poplar, birch, wild apricot, apple and walnut. Over 20 varieties of wild apples are found in Kazakhstan, as well as many varieties of walnut. Apples as well as tulips originated in the area. The Dutch annually buy hundreds of thousands of bulbs from the Kazakhs.

Kazakh is said to mean free rider. The culture is nomadic and agricultural, with wheat, cotton and livestock being produced. The country is the world's 7th largest producer of grain.

There are still snow leopards, wild goats, brown bears, foxes and eagles in the wild.

We enjoyed a traditional lunch in a soft, carpeted felt yurt outside the city at a ski resort. Horse meat, lamb and tongue with noodles, beet salad and cabbage were served. I found the meal quite tasty. Some of my fellow tourists did not agree.

The afternoon was spent in the National Museum, where I learned that the current country originated in the 1400's. In 1969 the Golden Man—the great treasure of the country—was found in the ruins of Indo-European men dating from the fifth century B.C. The people of Kazakhstan are very European in appearance, not oriental, and very attractive.

School is free for the first nine years, and the students attend school six days a week. The income tax rate is 13 percent, and there are casinos in the country. The government owns all the natural resources and minerals. If you are fortunate enough to own acreage, the government dictates what you grow. In the 1950's over 800,000 Russians were sent to Kazakhstan to cultivate the fields. Many of them returned to Russia after independence in the 1990's.

The evening meal in a local restaurant consisted of a beet salad with finely chopped potatoes, shredded carrot salad, soup with cabbage, and lamb and shredded veal with mashed potatoes as the main course. Caramel sponge cake with tea finished the meal. I came to prefer the green tea over the black. Both were light in color.

The following morning we visited the market, typical of the Sunday markets along the Silk Road. Everything from shoes, furniture, toys, clothing, fruit, vegetables, meat and the round, warm flat bread called nan was available. The smells and sights were a feast for the senses and the smiling faces of the vendors encouraged a taste or feel of the products. I ate apricot pits, figs, chocolate candy, roasted peanuts, smoked fish and fresh melon. A kilo, 2.2 pounds, of dried fruit cost about $5.

Down the road from the Sunday market was the cattle market, a flat open area where owners gathered to buy and sell sheep, goats, cattle and horses as well as tack. A milk cow sold for about $1,000, an Arab/cross horse for $1,200, a fat ewe for $110 and goats for $60. Most of them were quite shaggy and scruffy.

The road from Almaty to the border with Krygyzstan was a two-lane black top with no white line in the middle, rough and a bit ragged.

Honk if you married Sonja

We passed through fields of cotton ready to be harvested, irrigation canals and fields of drying corn. Gas stations and restrooms were absent. We stopped in groves of trees, men going one way, women the other to use the bathroom.

Before crossing the border we stopped for a picnic lunch at Torugart Pass, overlooking the Charyn River along the Silk Road. The Tien Shan Mountains surrounded us as we entered Krygyzstan, dragging suitcases from checkpoint to checkpoint. The sun was setting as we arrived at the Aurora Hotel, a resort on Lake Issyk-Kul, the Hawaii of central Asia.

Kyrgyzstan is often referred to as the Switzerland of central Asia. The highest mountain peak is 24,400 feet above sea level. The Tien Shan Mountains cover 80 percent of the country and the rest of the country is mountain valleys and basins. Over 8,000 glaciers are found in the country, and winter sports are popular, even snowboarding. The climate varies from dry continental and polar in the mountains to subtropical in the Fergana Valley. The country is landlocked, with the second largest high-altitude lake in the world, Lake Issyk-Kul. The lake is slightly saline with no outlet.

A new guide welcomed us at the border—Farhad, who spoke with a Texas accent. When I inquired where he had learned his English, he replied, "In Austin, Texas." It was a bit disconcerting to be in Asia with a blue jeaned, tee-shirted young man speaking Texas English.

Kyrgyzstan is half the size of Texas. The country has a population of five million and is the only central Asian country with Russian and American air bases. Military service is compulsory for one year.

Officially, Kyrgyzstan is secular, although Sunni Muslims dominate the society. Before the Arab conquest, the religion was Zorastrian. The country is poor, the average annual income being about $2,000 per year. It has suffered from economic difficulties since it gained independence. There is widespread corruption. Agricultural products, dairy products, wool, tobacco, cotton, livestock and fruit fill the country's bazaars.

Most of the power is hydroelectric, but there is a shortage. The resort hotel on the lakeshore turned off electricity from 10:00 in the evening until 4:00 in the morning. Candles and matches were provided in the comfortable rooms.

The sun had set before we arrived at the resort. Our evening meal was prepared—baked fish, eggplant and pepper salad, grilled potatoes and the familiar beets, carrots, cucumbers and cabbage.

The following morning I awoke with electricity and the racket of a hailstorm followed by the view of a spectacular rainbow over the lake. My Navajo coat of many colors served me well. It had become a talisman and good luck charm. It kept me warm on the long plane trips and was always a focal point of conversation. I could have sold it many times and was often asked if I had purchased it in the country through which I was traveling. The native symbols in the coat were universal.

The chilling walk to the restaurant tempted me for a good cup of coffee. No luck; again, it was tea. Breakfast consisted of the usual cold cuts, cheeses and fruit as well as chicken and mushrooms with eggs. The sun came out, the storm passed and the lake was blue and clear before we left to visit the petroglyph museum in the town of Cholpan-Ata.

The museum was a large unprotected field overlooking the lake and filled with boulders and stones covered in petroglyphs. Some had been found on the site and the others had been moved from various parts of the country. They dated from 800 B.C. to 500 A.D.

We continued our drive through Kyrgyzstan, stopping in a lakeside village to purchase illegally caught smoked herring from the lake. The Kyrgyz women string the fish from the trees along the road. Russian torpedo testing killed most of the fish in the lake, so fishing is outlawed. The fish were probably contaminated, but we ate them anyway. They were good.

The mountains and rivers covered the landscape as we made our way to Bishkek, the capital. Three mountain ranges cover central Asia: the Himalayas, the Tien Shan and the Pamirs. Over 5,000 rivers make rafting a popular sport.

We stopped for lunch in a small village and ate in the home of a retired school administrator. In addition to the smoked herring, rice, beef, eggplant with peppers and a noodle soup were served.

Following lunch we drove to a large field where a group of young Kyrgyz men on horseback demonstrated their equestrian skills. The game, known throughout Asia as buzkashi, consists of two teams of six vying for the carcass of a headless small white Angora goat. There was a lot of yelling and shoving and wrenching of the goat body. Once the winning team was determined, the riders displayed their skills riding full speed to pluck a small red ribbon embedded in the dirt. Very few missed.

Before reaching Bishkek, we stopped at the Buryan Tower, one of the only existing watch towers remaining on the old Silk Road. The area around the tower features a collection of ancient bal-bals, carved stone figures used as monuments. The towers along the Silk Road served as lighthouses for the caravans coming across the countryside.

Bishkek, being the capital of the country, has a population of over one million. The city was typical. The hotel was 4-star, large and quite nice, much less than the price of accommodations in Kazakhstan, about $50. After an evening meal of lamb and rice we were treated to a local cultural dance. The costumes were colorful and ornate; the headpieces consisted of owl feathers. The music was harsh and not rhythmic to my ears.

The following morning was spent exploring the city, visiting Victory Park, the Frunze House Museum and the State Museum of Fine Arts, featuring Kyrgyz embroidery, jewelry and unique felt rugs. We enjoyed lunch at a local restaurant where fresh water river fish, rice and lentil soup were served. Of course, there was also time for shopping at the local bazaar.

That afternoon, some of us with energy left to spare traveled outside the city to a park at higher elevations and went hiking to view one of the glaciers and experience the high mountain air and gushing clear streams. The view was breathtaking as the sun began to set, and we returned to the city for an evening meal at a local nightclub.

The club was crowded with young people dressed in current fashions gyrating to American rock and roll. We joined the smiling faces and danced beside them after a tantalizing meal of lamb, rice and the usual eggplant, beets, carrots, cucumbers and cabbage.

The evening drew to a close as we returned to the hotel to prepare for an early morning flight to Tashkent, Uzbekistan. The airport on the outskirts of Bishkek revealed the presence of U.S. military aircraft. Uzbeck airlines delivered us to Tashkent, the capital of Uzbekistan, after a short one-hour flight.

Tashkent is a city of two million. The city was destroyed in 1966 by a massive earthquake and was rebuilt with the aid of other Asian countries. After checking into the Tashkent Palace, where I hoped for a decent cup of coffee and was disappointed, we spent the afternoon visiting the decorated subway and a mosque and viewed the oldest copy of the Koran, dating from the seventh century. It was another Nescafé afternoon.

That evening, a Korean buffet was served in one of the many rooms of the Opera House, which survived the 1966 earthquake. Japanese prisoners built the Opera House in 1947. Dining in a massive empty opera house was almost spooky. Music from a practice session echoed in the vacant chambers. The meal was light and tasty—lots of noodles, chicken and assorted vegetables, followed by green or black tea.

Following the evening meal, I ventured onto the streets and found an Internet café in the basement of a popular coffee house. Internet access was quick and easy and my first opportunity to inform family that I was safe and unaffected by the earthquake that had rocked Krygyzstan several days before. The price for 30 minutes of Internet use came to about 16 cents.

Earlier that day I had exchanged $100 for some local currency, the som. I received 134,200 soms in return, a huge wad of money since the highest denomination was a 1,000-som bill. Three days passed before I shopped it all away. It was great fun with that giant roll of bills.

Since the city had been completely rebuilt in the late 1960's, there was not much of historical interest, mostly memorials—the Shahid Memorial in honor of the artists and leaders shot during Stalin's purges of 1938, the Courage Monument named for the workers who rebuilt the city after the earthquake and Independence Square celebrating independence. Most of the cities in central Asia contained at least one Lenin monument, but there were none for Stalin. They have been removed since independence. The Asians hated Stalin; Lenin they considered a part of their history.

And now came the part of the trip that I had been anticipating—the drive along the ancient Silk Road (The Golden Road) to Samarkand. We drove through cotton fields ready for harvest. The cotton plant is defoliated and the entire population of the area is expected to pick the cotton in the month of October. Cotton is king in central Asia. The Russians dug irrigation canals, seriously draining the rivers, to put hundreds of thousands of acres into cotton production. Even the schoolchildren are excused from school to assist in the harvest.

We drove through part of the Fergana Valley, the most fertile valley in central Asia, known as the cucumber empire. The valley is also famous for year-round fruit and abundant water. There are 27 million people in Uzbekistan, most of them under 25, and eight million live in the Fergana Valley. The remainder of the country, about 60 percent, is desert.

Mulberry trees lined the rough two-lane road; the leaves are fed to the silk worms in the valley. Along the road, we stopped at a local fish market. Carp, trout, perch and catfish, smoked and fresh, were available in huge piles.

Melons of every shape and size were also marketed along the road. We stopped and sampled the melons. A large one cost about $1.50. Most of them were referred to as Persian melons and were similar to the best and ripest honeydew ever eaten. The people have a saying that a good melon is better than any psychiatrist—easy to believe once the melons were tasted. We were cautioned to not drink any water for one hour after eating a melon, told it would make us sick. We followed the advice.

Apples of every variety as well as cotton blossom honey and pears were sold along the road and were almost as tasty as the melons. America does not purchase apples from these central Asian countries because of trade agreements that require us to buy apples from other countries rather than from those of their origin. What a shame.

The bumpy road took its toll on a shock absorber; the driver and guide changed it on the spot and we continued along the Silk Road to Samarkand, flanked by abundant vineyards. Samarkand produces 90 percent of Asia's raisins. We sampled them; the golden ones were my favorite because of their sweet flavor. The central Asian wines were bitter and young, but their beer was quite satisfying. Often it was not served chilled.

Previously, there were American air bases in Uzbekistan due to the close proximity to Afghanistan, but they were asked to leave. The American tobacco companies have a joint venture with the Uzbeks growing tobacco and manufacturing cigarettes for Asia. Cigarette smoking is rampant; a pack of cigarettes costs about $1. Chevrolet parts are also manufactured in Uzbeckistan.

At last we came through the arid plain to the rock formations signaling the entrance to Samarkand, the gates of Tamerlane. The city stood before us—2,750 years old.

That afternoon we discovered Registan, the 8th wonder of the world, the centerpiece of Samarkand. Three emblematic madrassahs frame the square and loom over the empty space in the center. It was this central space that gave the place its name, for "registan" simply means "place of sand." "Stan" means place. The blue and gold tile work of the mosaics was magnificent, and Registan was absolutely one of the most beautiful sights I have ever seen.

The Presidential Palace was home for the night. The evening meal was typical. I still had not found a decent cup of coffee and commented that a coffee-maker salesman could make a killing in central Asia.

After an early breakfast we drove toward the Tajik border. Our destination was the town of Penjikent, founded in the fifth century. As we approached the dusty border crossing, our guide pulled me aside and asked, "Would you carry my briefcase across the border?"

I didn't hesitate and took his briefcase. The border crossing was patience-challenging and slow. There were no questions asked. Arriving in Penjikent, I returned the briefcase. We visited the archaeological digs of the remains of the Shakristan, two Zoroastrian temples, the citadel fortress and ruins of an ancient city visited by Alexander the Great. Here he married Roxanna who supposedly came from Tajikistan.

We learned about the Sogdians and their domination of the Silk Road. We also learned the geography of Tajikistan and the arid steppes of the Pamir Mountains. Our Tajik guide described the 1979 bus that took us from the border into the town as better than waterboarding. The only toilets in Tajikistan were Asian—a small round hole level with the ground. Use your imagination and you will not be far from the truth.

Following a lunch of horse pilaf, soup, cucumbers, tomatoes and melon at a local official's home, we visited the Rudaki Museum, named after the celebrated writer of Tajik and Persian poetry. The guide gave a bit of central Asian philosophy. "It is easier to float with the clouds in the sky or spend 100 years in prison than to speak with a stupid person."

Later I communicated with hand gestures to a group of nursing students waiting for a bus. They were young, happy and attractive. Those that were married wore headscarves. Their dresses were colorful. Of course we visited the local market, sampling the fruits, strange vegetables and delicious chocolates.

The people were poor but friendly. The guide informed us that Tajikistan is the poorest country in central Asia, with the most rapidly growing population and largest unemployment rate—a country en route for drugs and other smuggled items. The country is 90 percent mountainous and borders Afghanistan. Grapes are grown on the ground. Potatoes are also cultivated.

The return crossing was repeated with me carrying the briefcase, and when the bus set out for the return trip, I quietly asked him, "What was in the briefcase?"

Honk if you married Sonja

"Money. I can't risk losing my visa status in the 'Stans.' Guiding is my livelihood." He held an Uzbek passport.

We returned to Samarkand in time for some Uzbek dance lessons. The music is discordant; the dance uses minimal footwork and is very elaborate with graceful hand gestures and twirling. I did not find it difficult but had trouble synchronizing the hand movements with the footwork.

The following morning, we set out on foot to walk the city. The flowers were in full bloom—roses, marigolds, canna lilies, petunias, mums and salvia. We visited the Bibi Khanum Mosque, the Gur-Emir Mausoleum, where Tamerlane, Ulug Bek and some of their family are buried and, of course, the local bazaar.

In the afternoon, we found ourselves at a row of tombs and mausoleums collectively called Shah-I-Zinde, which stretches from the present to the past. The cousin of Mohammed is buried here and is a second pilgrim site for the followers of Islam. The mausoleums and tombs are shady and cool, with colorful mosaics and blue tiles. We continued to the observatory of Ulug Bek, son of Tamerlane. He was an emperor but also a famous student of the skies.

Samarkand was Persian before being conquered by Alexander the Great. The canal in the city dated from the time of Alexander. There was some Buddhist influence in the city's history. In the seventh century the Arabs, who brought Islam, conquered the city. Then came the Samanids, who were Tajik. In the 13th century the Monguls captured the city. Tamerlane died in 1405.

That evening we attended a style show featuring modern clothes in traditional fabrics. The music and models were very dramatic, and of course, I purchased a silk outfit at a nominal price. Tea, nuts and dried fruit were served. Still, no coffee.

We visited a carpet factory owned by a Turkmen family who fled to Afghanistan when the Soviets conquered the country. Following independence they returned, and their factory became a joint venture with the Uzbek government. The 92-year-old uncle was in charge of the vegetable dyes for the silk and wool threads. Sacks of dried pomegranate peels, walnut shells, dried indigo and other materials ringed the giant iron kettles outdoors, where the dyes are cooked over wood fires. The factory employs 1,900 people at several locations, employs no children and awards all employees full benefits. They have been given awards from

UNESCO for their labor relations. And, of course, I purchased a small carpet.

Following a tour of the facility given by one of the family who elaborately described their training and employee hiring standards, he asked the question, "What do you think is the most important factor in hiring someone to weave a carpet?"

Many answers were forthcoming. "Dependability." "Attitude."

I answered, "Passion." For the correct answer I was given a small hand woven carpet. I treasure it.

That evening we attended a classical music concert held in a Russian Orthodox Church. The private concert featuring a top soprano in Uzbekistan was for the benefit of some Israeli tourists, but our guide piggybacked us in for $7 each—5,000 soms. Bitter wine was served and the first song was "Ave Maria." How ironic: A Russian Orthodox church, an Uzbek singer, Israeli tourists, a Texan and a Catholic song. The soprano was accompanied by a cello, piano and flute. It was an inspiring evening. We walked back to the Presidential Palace Hotel in the late evening hours, perfectly safe on the streets of Samarkand.

The Silk Road to Bukhara was next.

The road from Samarkand to Bukhara led west through more fields of cotton, apple orchards and grapevineyards. Desert soon replaced the irrigated fields. The road was paved but pitted with holes, and progress was slow. Appropriately, we paused for a picnic lunch near the ruins of a caravanseri, a stage post along the Silk Road. The gates to the shelter still stand as a beacon for travelers seeking rest and water. The Red Desert is to the south.

We halted at a ceramic factory on the outskirts of Bukhara. The same family had produced the colorful blue pieces for six generations. A lunch of fish and lamb kabobs was served. The skewered chunks of lamb were alternated with squares of pure fat. The meat was tender and juicy.

Bukhara, an oasis in the desert, offered cool shade and rest to the camel caravans that traversed the Silk Road for hundreds of years. The city of 250,000 is as old as Samarkand and has more cultural sites than anywhere in Uzbekistan. The ancient architecture and design have been preserved to give the Old Town a unified feel, with a reflecting pool and plaza in the center.

We stayed in the Old Town at a small hotel that dated from the 1640's. The rooms surrounded a charming flower-filled courtyard. To welcome us as though we had been on a long caravan trip, apple champagne, dried fruit and nuts were served.

Beautiful mosques, madrassahs, bath houses and caravansaries dotted the Old Town. Shops lined the sidewalks, offering handicrafts for sale. We visited the Ark Citadel dating from the fourth century B.C. and visited the monuments ringing the Old Town as well as the Zindan Prison, site of a well-known episode in the 19th century. Two British spies posing as explorers were imprisoned and executed when the "Great Game" was being played between Russia and England vying for control over central Asia and access to India. The prison was located below the stables so that the debris from cleaning the stalls fell into the prison. The last emir was known for his brutality.

We visited the mausoleum of a 12th century Samonid ruler and observed the canals that furnish water to Bukhara from the Amu Darya (Oxus) and Zarafshan Rivers. Many of the 16th century structures are now used as craft centers. Under the Russian regime, the buildings were used for hotels, restaurants, shops and storage.

We visited Bukhara's Ark Citadel—the original fortress that dates back over 2,000 years. Like the medieval castle complexes of Europe, the Bukhara Ark served the emirs of Bukhara as a residence and audience hall and as protection from neighboring enemies.

The summer palace of the last emir is on the outskirts of town. The palace and surrounding gardens have been well restored. The emir ruled until 1920, when the Russians absorbed the country. We enjoyed lunch in one of the bathhouses of the Old Town, sitting comfortably on the floor on plush cushions. We dined that evening in the courtyard of a caravanseri, entertained by dancers, music and a style show.

While Bukhara has preserved its ancient sites, the city continues to expand. Beyond the perimeters of the Old Town lie textile factories, a pharmaceutical plant, a silk factory and the largest oil refinery in central Asia.

From the 6th to the 17th century, the road to Bukhara was one of the most difficult parts of the Silk Road. Caravans consisted of thousands of people and animals. The leader governed the caravan, assisted by veterinarians, doctors and astrologers. The rise of shipping spelled the end of the caravans. The transport of goods was faster and cheaper by sea.

Sonja Klein

I was reluctant to leave the safety and comfort of the walls of Bukhara. Life in the Old Town was pleasant and relaxed.

We continued westward through the region of Uzbekistan through Karakalpakstan, an autonomous region of Uzbekistan, inhabited by 2.2 million Karakalpaks who speak the Turkic language. The area is mostly desert, the people are nomadic and the territory contains gas and oil reserves. The Aral Sea is in Karakalpakstan and has receded drastically due to the Russian irrigation canals along the Amu Darya River. The Russians also conducted biological testing on an island in the sea, which has affected the fishing and livelihood of the natives who live along the shores. The country currently has a plan to restore the sea and discontinue significant cotton production in an effort to reduce the salinity of the soil and rivers.

The desert became more severe as we approached Khiva, one of the best-preserved cities along the Silk Road. Legend says that the oasis of Khiva was founded at the place where Shem, the son of Noah, discovered water in the desert and that the city got its name from Shem's joyful shout, "Hey va" at discovery. The well continues to supply water.

Khiva has been inhabited since the fifth century B.C. and for hundreds of years was a fortress town and stop on the Silk Road. In the 16th century the city became the capital of the Khorezm Khanate, who ruled for more than 300 years. It was a well-known slave-trading center.

The markets and minarets of Khiva are beautiful and elaborate. Within the inner city, called Ichon-Qala, we visited the Tash Hauli Palace containing 165 rooms built in the 19th century for the reigning Khan and his four wives. We entered the Dzhuma Mosque, with its interior forest of carved wooden pillars and the Kunya Ark, the original residence of the khans, partially destroyed in the Persian invasion of the 18th century. The earlier palace held 100 rooms. Strolling through the space and courtyards was a trip into the past. The harem was well preserved.

Leaving the security of Khiva we journeyed to the Turkmenistan border. Again we endured the routine of dragging suitcases from building to vehicle. Because our Uzbek guide, Jamshid, was of the same tribe as one of the border guards, the x-raying of the luggage was bypassed. Two bottles of scotch sweetened the deal.

Honk if you married Sonja

From the border we continued to Tashauz, where we boarded a Boeing 717 specially designed for Turkmenistan, flew over the Kara Kum Desert and arrived in Ashkabat, the capitol of Turkmenistan.

Turkmenistan is comparable in size to California and boasts a population of 5.1 million, 85 percent Turkmen. The Kara Kum Desert covers 80 percent of the country and borders the Caspian Sea to the west. Turkmenistan shares a 600-kilometer border with Iran and a 1,000-kilometer border with Afghanistan. Genghis Khan invaded in 1221. The Russian czar conquered the country in the 1880's. The country is rich in resources. Natural gas reserves rank in the world's top 10.

From its independence from Russia in 1991 until 2006, Saparmurat Niyazov, known as "Father of all Turkmen," dominated political life. He announced a policy of permanent neutrality after September 11, which translates into isolation. His absolute power ended with his suspicious sudden death, bringing to power Burganguly Berdimuhammedow, who is undertaking the building of a gas line to China, improving the health and educational systems and reforming the currency. The unit of currency is the manat, 14,000 to the dollar, and the largest bill was 10,000 manats. Changing $100 filled my wallet.

Native Turkmens receive free electricity, water and natural gas, can fly anywhere within the country for less than $20 and purchase 100 gallons of gasoline for $15. Each citizen must plant two trees a year. In the 1960's the Russians built a 1,300-kilometer irrigation canal from the Amu Darya River to the Caspian Sea. The country grows one million tons of long staple cotton per year.

The flag of Turkmenistan portrays the rug patterns of the five major tribes. The population is half nomadic. The first mosque in the country was built in 1996. The new mosque, which is a copy of the Blue Mosque in Istanbul, was completed in 1998 at a cost of $40 million.

Ashgabat, the capital of Turkmenistan, has a population of 650,000. An earthquake demolished the city in 1948. A tour of the city included the National Museum of History and Ethnography, with a collection of carved ivory drinking horns from Nisa and a helmet of Alexander the Great. We also visited the Museum of Carpets and Textiles and viewed the largest carpet in the world. It covered the entire wall of a huge hall.

That evening we dined in a Chinese restaurant. As we entered the dining room, "Ave Maria" was playing. That song was followed by a Jewish song and then "Hotel California"—another example of global integration.

Sonja Klein

The food was excellent—whole baked fish, lamb, chicken and an assortment of vegetables and noodles.

A visit to Nisa, the capital of the ancient Parthian Kingdom, set amidst the beautiful views of the Kopet-Dag Mountains in view of Iran, took place the following morning. The 500-year empire existed until 300 A.D. The Parthians defeated the Romans. The Mongols arrived in the 13th century and laid siege to the city. Today the once-magnificent structures of Nisa are only vague dusty shapes. Archeological excavations continue to reveal more about the ancient city.

The Parthians were great warriors who charged the enemy on horseback, wheeled their horses around and let go their arrows. From this battle technique comes the term "parting shot."

The earliest religion was Zorastrian, followed by the Nestorian Christianity. The Parthians took Buddhism to China, and the Arabs brought Islam with their conquest in the seventh century.

An entire morning was spent at the Tolkuchka Oriental Bazaar, one of the largest bazaars in central Asia, located on the outskirts of Ashgabat. on the Silk Road. Tolkuchka literally translated means "a lot of elbowing."

We first stopped at the camel market, where animals of every variety were for sale. The Turkmen claim to have the best horses in the world. Sheep, goats, turkeys, chickens, ducks and camel milk were also for sale. It was a colorful place, delighting the senses with the smell of kabobs and animals. Shopping at Tolkuchka was great fun and bargaining was compulsory.

The buildings in Ashgabat were of white marble. The hotel was luxurious with the rooms costing about $50 per night. Construction of an Olympic Stadium is under way. Many skyscrapers are being built and the cranes are lit up with colored lights at night. The city is referred to as "The Russian Disneyland," even though it is no longer a part of the Soviet Union. There was even a monument to a great Turkmen writer who authored a book about the Turkmen soul. The monument was in the form of a 20-foot marble book whose illuminated pages turned magically.

The trip to central Asia was mind transforming. At one moment in an open market in Tajikistan I was sampling honey when a man asked, "Americky?"

I replied with a nod, "Americky, Texas." His face went blank, and in that instant I realized there were people who had never heard of Texas. I had finally broken the rubber band that connected me to Texas and my world. It was the defining moment of the trip, accentuating the provincial attitude that dominates many Americans. The beautiful area of central Asia is vast, ancient, alluring and important for its natural resources and rugged scenery. I have never felt threatened or disliked for my nationality. Smiles are a wonderful form of communication when words fail.

While the five "Stans" are predominately Muslim, I never saw veiled women or heard the call to prayer. A structured religion such as Islam is difficult to maintain in a nomadic country. The Russians governed the countries for 70 years and did not encourage religion of any sort.

The young people dress in western style. There are Internet cafés, except in Turkmenistan, which is more oppressive.

I do not believe that central Asia harbors terrorists or is inclined to inflict the laws of Islam on its people. Instead these countries are in transition from Soviet rule towards democracy and the freedoms we enjoy. I might also add that I did not see any aluminum cans or franchise restaurants, though food and western products were plentiful. Recreational sports are popular, and tourists are welcome. My worldview was altered forever. I simply loved central Asia and its people. I never found that good cup of coffee, but then it didn't matter anyway.

31

The perfect day

I was playing bridge with the couples club, substituting for the wife of a recent widower.

"Why don't you drop by sometime?" said the widower. "Maybe you would like to play bridge with me at the Adult Activity Center in Uvalde. They play every Thursday."

"I stay pretty busy."

"What do you do every day?"

"Well, I usually get up around 5:00 or 6:00, put on a pot of coffee and write at the computer. Then I eat some fruit and oatmeal and do ranch work."

"What do you write?"

"I write newspaper articles on my travels. I write essays, short stories, poetry, books and movie scripts—nothing for money or fame, just because I have to write. It makes me happy. I've had some minor work published in literary journals and magazines and have won a few contests, nothing serious."

"What kind of ranch work? Do you have any help or anyone living on the place with you?"

"Don't want anyone living on the place. I have a vegetable garden, grow herbs and flowers. Then I feed the sheep and throw out a coffee can of corn for the deer, check on food for the dog and cat and mow and weed eat. When I get tired or it gets hot, I quit and come up to the house and take a shower. Sometimes I read. In fact, I read a lot. My biggest vice is ordering books.

Then I cook in the afternoon, put on some music, dance around the house and watch the evening news, go to bed early with a good book and start all over again the next day. You know how it is living in the country; there is always something to do. Besides I have three houses at the ranch to take care of; something is always breaking or needs fixing."

"Don't you ever get tired or lonely?"

"Nope, Mother Nature provides all the company I need. I've got lots of animals and birds around. Just keeping the bird feeders filled and the bird bath full of water furnishes a daily symphony of songs. The axis deer call, the insects make all sorts of noises and the seasons give variety. The sunrise and sunset are always a treat; the stars are a wonder to behold and the night sounds are intriguing. I never get lonely; I can always find company. I get along best with myself. And of course I do my adventure traveling a couple times a year, plus kids and their friends come and I go down to Houston to see my mother and brothers."

"How many brothers do you have?"

"Three."

"Where do they live?"

"Two live close to my mother, north of Houston. One lives at his ranch out of Crockett, but the other two also have ranches: one in Crockett next to my oldest brother and one in New Mexico, between Las Vegas and Santa Fe. We all visit each other at our various places. I have a great family."

"What about your children?"

Daughter is in Alpine finishing her master's degree. She comes with friends to the ranch. Son and daughter-in-law live north of Tomball and come to the ranch with friends too. Oh, by the way, do you dance?"

"Oh, no. I haven't danced in years. Besides my knees are bad."

"That's a shame."

"Do you dance, that is besides around the house?"

"God, yes. I'll drive 500 miles to dance. I especially love to waltz. No month is complete unless I have the opportunity to waltz."

"Where do you go to dance?"

"Sometimes a bunch of us go to the Lone Star in Uvalde. I only go if I have someone to dance with. It's no fun going to a dance and just sitting there like a wallflower waiting for some cowboys to get drunk enough to work up the courage to ask after they're too drunk to dance. Then once a year I go to the Terlingua Chili Cookoff out in Big Bend. We camp out and dance every night whether it's cold, hot or raining. It's a great Texas party."

"I think I'm too old for all that."

"You're never too old."

"Don't the evenings get long? That's the worst time for me."

"Sometimes in the hours before sunset, I go out to the fire pit, burn some cedar and brush and aromatic plants and enjoy the shift change, that time when the daytime noisemakers retire and there is that still time before the night sounds begin. I love that time of day, a good time to reflect. Then I watch the stars pop out, waiting for the first one to appear. The night skies are awesome."

"It wears me out just hearing what you do. You must have a lot of energy."

"Nature energizes me. That's why I live out in the middle of nowhere. Cities drain me with their chaos—all the vibes and noises."

"Do you really like to cook?"

"Oh, yes. I love cooking."

"I hate having to cook for myself. My wife was such a good cook. Besides I don't like leftovers. What do you cook just for yourself?"

"I only eat fresh or what I raise on the ranch. I don't eat processed foods and only meat raised or killed on the ranch. I do buy bacon, but I don't eat chicken or lunch meat."

"Gee, you're going to live to be a hundred and ten."

"I hope not."

"Why not?"

"Who wants to live that long and lose mobility and freedom? I hope I go before that happens."

"No one wants to suffer that type of indignity. I agree."

"I just try to live each day like it would be my last, leave nothing left undone or unsaid."

"Do you go to church?"

"Sometimes. My God doesn't live in churches; he's with me all the time, along with my guardian angels."

"You have guardian angels?"

"Sure, two of them. They're real cute guys and they go everywhere with me; they take good care of me. Remember the Bible says there are legions of angels and the Koran says your guardian angel is never any farther away than your throat."

"What church do you go to?"

"I go to House of Praise; it's nondenominational, somewhat charismatic. I go to hear Little Carrol; he's very spirit-filled and the music is great, quite inspiring."

"Well, I'm Episcopalian, but I don't go much."

Honk if you married Sonja

"I was raised Missouri Synod Lutheran, then became Episcopalian and now just try to live my life in the spirit and manifest my God's love in everything I say, think and do."

"Sounds pretty simple."

"In a way it is. The two greatest commandments are to love God and love your neighbor. I try to see God in everyone I meet."

"You really seem to have it together."

"I've made a lot of mistakes, most of them expensive either money-wise or emotionally draining. My past is a bit checkered, but even the creek needs the stones to sing. I try not to spend my time rearranging the rocks in the river. What do you do every day?"

"Oh, I don't know. I just kind of putter around missing my wife. I'm really quite lost with lots of time on my hands. I talk to friends, play some bridge, get on the computer, try to stay busy. I suppose you could say I'm lonely."

"When John died, I knew where he was, but I didn't know where I was. I grieved alone until it played out, and then I decided I could either die or live. I chose to live. Losing someone is rough; there's a process we all go through and it's not fun. The journey is a solitary one. You'll make it. Time helps; the wounds heal, but the scars remain. Pain is inevitable, but suffering is optional.

"I know those are platitudes and I can spout them all day long. Nothing helps much. There's a saying that goes something like this: 'He couldn't change reality with drugs, alcohol or anger, so he changed his mind.' I know it's a simplistic view, but you have the gift of life. You can recreate yourself and be anything or do anything. Design a new lifestyle, ride on the front of the train, see what is in front of you and design the perfect day. Think about it, create in your mind the perfect day and set out to achieve it—conceive, believe and achieve."

"What is your perfect day?"

"Easy. Arise naked 5 A.M. , brew some pecan-flavored coffee. Fix the bed, weigh, brush my teeth, get dressed and pour that first cup of coffee. Season it with red pepper, dark powdered cocoa, and vanilla soy milk. Sit down at the computer and read emails from friends and family, replying where necessary. Write an essay or short story or poem or work on a book in progress until about 10:00. Eat some fresh fruit, maybe a bowl of oatmeal and stretch. Attend to phone calls or paper correspondence, thaw out some deer meat or lamb from the freezer and dress for outside work. Feed animals and birds if needed, drive down to check garden, feed sheep and deer and do work as necessary.

"Return to the house early afternoon, shower if needed and cook—maybe smothered okra or squash from the garden, perhaps cabbage, beets, turnips or Brussels sprouts, maybe put a sweet potato in the oven. Season the thawed meat and bake it with garlic and herbs. Meanwhile have some country music playing and dance while cooking. Once the meal is underway, lie down and read, meditate for a while and take a power nap. Eat the bounty from the kitchen and go out to the firepit for the shift change, lighting a modest aromatic cedar fire. Return to the house, eat some more, watch a news channel and go to bed naked with a good book—the perfect day."

32

Anger management

I never heard of anger management while growing up with three
brothers. Whatever our emotions dictated, we conformed to
acceptable behavior due to fear of punishment. We knew right from
wrong and how to control our feelings.

And then came the 60's, 70's and 80's—the touchy, feely, me first,
give me a hug and fuck you years. "You don't feel good? You must be
depressed. Take a pill, smoke a joint, have a drink, see a counselor. It's not
your fault."

Even elementary schools furnish counselors for every malady imaginable.
Parents started telling their children they loved them. No one ended a
phone conversation without saying, "I love you." Church services devoted
special time for everyone to hug each other. Restaurant servers trained
to bond with the diners.

"Hi, I'm Don, and I'll be serving you this evening."

Hell, I knew my parents loved me. It was a given fact. I knew my
aunts, uncles and cousins and brothers and friends loved me. I didn't
have to be told.

And then everyone became angry. Television became violent, movies
were scary and action packed. People started shooting everyone in
cafeterias, fast-food restaurants, post offices, along the freeways. Wars
broke out around the globe—insurgents fighting each other, countries
encroaching on neighboring territories, families abusing their children.
Societies turned angry and anger management came into focus.

People held nothing back. They struck out. "Oh, you staged a fit.
Now you have to go to anger management." Instead of taking
responsibility for one's actions, anger management courses were
prescribed as the punishment, along of course with a few pills to quiet
the raging beasts we all had become.

I personally thought it all baloney until one day working in my
garden, hoeing some weeds. When I encountered a small garden snake I

hacked it to pieces in front of my son. He silently watched me shatter that small reptile into shreds.

"Mother, do you have an issue with anger?"

The emotion of the moment calmed. "Well, I guess I do. But now I feel much better."

Reality checked into my mind. Now whenever I find myself a bit anxious, I go cut brush, crank up the weed eater or till the garden and feel much better for the effort. I don't need anger management. I just need to get out and do a little physical work.

33

The classy porcupine

I drove down to the guesthouse on the ranch. My daughter came to the door. "Oh no, there's a porcupine in the yard," I said. "Grab the dog."

"Calm down, Mother. You're going to excite Easy and make it worse. I've got him."

We were moving Molly's stuff into the house. She had moved home after her recent boyfriend breakup. Standing safely within the screened porch, we watched the mottled gray, lumbering porcupine make his way across the yard. Molly grabbed her camera and carefully walked toward him.

"Stay away from him; he might shoot quills at you."

"Mother, they don't do that."

I cautiously followed her, leaving the dog on the porch. Molly aimed her camera as we watched. He wasn't bothered by us, didn't even hurry. His face was grizzly, wrinkled with age or disease. The old fellow would take a few steps and then pick up his paws as if to shake something off of them. His body swayed back and forth as he padded toward the gate, rolling his body from side to side.

Molly snapped pictures until he stopped, turned around and faced her with no fear, as curious as the two women tracking him.

"He must be the porcupine that ate the bark off the peach trees. Oh, and remember the one that fell out of the tree that David clubbed to death. He had those tumors on him and was probably diseased."

"Well, now we have another one. I hope he stays out of the yard. I don't want to have to take Easy to the vet again and pay $130 to sedate him so Dr. Herndon can pull the quills out of his mouth, nose and gums."

The week passed swiftly as we continued settling Molly's stuff into the house—until one day when we were feeding the goats in the pen that joined the yard. There he was again, strolling through the enclosed trap and walking with the distinct air of an animal that has no enemies. The goats didn't seem to notice him, in fact, paid no attention whatsoever.

"We're going to have to do something about that porcupine. He's obviously staked out the yard and this area as his territory. You're going to have to shoot him, Molly."

"Mother, I'm not going to shoot some old porcupine that's about to die anyway. Can't you see how old he is?"

The remodel of her house was underway. She moved up to my home on the hill overlooking the creek valley below while the contractor and his crew began work. After the first week, the contractor remarked, "Did you know there's a porcupine that hangs out around the house?"

"Yeah," Molly told Rudy. "He's harmless. Please keep the screen door to the porch and the windows closed. I don't want him or any other varmint getting in my things." The porch was littered with boxes of dishes and pots and pans from the kitchen cabinets that were being replaced.

One hot afternoon, sitting in the cool of my air-conditioned house and smelling a pot of deer sausage and beans simmering in the crock pot, I picked up the mammal reference book that I keep close at hand. Turning to the section on porcupines, I read aloud to Molly, who was enjoying the view of the cliff opposite the valley. "'The solitary common porcupine is active year-round.' Oh, great.

"'Primarily nocturnal, it may rest by day in a hollow tree or log, underground burrow or treetop, for it is an excellent climber. Yet, the animal occasionally falls.' We know that. 'About 35 percent of museum skeletons examined show healed fractures. On the ground, it has an unhurried, waddling walk, relying on its quills for protection against more agile predators. The common porcupine has 30,000 quills on its body.' Just what I wanted to know, a quill count."

I read on. "'While a porcupine cannot throw its quills at an enemy, when forced to fight it erects them, lowers its head and lashes out with its tail. If the tail strikes the enemy, the loosely rooted quills detach easily and are driven forcefully into the victim, whose body heat causes the microscopic barbs on the end of each quill to expand and become even more firmly embedded.

"'A strict vegetarian, the porcupine feeds on leaves, twigs and green plants. The porcupine has a great appetite for wooden tool handles that have absorbed human perspiration through use. The animal may kill trees by stripping away the bark, and its gnawing may damage buildings and furniture.'

"Molly, you're going to have to shoot that porcupine," I said. "I don't think we can keep him out of the yard."

Molly replied, "Let the contractor deal with him. Maybe the porcupine will drink some paint and die on his own."

Molly drove to Austin for a dentist appointment and to have her car serviced while I kept the dogs up on the hill. The contractor didn't show up for a few days, so I went down the hill to check his progress. As I entered the house, I detected a smell, unmistakable to a country dweller. Something nearby was dead. Not wanting to deal with a dead animal, I left, determined to play dumb when the discovery took place.

Rudy the contractor called from the phone in the house the following morning. "There's a dead porcupine in the box of dishes on the porch. It really smells down here."

"Get him out of the dishes and put the carcass out in the pasture. We asked you to keep the screen door closed, Rudy."

"I must have left it open. It really smells bad and there are maggots."

"Well, please clean it up; Molly's coming home today and you know how weird she is about smells and her stuff."

The rotting smell drifted over the site; the southern breeze that drifts through the canyon carried the odor for a few days until the turkey vultures cleaned the rotting carcass.

Molly was livid, angry that Rudy had left the screen door open and revealed in an instant, "Mother, the porcupine body fluids and maggots are all over Grandma's china. What are we going to do?"

"Well, we can't throw away the china. Guess we have to clean it."

"Ugh! You know I can't handle that kind of stuff, makes me nauseous."

"Well, we'll just let it dry up and season, and then we'll clean it."

The following day Molly disappeared, went down to her house and spent the day. She came back up the hill tired but with a satisfied light in her eyes. "Mother, I started cleaning the dishes. It's nasty. I used the feeding tubs from the sheep pens, made a Clorox bath and a soap bath and have most of it done. Can you believe not one dish was broken? I wish I could make Rudy clean the dishes, but he'd probably break them. It's all his fault."

I helped her the next day. We finished the job in the yard and washed the dishes once again, this time in her new dishwasher, and placed them in the new kitchen cabinets. Grandma's china was safely home again.

Sonja Klein

As we prepared a first meal in her restored house, I reached into the cabinet for the china dishes. "Mother, I don't think I can eat on those dishes yet, maybe later."

Determined, I picked up a bowl and then put it back. "You know, Molly, I don't think I can either."

34

Australia and New Zealand

Eight hours in a cold and frantic Los Angeles airport on New Year's Eve waiting on a delayed flight to Fiji was not an auspicious beginning for a trip down under. An empty plane with room to lie down was a welcome relief. Though the colorful, noisy band in the airport at Nadi, Fiji, brought a smile on my birthday, New Year's Day had been lost mid-flight. The tropical island shone green, leaving winter behind and forgotten. The journey had begun and this one was not solo. With me were my children—my son Joe and his wife Carla and my daughter Molly.

From the short layover in Fiji we arrived in Sydney, a large bustling city on the coast of Australia in the state of New South Wales. The summer warmth refreshed our spirits as we traveled to the Grace Hotel in the heart of the city. The hotel had been the headquarters of General Douglas McArthur during the Pacific campaign of World War II. The Sydney Opera House and port stood in full view.

I had engaged a private guide for a city tour. He was a retired school teacher and picked us up at the hotel for an informative day.

Frank was full of facts and stories. Sydney's population of over four million sprawls the hills sloping to the Tasmanian Sea. The explorer James Cook discovered the continent and charted it in 1770. It was settled in 1785, when the first fleet of ships from England arrived, bringing over 800 convicts. England had lost the American colonies in our war of independence and needed a new location for their prisoners.

The nine-month voyage must have been awful for the prisoners—men, women and children. Their ages ranged from 10 to 83. The Australian colony nearly starved in the early years; punishment, debauchery, graft and hardship took many lives. Rum was the currency and American ships visited the busy harbor selling it.

Coal, wool and timber soon made the colony rich, and it has been said that Australia grew on the backs of sheep. The climate and grass suit sheep ranching. The country went through an era of prohibition in the

1920's, and instead of the speakeasy, they developed sly grog shops, so entitled because the customers visited the shops on the sly.

The average income in Australia is $41,000 and apartment rentals for a two bedroom, two-bath apartment cost $1,200 per month. The average house is priced at $350,000. Gasoline, beer, bottled water and pizza are much higher than in the states. The minimum wage is $12.50 per hour and unemployment is close to zero. In fact, there is a labor shortage in the agriculture industry—no workers to pick the grapes, kiwis and other food products. Voting is compulsory; failure to vote incurs a $180 fine and continued absence at the polls can result in jail time. What a great idea for our low voter turnout.

Australia is currently suffering drought conditions and the cities enforce water rationing. Health care is free, and there are no property taxes on one's primary residence. I saw few if any pickup trucks and no mobile homes. Sydney is clean, the people friendly, open and energetic.

Australia was one of the last continents to be explored by the Europeans, being settled primarily by 160,000 convicts. Historically, Australians have borne a sense of shame about living in a convict colony, but the trend now is to be proud of having an ex-con in the family tree.

The discovery of gold in 1851 added increased prosperity to Australia. The British government never forgot the loss of the American colonies and learned a valuable lesson. They gave the vote, freedom and the ability to tax to each of the six states that formed Australia and became united in 1901.

The Australians are sports-obsessed—horse racing, camel racing, sculling, rowing, soccer, football—most likely due to having been a male-dominated society. The male convicts outnumbered the females 7 to 1, and the gold rush generated a male-dominated populace.

The total population of Australia is about 21 million and culturally the country is European. Australia is closely allied with America; Vietnam was the first war that Australia fought without being a British ally. Wool was their main export in the past. Now Australia is the world's main exporter of iron ore. China has replaced Japan as their main trading partner.

We found their descriptions quite humorous. Instead of yield signs on the road, they use "Give Way." The symbol is the same. Putting on a coat is translated as "rug up."

Honk if you married Sonja

Australians drive on the left side of the road and use the metric system. I soon learned to convert the temperature. A temperature forecast of 22 degrees converts to approximately 74 degrees. The simple formula is to double and add 30.

The kangaroo and the emu symbolize Australia; neither animal can go backward. Australia looks forward, always moving ahead. The flora and fauna are quite unusual; species found in Australia live no other place in the world. We visited the aquarium in Sydney Harbor and observed platypus, penguins, strange-looking sharks and many other varieties of aquatic species.

Beaches surround the city of Sydney; the waves looked inviting but treacherous. We visited the famous Bondi Beach area, an eclectic surfing community. The famous Harbour Bridge, built in 1932, connects north and south Sydney. An amazing excursion is offered. For about $100, a person can be attached to the railing, receive a safety lecture and walk a catwalk above the Harbour Bridge. From the base of the bridge, they looked like ants far above the shore level. The adventure takes about four hours. I told my children before they asked that the answer was no, just like it was for bungee jumping.

Sydney offers a variety of activities for tourists. An area called the Rocks, home of Sydney's first European settlement, is unique, with many restaurants, old buildings and shops. Harbor cruises are available, and there are many interesting museums to visit. Whether it's jet boating, rafting, kayaking, bushwalking or helicopter riding, Sydney has something for everyone.

After visiting the Sydney, our adventure took us to the interior of Australia. The flight from Sydney to Uluru was short by comparison to our earlier flight, only four hours. We observed the dingo fence far below as we flew across the vast Australian country. The dingo fence is the longest man-made structure in the world and crosses Australia from north to south, supposedly protecting the eastern Australian ranchers' livestock from destruction by the dingoes. Dingoes are dog-like predators about the size of a collie.

Mid-flight we were instructed to move our watches one and one-half hours forward or backward. I don't remember which, except that I didn't do it. I thought it was a joke; I was wrong. The change was time zone and daylight savings combined.

As I stepped off the plane in Uluru a hot wind blowing like the highest setting on a hair dryer hit me. The temperature was 112 degrees

Fahrenheit and the humidity was 5 percent. A short ride to the resort and cooler air was encouraging but not for long. We were told to drink a liter of water every hour. With water costing $3.50 for half a liter, I told my children I would soon be bankrupt. Thankfully we discovered a free water fountain and kept our bottles refilled.

The resort was in the middle of the Northern Territory, one of the six states of Australia. In the distance I viewed Ayers Rock, a giant red exposure.

Ayers Rock has been exposed for 300 million years, measures eight kilometers around, and is five kilometers deep and 300 meters high. Ayers Rock is in Kata Tjuta National Park, which spans 1,325 square kilometers and was returned to the aborigines in 1985. They in turn leased it to the government for 99 years. The park is aboriginal land, the home of the Anangu. The aborigines receive income from park entrance fees.

The dirt of the desert around the rock is red iron ore and the shrubbery is sparse—similar to the Chihuahuan Desert. Rainfall averages about 12 inches per year. The resort was busy, not quite full, with most of the tourists being Orientals. After a $20 pizza, salad and lots of water, we felt prepared for a camel ride.

Joe, an Australian, picked us up at the resort for a short trip to the camel center. Before leaving the van, I signed my life away with trepidation. There were about a dozen hearty souls who had also signed the waiver and joined us for the adventure. Camels were brought to Australia to assist in building the railroad because a mature male camel can carry up to over half a ton of cargo. A camel caravan was capable of transporting 100 tons of trade goods.

The Afghans trained and brought camels to Australia. When the railroad was complete, the camels were set free. Close to a million wild camels now roam central Australia. They have become a nuisance to the ranchers because they can drink an inordinate amount of water in a short time. Forty wild camels will drink a stock tank dry and also tear up fences. The ranchers shoot them.

Joe, our guide, gave us a camel lecture. The camel lovers that conduct the tour trap the wild animals, castrate the males and charge the tourists to ride them. A camel is smarter than a horse, lives about 45 years and stores water in his blood. Today mid-easterners pay as much as a million dollars for a single camel to use as breeding stock and for popular camel racing. Camels have long memories and are not forgiving. They do not smell and do not spit; instead they projectile vomit upon those who mistreat them.

The "How to Get on the Camel" lecture was succinct, "Put your foot in the left stirrup. Hold onto the front of the saddle with both hands. Swing your right foot over the back of the saddle. Do not hold on to the back of the saddle. Your foot will not go through your arm. Remember that the camel behind you will not forget if you hit him in the face with your foot while swinging it over the saddle. Do not put your right foot in the stirrup or try to adjust it. We will do that. I don't want you kicking or hurting my camels."

Several of the Japanese tourists either were not paying attention or could not understand English. Instead they chatted among themselves. Joe gave them no slack. "Pay attention. I do not want my animals mistreated."

The rolling gate of the camel and security of the saddle abolished the oppressive heat. The long ride to a spot overlooking Ayers Rock for the sunset was absolutely one of the high points of the trip.

Darkness ended the ride at the camel center, where we drank ale and ate camel and kangaroo. The camel meat, served in small square chunks, was dark red with some marbling and tasted a bit like elk or beef. A bowl of horseradish sauce was nearby; I chose not to dilute the flavor. The kangaroo meat was not quite so dark, served in slices with a coarse light brown bread and did not taste like chicken, rather like young pork or veal. Both meats were quite tasty. Sheep cheese was also served—one of my favorites.

Before leaving I read some of the comments in the guest book. One of my fellow riders had written, "Why are you so mad?" Obviously they didn't get it. These people loved their animals, trained them and took excellent care of them. Not everyone can appreciate dry humor.

Before daylight the following morning, a park ranger picked us up for an eco tour of Ayers Rock. Surprisingly I was not sore from the camel ride since their backs are narrower than that of a horse. We drank lukewarm tea as the sun arose. The rock was illuminated in colors from red to pink to pale yellow. The temperature was bearable and the beauty was almost unbearable, the quiet inspiring.

Ayers Rock is sacred to the aborigines, who believe that all animals were once people. Each aborigine has an animal totem and is forbidden to eat the flesh of his totem. There are seven sacred sites around Ayers

Rock, and no photographs are allowed of those sites. The men and women have separate sacred sites and ceremonies. The stories of the aborigines continue for miles across Australia. In many of their tales, the people change to animals and vice versa.

There are water holes around the base of Ayers Rock but no springs. The water holes contain ground water that seeps from the rock. Several of the water holes never go dry.

Today the aborigines have chosen to live in seclusion. There is a small village of about 200 near Ayers Rock. It is off limits to visitors and rangers. They will not have their pictures taken and do not go to school but rather prefer to live the old way. They are not nomadic and are exposed to television. Yet they attempt to minimize the influence of civilization. As many as 250 different aboriginal tribes and languages exist. About half a million claim to be aborigines, 2.5 percent of the population. Our guide said, "There's probably 50,000 pure aborigines left." Australia is so big it is hard to realize there are only 20 million people living on a continent as big as the U.S.A.

The ranger guide told a story about one of the aborigine mothers in the village who decided to start a school in her house. Her children had watched television. One of them wanted to be a helicopter pilot and the other wanted to be a firefighter. She realized that to fulfill those dreams her children required education. The other children in the village disrupted the school she had begun in her home until she petitioned the elders of the village to allow a fence to be built around her house. They refused; their ruling was absolute, and the school and hope was abandoned.

The aborigines suffer the same social problems as all indigenous peoples—wife bashing, sex crimes, alcoholism and lack of education. Alcohol is forbidden in the park or at the resort unless you can produce your room key.

Uluru is the small resort area that joins the park. The population of several hundred is composed mostly of workers and shopkeepers. The main courses on the dinner menu started at $28. There was only one small store and three television stations, none of which entertained or made any sense. The isolation of Uluru is compelling and real. The nearest town is 280 miles away—Alice Springs with a population of 30,000.

Honk if you married Sonja

The road signs continued to amuse us. "Do it up" means buckle up. The symbol of the seat belt remained the same. "Way Out" means exit.

The flight back to Sydney was turbulent. From there, we planned to continue around the southern coast through the Bass Strait by ship to Melbourne.

Again I had engaged an informative guide. Melbourne, the second largest city in Australia, is in the state of Victoria, located in the southeastern portion of the country on Port Phillip Bay. The population is 3.4 million. John Batman, a Tasmanian in search for a pastoral settlement, purchased land from the aborigines in 1835 and named it after Lord Melbourne, Queen Victoria's prime minister. The gold rush in the 1850's made it the richest city in the world; and the city contains many botanical gardens and parks. Parking lots are designated "car parks." The annual rainfall is about 30 inches, and the Dandenog Mountains are located a short hour and a half north of the city.

The trip to the mountains was over a wide freeway, and the terrain changed from the sloping, verdant hills to almost tropical forests with large fern trees and the ever-present eucalypt tree, a variety of mountain ash. There are over 750 varieties of the tree in Australia. In the forest we observed and fed cockatoos, rosellas and kookaburras. The kookaburras make unique jungle sounds. A 100-year-old steam train called Puffin Billy took us on a ride through the forest over the Yarra River to Menzies Creek.

Australia has many beautiful flowers, but the purple and white agapanthus grows wild and lines the roads and hillsides. Jacaranda and hydrangea are also common. We drove through the Yarra Valley, famous for its vineyards that produce chardonnay and pinot noir. The Italians and Greeks brought their grapevines to the area after World War II.

The valley was lush with fields of blueberries, raspberries, apricots and strawberries. As we drove past a dead animal in the road I asked what it was.

"It's a wasa."

"A what?"

"Was a rabbit."

Rose bushes are planted on the fringes of the vineyards to signal the presence of insects harmful to the grapevines. The insects infest the rose bushes before they attack the grapevines. White roses are planted near the white grapes and red roses near the dark grapes.

A lunch of grilled steak, chicken, pork and beans, various salads and condiments was served at Lilydale Vineyards. The weather was cool and pleasant as we dined on the patio overlooking the gently rolling hills.

The highway signs continued to entertain—"Drowsy Drivers Die." Dangerous road areas are called black spots.

Visiting a wildlife sanctuary established in the 1930's occupied most of the afternoon. On the site was a hospital for treating diseased and injured animals and birds. Koalas sleep 20 hours a day and eat a kilo of eucalypt leaves each day, which also provides their water. The Tasmanian devil is currently endangered due to facial cancer. The researchers have not determined a cause or cure.

Melbourne was a large city. The close proximity of the mountains and forest and the countryside lush with farms, vineyards and orchards make Melbourne an appealing destination. There are also ski slopes north of Melbourne, and the beaches were crowded with vacationers.

Our ship took us next to the island of Tasmania, which the Dutch explorer Abel Tasman discovered in 1642. The Dutch and the Portugese were among the world's hardiest explorers and shipbuilders but did not have the capability of settling vast areas of land. They simply did not have the population to export. The English settled there in the early 1800's with shiploads of convicts. Tasmania is one of the six states in Australia and the residents enjoy a competition with the mainland of Australia, referring to it as the North Island. Australians on the mainland refer to the Tasmanians as rednecks or country cousins. Tasmania has been voted one of the top islands in the world to visit. Nearly a third of the island is protected through 14 national parks. There is an overnight ferry from Melbourne that runs every day.

Again a local guide provided us with much information. Devonport is the third largest city in Tasmania, with a population of 30,000, and is located on the northern coast of the island. The population of Tasmania is 500,000. There is currently no drought in Tasmania and there are no water restrictions. Hydroelectric and wind power furnish all the electricity and the excess is sent to the mainland. Tasmania is an agricultural state producing apples, potatoes, onions, pumpkins, carrots, cherries, raspberries, strawberries and poppies. Acres of poppies are grown for the major American pharmaceutical companies to produce morphine and other opium derivatives. The potatoes from Tasmania furnish McDonald's in

Honk if you married Sonja

Australia. The Fuji apple is exported to Japan. The major export is wool. Forestry is also a major industry and pine trees dot the hillsides.

The Great Western Tiers is the predominant mountain range of the island, and one third of the state is up on the plateau. Fishing, skiing, hiking, biking and the beaches attract tourists from all over the world.

A trip to the countryside and the mountains was enjoyable. We visited a honey farm and tasted honey from the leatherwood tree. The farm had over 50 flavors of honey, ranging from chocolate to mango. The exotic flavors were infused into the honey. After tasting them we were hooked. They served honey ice cream and sold a variety of cosmetic and medicinal products. I was on the verge of buying a variety package of their honeys when I was disappointed to learn that none of the honey could be taken to New Zealand due to custom restrictions, but I did obtain their website and later ordered some of their honey.

Aberdeen and Friesen cattle grazed the hillsides. The grapes grown are the chardonnay and the pinot noir because Tasmania does not have the heat of the mainland. There are no dingoes in Tasmania, and the finest Merino wool produced on the island can sell for as much as $3,000 per kilo. The Japanese and Italians purchase it for their fine wool clothing. My children remarked, "Mom, maybe you should buy some Merino sheep."

Hobart, the next town we visited in Tasmania, is the largest city on the island, with a population of 200,000, located on the southern end of the island. The city has always been the center of the Southern Ocean whaling and seal trade. The island is one of the most mountainous islands in the world. While the northern coast has an annual rainfall of about 25 inches per year, the west coast receives 10 feet of rain and hosts the largest temperate rain forest in the world. Forty-three percent of Tasmania is reserved as a world heritage rainforest. Copper, zinc, lead, tin, gold and coal are mined. Timber and farming are also major industries. I observed hops growing as well as grains and berries.

Accompanied by a forest ranger, we took a walk through the rain forest among giant trees and abundant birds. We even saw padymillas—a small species of kangaroo—hopping and munching leaves. Waterfalls and ravines abounded in the forest and the summer temperature was in the 70's. We visited a wildlife sanctuary, petted koalas, wombats and even a baby Tasmanian devil.

The phrases in Tasmania continued. "Throwing it down" means rain. Food to go was called, "takeaway" and something was described as "puffed up like a poisoned dog." TV commercials advertised for "Mum and the cubs" and "men's tops," otherwise known as shirts.

I found that Tasmania lived up to its description as one of the best islands in the world to visit. The people were open and friendly, rural in philosophy and responsible to the environment. The cost of living was less than on the mainland and the pace of living slower, more relaxed and in tune with nature.

From Tasmania, the ship made its way to New Zealand. A magical fairyland emerged from the mist as we cruised beautiful Milford, Doubtful and Dusky Sounds. I half expected to see a hobbit or two waving from the shore. The fiords of the southern island of New Zealand are deep inlets caused by glacial migration. A sound, found on the northern island, is caused by erosion and changes in water levels. A fiord is formed by gouging caused by glacial retreat. Even though the fiords are called sounds, they are still fiords. The morning fog hung on the mountaintops and the dark green flora extended to the water's edge. As the ship maneuvered through the fiords, each view was even more breathtaking.

Captain James Cook discovered and explored the area in 1770. The vertical cliffs and mighty waterfalls plunging over sheer rock faces are spectacular and one of the best examples of New Zealand's renowned classic landscape of steep granite peaks framing glacier-carved inlets with mirrored reflections on dark waters.

A local guide toured the city with us. Dunedin, New Zealand, is touted as the Edinborough of the south with a population of 110,000. Pronounced "do-neé-din," the city is a university town. The natives of the South Island refer to themselves as the mainlanders as opposed to North Islanders.

While the New Zealanders, who call themselves kiwis after the bird and not the fruit, have a friendly rivalry with Australia, they also have an open border or open ocean. Citizens can travel and work freely between the two countries. The Australians claim that they have more fun because their country was settled by convicts of English and Irish ancestry, while the Scottish Presbyterians colonized New Zealand. Indeed, the accent in New Zealand has more of a Scottish brogue, while the Australians' accent is less pronounced.

Honk if you married Sonja

Fishing is a big industry—flounder and salmon. Timber is also important. The eucalypt trees are imported from Australia and planted on the hillsides. A specially designed plane called a Fletcher applies fertilizer from the air. Phosphate is imported to manufacture the fertilizer.

Rhododendrons and azaleas were blooming in abundance, and the Presbyterian churches were numerous. Cypress trees also grow there. There was a gold rush in New Zealand between the 1860's and 1890's. New Zealand has no native animals or snakes. The birds on the islands forgot how to fly because they had no natural predators. Since the sheep also had no enemies, vast numbers of them populate the islands. In fact the natives claim that sheep outnumber people 20 to 1 and brag that if you hear a noise outside, the odds are that it is a sheep making the disturbance.

Rabbits were brought into the country and caused a problem eating the grass. Two rabbits eat as much grass as a sheep. Weasels and stoats were imported to kill the rabbits. When that didn't work, a virus was introduced to kill the rabbits. The introduction of possums precipitated more difficulties. The possums, unlike our possums, killed the trees. Their fur is used for garments and blankets and is quite soft.

We toured the harbor of the Otago Peninsula in a small boat and observed sea lions, penguins and albatross, who have a wingspan of 10 feet. They were quite graceful and nested on the cliffs. As I booked the harbor tour I realized that the New Zealanders referred to me as an "oldie," and I received a discount.

Our next stop was Christchurch, population 340,000. The port of Lytteltown is near Christchurch. When the colonizers arrived in the 1830's and hiked over the mountain to find higher more productive ground, they gazed at the valley below after climbing the rugged hills and said, "Christchurch," and supposedly that is how the city was named.

Agriculture dominates the economy of the area known as the Southern Alps. Potatoes, peas, wheat, barley and oats are grown. Greenhouses were in abundance. Flowers bloomed everywhere—roses, marigolds, agapanthus, azaleas and zinnias. Two types of horse racing are popular—trotting and galloping. Snow falls in the winter and snow skiing is a favorite sport.

We traveled across the alpine mountains to Flock Hill Station, a 35,000 acre sheep ranch high in the mountains. Scenes from *The Chronicles of Narnia* were filmed there. Annual rainfall at the station is 18 to 24 inches. The ranch runs 30,000 Merino/Romney crossbred sheep and 3,000 cattle.

Lunch at the ranch headquarters was tasty, a lamb stew with chunks of baked sweet potatoes, feta cheese and herbs. Following lunch, a four-wheel-drive vehicle carried us across the high ranges of the ranch down into a gorge, where we boarded a jet boat. Jet boats were designed in New Zealand by Bill Hamilton. The boats move over 40 mph and can do so in four inches of water. The jet boat ride through the Wataka Gorge was breathtaking and exhilarating.

We next visited Picton, located on the north end of the southern island in the Marlborough District. A three-hour ferry ride from Picton delivers passengers and vehicles to the North Island. The population of Picton is 4,000, and the town is known as the gateway to the South Island. There are 400 mussel farms in the area as well as salmon farms. Boat building, farming and timber are the main industries. Deer farming has also become quite popular and the meat is sold in supermarkets all over New Zealand. Red deer are the most popular. Vineyards dot the hills; there are over 200 wineries in the area. Vineyards are gradually replacing sheep farming. An acre can support 750 vines and the profits can be as much as $50,000 per acre.

The scenic harbor was full of sleek yachts and sailing vessels. The tallest mountain is about 9,000 feet, and the snow skiing, trout fishing, duck hunting and hiking attract tourists year round. The area is known as the gourmet region for the fruits and berries. Rainfall is 25 to 30 inches per year and the gardens in the area are lush with roses, dahlias, clematis and begonias.

While my family went kayaking and bushwalking, I visited a 1,800-acre sheep farm with 3,500 Merino/Romney/Corriedale sheep. Dogs do most of the work and a trained one costs $10,000. The dogs also work cattle, goats and deer. A two-year-old ewe is worth $80 to $100. New Zealand's rate of exchange is about 84 cents to our dollar. Shearing is done only once a year and produces four kilos of wool per sheep. Where the climate is wetter, they shear twice a year. Here I learned that an unpaved road is called a "shingled" road.

The rainfall at the sheep farm was about 30 inches per year. Shearers are paid $1.20 per head. The sheep averaged in weight about 65 kilos and the ranchers try for a 160 percent lamb crop. There are no predators. A gutted, skinned sheep sells for $1.40 per pound.

Honk if you married Sonja

Water rights are important in New Zealand, and there are different types of water permits, all of which are valuable and essential for the agricultural economy. I prefer the South Island with its majestic scenery and rural atmosphere to the North Island.

We continued by ship to the town of Napier, population 14,000, located on the eastern coast of the North Island. Napier is known as the Art Deco Capital of New Zealand. When the city was rebuilt after a major earthquake in 1931, art deco dominated the architecture.

The Hawkes Bay area is famous for its geothermal hot springs and its wines and fruit—citrus, apples, peaches, berries. Lavender farms, pine forests and orchards dot the countryside. We traveled to the wild and scenic Mohaka River for a day of rafting. On the way we passed the famous Tepohue golf course, the greens and course maintained entirely by sheep.

The rafting trip through the gorges of the Mohaka River was not as challenging as we had hoped. The river level was down, but there were sufficient rapids to keep us busy.

In Napier the Kiwi House is the only place in the country where it is possible to actually touch and feed the indigenous flightless bird that is the symbol of New Zealand.

We next visited Tauranga, which means "safe harbor." On the Bay of Plenty, discovered by James Cook, Tauranga is the fastest-growing area on the North Island. Its population is around 70,000.

The port is an important shipping center, shipping tons of kiwi fruit all over the world. We toured a kiwi farm and discovered that there are three varieties of kiwi fruit—gold, green and newly developed red. Kiwi fruit grow on vines and are grafted onto the same rootstock as grapes. Kiwi vines produce fruit for up to 40 years and the profits are immense. The fruit has a long shelf life and is quite tasty. We sampled kiwi brandy, kiwi wine and kiwi milkshakes.

The jet boat ride on the South Island had been so much fun that we arranged for another one up the gorge out of Tauranga. With more maneuvering room, we sped through the forests and over the rapids and around the rocks, where there was turning room for doing donuts, quite a back jerk and splash, but great fun.

Much of the area around Tauranga played a significant role in New Zealand's history. In the early 1860's many of the wars over Maori land were fought nearby. The Maoris (pronounced "Mow"—rhymes with cow

—"ree.") are the indigenous population. After the Treaty of Waitangi, in which Maori chiefs acknowledged British sovereignty, Tauranga started to become a thriving farm community and port.

Auckland was our last stop. Sprawling across a narrow isthmus, Auckland and its far-flung suburbs are divided by two magnificent harbors. With a population of over one million, Auckland is New Zealand's largest city. The "City of Sails," as it is called, boasts more boats per capita than any other city in the world. The balmy year-round climate encourages water-oriented recreation. Auckland's cosmopolitan flavor is enhanced by its large Maori community. Asian, European and Pacific Island immigrants exert an international influence upon the city.

After an overview of the city, we met with a Maori cultural guide who drove us to the top of a hill located in the heart of the city, the ruins of a Maori fortress. From there we viewed the city and began a walk down the hill as he told us of his people's history. Maoris currently compose 17 percent of the population of New Zealand and after years of legal battles have regained some of their most valuable land. They are integrated into society and intermarriage is common and not disgraceful.

There was a time in the 1950's and 60's when they suffered discrimination. Historically, the Maoris were cannibals and ate their enemies to debase them and conquer their spirit, not because they liked the taste of human flesh. They were valiant warriors and their women often fought with them. With the influx of foreigners and colonization, the Maori chiefs made peace with the colonists and sold them land, choosing to live with them. Relations between the two cultures appear to be affable, and New Zealand boasts that they are "Two Cultures, One Country."

I found Australia and New Zealand to be prosperous, thriving, free and friendly. The people are energetic and open. I felt a special kinship with the Australians. Their land is harsh and hostile. The plants had stickers, the insects were painful and the animals dangerous—in many ways Australia is a lot like Texas.

35

Hurricanes

M y mother was insistent. She called my brother, "David, I want you to call somebody and have my electricity turned back on."

"Mother, we're in the middle of a hurricane."

"The winds have calmed down. I need my electricity."

"It's just the eye passing over. Stay put. The worst may be coming."

In 2008 Hurricane Ike ravaged Galveston and Houston. Millions of people were without water or electricity. Cell phones ceased to work. The transmission towers succumbed to the Category 2 winds. Streets flooded; trees and debris littered both the roads and the freeways. Thousands of residents evacuated; just as many remained hunkered down, determined to weather the storm.

Three hundred miles west I spent a calm day under blue skies and mild breezes, disappointed that the storm moved east, sparing me the adrenaline rush of extreme weather.

I broke my rule, turned on the TV at 5:30 A.M. , watching Geraldo the evening before on the seawall of Galveston. Little was being filmed live. I saw him fall in the turbulent surf. The hurricane had crossed the coastline in the early morning hours and was hammering the Houston area. I thought of my family. My son Joe is a firefighter, manning the Emergency Operations Center in Missouri City. I knew he was safe; he was a trained professional. I did fear for the long hours and emergencies he would face in the coming hours.

Aunt Stella and her family lived in the Clear Lake area. I prayed their homes would withstand the winds and that the drainage ditches would be adequate to prevent their homes from flooding. I knew my brothers were safe on their ranches near Crockett, equipped with generators. My daughter-in-law Carla was safe with her parents. They too had a generator and water supply. I felt little concern for property damage— insurance would take care of that.

I had spent the week preparing for the storm that did not come. I stored extra water, visualized making coffee and cooking on the propane stove down in the hunters' cabin. I pictured myself showering in the newly tiled bathroom, even planned on being flooded in by the rising creek and experiencing the joy of physical isolation—a memory that took me back to the days when my husband John was alive and local flooding would strand us for weeks. I fondly recalled bathing in the creek, sloshing in the mud and not caring about anything but the moment. I am an extreme-weather junkie and reluctantly came down from the high that would not be refueled.

Instead, I spent the day in contemplation, cooking greens and baking part of a wild hog I had trapped, eating fruit and returning to the pictures on the old TV that I had muted.

I remembered my first hurricane, Carla, back in the early 60's. I was a university student and had been in Pasadena having dinner with a boyfriend. My parents advised me to stay put, that the storm was coming. I spent the night in the bedroom hallway with his parents and younger brother.

The wind sounded like a freight train as the storm raged in the darkness. The roof blew off, and when daylight glimmered, the water was within a few feet of the front door. The street was a dirty river but the cars near the house were high and dry. Two days of cooking on a barbecue pit and sharing a nasty bathroom with him and his family brought me to the realization that he was not the man for me. I finally escaped to home north of Houston, not having missed too many classes in Austin.

I remembered the early 70's, living on Lake Livingston, divorced and childless from a failed marriage. I was bitter and angry and somewhat broke. The hurricane had come through Houston and headed directly for the beautiful big lake north of Houston. The waves splattered my picture window and the winds left the bulkhead and dock in shambles, the surrounding grounds littered with limbs and fallen trees. Stored water and the barbecue pit sustained me until power had been restored.

As I continued to watch the muted TV, I saw Anderson Cooper from CNN standing in muddy water in hip boots like a fool, broadcasting live from Bridge City near the Texas-Louisiana border. He looked ridiculous, his hair sprayed to perfection, overly dramatic. "I'm live from Bay City; this is the town of Bridge City; Bay Harbor is under water."

He obviously didn't know that he was standing in the ditch. Only when a dog splashed through the water to him was it apparent that the road was only covered in a few feet of water. In the meantime Geraldo was still sleeping it off in the high-rise hotel in Galveston. His broadcast would come later.

Memories flooded my consciousness—the 1980's with two children in Louisiana, Hurricane Danny and an absent husband. Our plantation home was on the Bayou Teche. The winds blew, and the water came up the slope near the house. The party-deck boat rose in the boathouse to the roof. I waded out and freed it in time to keep it from lifting the roof and tied it to a large cypress on the banks. The filthy bayou water rose almost to the swimming pool before it receded.

The children and I were snug and safe under the slate roof and inside the sturdy home built in the 1930's. The natural-gas generator provided us with electricity. It was fueled directly from the gas fields of the previous owners and was started with a battery that I kept charged for such emergencies. It was easy to remember the name of Hurricane Danny because my daughter Molly found a puppy in the days after the storm. Molly had gone out to the road to get the mail and heard him crying. We named him Danny and he was a constant companion to the children as they grew to maturity.

Later that afternoon I called family and friends. They were all safe and had minimal property damage but were without electricity and water. The authorities predicted it would be days before power would be restored. Evacuees were cautioned to stay put, not to return until the flooding had passed, the power was restored and the infrastructure was repaired.

By the third day I imagined short tempers, impatience and indignation over the loss of comfort. I had experienced the high. That was sufficient. My mind had experienced the storm and my body had missed the suffering. There was always the next year and the next hurricane season.

36

How to make it rain in west Texas

L iving in west Texas, where water is important requires a surrender to the weather junkie phenomenon. Weather is the main topic of conversation, the opening line and the ending words.

"Has it rained up your way? How is the creek running? How cold was it this morning? How high did the temperature get? What's the latest forecast? I sure hope this wind lets up."

The bottom line though has to do with rain. There is never enough rain. Water is becoming a big issue in Texas and all over the world—clean water, desalinization plants, urban waste, gray water, purifying sewage water, cloud seeding, water catchment.

Most of our ground and surface water comes from rain, the old-fashioned stuff from the clouds and sky above. Rural inhabitants look forward to and depend on rain. I have always loved rain because when it rained I didn't have to work outside. Rain drove me indoors with a good book, sex, a card game, music or the challenge of cooking some good food.

Ranchers who depend on the land for a living have secret techniques to cause rain. The once-a-year pickup truck car wash and cleaning is a standard. Leaving sacks of feed and hay overnight in the bed of the pickup is another. Those two are relatively cheap and emotionally light. Fixing the water gaps (fencing that crosses a dry creek bed or running water) is a more severe method. I have gone years without repairing the fence across a water bed. As soon as I make plans to fix the fence a flood occurs. Grading the rough caliche roads or actually repairing the water gaps is a guarantee for a gully washer.

Absentee ranch owners however provide the best insurance for rain. Repeatedly I have seen owners from Dallas or Houston purchase property and begin to contour the terrain to suit their inflated egos. One man brought in heavy equipment to build a crossing over the creek using culverts and concrete. Within a week the most destructive flood in history came raging down the creek and destroyed his efforts.

A man from Houston purchased a ranch down the road, cleaned the creek banks, dredged out the creek and created a picturesque park. Within a week, the heavens let loose and washed away his scenic world. Not to be dismayed, he restored the area and in less than three days, another flood came down. He continued to configure the rough land until we had the wettest year ever, 48 inches of rain in an area with an average rainfall of 22 to 24 inches per year. I was sad to see him, spirit and bank account broken, abandon his ranch and go back to Houston, leaving the ranch to a part-time caretaker, only to return and reconfigure the creek once again.

The weather forecast is not a reliable source of information. I have witnessed the San Antonio weather radar scanning my county and showing not a drop of rain when rain was falling. I believe that sometimes the television stations show file footage.

The current year has been one of the driest in recent memory. The little moisture we have received has been due to my strenuous efforts and exercises. I washed my pickup and produced almost half an inch. I talked about repairing my water gaps and the skies dropped a quarter of an inch. My best results were leaving a bale of alfalfa, a sack of pellets and a sack of corn overnight in the bed of the pickup. Though no rain was forecast, a thunderstorm appeared out of nowhere and left an inch of rain.

I think if I grade my roads, fix the water gaps and spend a few thousand dollars in the process, the area will probably be free from drought conditions for the year—a cheap price for rain.

37

The full moon

A calendar does not alert me to that time of the month when the moon is full. Instead my body and Mother Nature inform me silently. The first indication is sleeplessness. Chastened with being wide awake, I simply look out my window. There it is: the approaching fullness of the moon resting lightly outside over the head of my parent's four-poster bed.

The scale is the next prime example. Though my eating habits have not changed, I have managed to gain at least two pounds. Throughout the next few days, no amount of fasting can shed the weight. As the moon wanes, so does the weight.

And then the animals have their turn. They graze by the full moon. The sheep and the deer are out in large numbers. A trip home to my ranch by night reveals all sorts of activity along the winding roads. Porcupines are on the move. Skunks, raccoons, foxes, bobcats, hogs and all sorts of hoof stock are darting across the black pavement.

The news presents violence and crazy events. Chaos reigns. Long lost friends call. Marriages dissolve. New relationships evolve. The world becomes animated. Energy permeates the atmosphere.

Planting by the moon achieves splendid results. Seeds placed into the warm earth produce flourishing greenery, provided they bear above the ground. Seeds that produce below the soil are best planted in the new moon.

Postholes dug in the time of the full moon are easily filled with excess dirt. Those dug during the new moon remain cratered.

Ranchers and those who are savvy consult the phase of the moon to determine the appropriate time to castrate animals or to schedule surgery. Healing occurs more rapidly in the time of the new moon. Cuts and scrapes endured during the full moon linger with aggravation.

A walk during the night of the fullness of the moon doesn't require a flashlight, and the sounds of wildlife crashing in the thick cedar of the canyon country are reassuring that Mother Nature is once again having her way with the sentient beings on this lovely planet called Earth.

38

No such thing as a free dog

The phone rang. It was my daughter Molly.

"Hi Mom, I'm home."

"Great, I heard you come through the bump gate. Is everything okay down there at your house?"

"Yeah, all is well."

"How was the drive?"

"Oh you know, long but scenic. I came through Del Rio. I don't like the interstate from Ft. Stockton to Sonora."

"Me either. Your dog Easy is waiting."

"I heard him howling when I drove up."

"Molly, I thought I heard some dogs barking."

"Well, I was going to tell you later."

"Tell me now. I'm in a good mood."

"I hope you're in a real good mood."

"Not that good."

"I brought home two puppies. They were beside the road. Obviously, someone dumped them. They're real pretty. Look like a cross between an Australian shepherd and a Catahoulla, a boy and a girl."

"Molly, we don't need any more dogs."

"They're so cute."

"Leave them down there when you come up for dinner. I cooked some gumbo."

"Great, give me time to unload. I'll bring Easy back down after dinner and introduce them. He'll get along fine."

"You know how he is with other dogs."

"Trust me, he'll be fine."

"See you in a little while."

My daughter drove up the hill to the ranch house overlooking the creek bottom where her house lies snug on the floor of the rugged canyon. Over a glass of wine before dinner, we talked animal talk.

"Mom, the puppies are so cute. One has blue eyes."

"Are they short-haired?"

"Of course. I know better than to bring long-haired dogs to this country."

"What about shots and all that?"

"Don't worry, I'll take care of it, like I always do."

"Yeah, remember the free cat."

"You love Parlay. He's a great cat and a good mouser."

"After $178 for all his shots, being neutered and Frontline every month at no small cost."

"I'll pick up the stuff at the feed store."

"And charge it to the ranch account."

"You can afford it."

"You can't."

"Oh, Mother. Don't be that way."

After an enjoyable meal, Molly drove down to her house, taking Easy, the 120-pound Bull Arab that we both claimed.

My morning coffee on the porch was disturbed by the yelping of a puppy.

Not long after, the phone rang.

"Mother, Easy bit one of the puppies. His head is bleeding. I cleaned it up. It doesn't look too bad. I think he'll be okay. I can't believe I let that happen."

"I'll come down and get Easy."

"No, I think it'll be okay. I read him the riot act. He learned his lesson."

"I hope so."

I left her alone to become one with the solitary sounds of nature, on which we both thrived.

For the second morning in a row, my coffee ritual was interrupted.

"Mother, the puppy's head is all swollen. I think I need to take him to the vet. I called and have an appointment this afternoon. Can I take the truck?"

"Sure. Better bring Easy up here before he hurts the other one."

"Okay. I'll bring him up before I leave."

She returned home that evening, worn out from the 120-mile round trip drive to Uvalde. The puppy was fine after $156 of vet expense.

Molly came up for a visit and took Easy down to her house. And again for the third morning, my coffee moments were soured. "Mom,

Easy bit the other dog in the jaw. There's blood everywhere. I have to take her to the vet. I'll bring Easy up to you."

"Okay."

"Thanks for being so understanding."

"No comment."

"I dreamed about Grandma last night. I really miss her."

"Me too. . . . I dreamed the composter was full."

"Mother, you need to get a life and dream about something other than a composter."

"Pretty hard to get a life living in the middle of nowhere."

"I'll see you in a little while."

"Sure."

That evening she returned again. "Mother, Easy broke her jaw. They operated on her and wired it together. The bill was $286. I had to pay. My bank account is overdrawn. Do you think you could run into town and put some money in my account in the morning? I'm sick of the road."

"Those free puppies are getting a bit expensive."

"I don't want to hear it."

"Talk to you later."

The following day I had a visit from some hunters who lease the hunting rights on an adjoining ranch. Over drinks, they remarked, "I saw two puppies down at your daughter's house. What are they?"

"Australian Shepherd-Catahoulla cross, we think. My daughter picked them up beside the road. Would you like one or both?"

"Funny you should ask, our dog died last month, and my wife is talking about getting another dog."

"How about two?"

"Are you serious?"

"Dead serious."

"Great. I'll pick them up in the morning when we leave."

"Super. Of course you know there's no such thing as a free pet."

"Goes without saying. Thanks."

39

Mom

I visited my mother's grave for the first time since the funeral.
"Hi, Mom. How's it going? This place is a mess. I know you must not like that."

The wind was blowing lickety split. I attempted to right the light black metal stands that had held the floral wreaths. The circles of flowers were no longer attached. I plucked some greenery that had not turned brown in the three weeks since the funeral. The pain of the slender thorns was welcome. I wished it more severe, hurting so it would overshadow the emotional pain.

I stood at the foot of her grave feeling so weak and helpless. My strength had gone underground with her body. I stood there in the quiet afternoon, feeling the presence of my ancestors hovering in the small family cemetery. Aunts, uncles, grandparents, cousins, great-grandparents and a nephew were all there. I strolled between the rows of graves, reading inscriptions on the carved headstones.

I felt her presence when I returned to her home. The clock in her office had quit working and the hands were quaking back and forth erratically. My brother had replaced the batteries, but the clock continued to malfunction.

"Allan, Mother's messing with us, letting us know she's here."

Allan explained. "The hand is bent and keeps hitting the other one. There must be a way to take the back off this thing. Let me see. We need a screwdriver."

"I'll fix it tomorrow," I offered. "Leave it on the chair."

We played bridge that night at my brother David's house. Tuesdays were bridge days. Two of my brothers and a nephew routinely ate dinner and enjoyed an evening of cards with Mother. It was a 10-year ritual and one not easy to abandon.

Mostly we talked, sharing our grief. We knew she was tired and ready to go. She indicated that on many occasions. We agreed that our love kept her alive longer than she wished. We missed her horribly.

Allan met me downstairs the next morning. As we went into her office, I remembered the clock and left to find a screwdriver. Allan picked up the clock as I returned.

"I see you fixed the clock, Sonja."

"No, I forgot. See the screwdriver in my hand. I just remembered and went to get it. I guess Mother fixed it."

"Maybe so." He hung the clock back on the wall.

The movie reel in my head that had begun playing after her death continued. It never stopped—childhood, memories, the funeral, words, pictures, Daddy. I could not focus because of the movie. In the weeks and months that followed, I lost mail to the wastebasket; thought the oncoming season was fall instead of spring. I could not focus, tilted on the edge of a cliff, craving physical pain.

I found it, hit my eye so hard on the door that it hemorrhaged and I lost vision. A trip to a specialist in San Antonio assured me that the retina was still attached, but the eye was full of blood. Steroid drops and a shot were delivered with the promise that the vision would return slowly. In the meantime, I was to take it easy.

How could I? The drops produced mood swings and insomnia, just what I needed when my brain was trying to archive the data in the movie that continued to play night and day. I had experienced a crazy period when my husband died, but this was worse, intensified by the eye drops. In addition, I was told to sleep sitting up so gravity would help diminish the blood in my eye. The full moon did not help.

I fled to books, seeking escape. I began to reread the sequel to Gone with the Wind. No help there. Scarlett and I were both dealing with death and loss. We joined forces and still no help. She just aggravated me.

And then somehow before a year had passed, I arose and knew where I was, still feeling my mother's absence, but having formed a new relationship with her, a spiritual one. Her energy was with me and in me.

40

The Balkans

This adventure carried me down the Danube River through the Balkan countries in southeastern Europe. My means of travel was a comfortable river barge built in Holland and designed to go under the many bridges and through the locks along the blue Danube, which incidentally is not blue but rather black. The river barge accommodated about 120 passengers but was not full, due to the world-wide recession. The majority of my fellow passengers were a bunch of rowdy and fun-loving Australians, along with some Mexicans, New Zealanders, Germans and very few Americans.

The Danube is the only major river in Europe that flows east. In the 1990's a canal connected the Main River to the Danube, thus connecting the North Sea to the Black Sea. The Danube flows 1,780 miles through 10 countries—Germany, Austria, Slovakia, Hungary, Croatia, Serbia, Bulgaria, Romania, Moldavia and the Ukraine.

Vienna was for centuries the capital of the Holy Roman Empire and is still the great cultural capital of central Europe, with about 1.7 million inhabitants. The country of Austria has a population of 8.2 million. I spent the first day exploring Vienna, walking through the grounds and rooms of the Hofburg Palace, which dates back to the 13th century and was the historic winter residence of the royal Habsburg dynasty.

The Opera House, built by the Emperor Franz Josef, was 140 years old. Johann Strauss composed the "Blue Danube Waltz" in Vienna. Mozart was at the height of his creative powers when he lived in Vienna. Before visiting St. Stephens Cathedral, I walked through the house where Mozart lived.

There are more than 800 parks and gardens in the city. Sidewalk cafes are in abundance. Austria is a neutral country and the headquarters of OPEC are located in Vienna.

Schonbrunn Palace was the summer residence of the Habsburgs and is a stunning palace rivaling Versailles, the palace on the outskirts of Paris. When the empress Maria Theresa began her reign in 1740, she completed the work begun by Leopold I, enlarging it perhaps to accommodate her 16 children. The palace grounds contain the world's oldest zoo.

The next stop along the Danube was the city of Bratislava, straddling both banks of the river. The city is a melting pot of cultures and architectural styles, including gothic, baroque and art deco. Bratislava is the capital of Slovakia, and the seat of government is housed in the restored 17th century palatial residence of a former Archbishop.

Both Romans and Celts settled the area, and when the Slavs arrived in the fifth century, their leader Bretislav gave his name to the town. By the early 900's Bratislava was a river trading town and by the 12th century, a large city.

I visited Bratislava Castle, a beautiful medieval castle enjoyed by Maria Theresa. It was once a Hungarian stronghold and fort. She had the steps to her quarters designed so that she could ride her horse to her living rooms. From the castle grounds, the stunning view included the countries of Hungary, Slovakia and Austria.

Maria Theresa married Prince Albert of Saxony. It was said to be a love match. With 16 children, they must have been somewhat compatible.

On foot, I walked through St. Michael's gate into the medieval city past Mirbach Palace and the Primatial Palace, where Napoleon reluctantly signed a peace treaty with Prussia in the 18th century. I visited St. Michael's Cathedral, where many kings of Hungary were crowned. The cobbled streets of the old city are embedded with gold crowns, one for each of the 11 kings and 8 queens crowned in St. Martin's Church. I visited an 18th century chocolate factory along the way.

Slovakia is a parliamentary democracy and has a population of 5.2 million. The amber trade route crossed the Danube, and in Slovakia the beginning of the Carpathian Mountains can be seen.

Originally Slovakia was part of the Moravian Empire. Rome never went north beyond the Danube, and in subsequent centuries, Slovakia was part of the Hungarian Empire, the Austro-Hungarian Empire and Russia. Russia tried to combine the Czechs and the Slovaks, but after the fall of the Soviet Union there was a peaceful separation.

Bratislava has half a million inhabitants and eight colleges and universities. It was the capital of Hungary for over 200 years and a barrier to invasion from the Turks, as was the Danube River. The Danube was the border between the civilized world to the south—Greeks and Romans—

and the barbarians from the north—the Huns. Bratislava is lively, and the people are stylish and have a great sense of humor, always smiling.

Budapest was the next stop along the blue Danube that isn't blue. This capital of Hungary is made up of two parts—Buda (the hills) and Pest (the flat lands)—divided by the Danube River.

Along Castle Hill on the Buda side are more than 170 buildings, many of which date back to the 13th and 14th centuries. A statue near St. Matthias Church commemorates St. Stephen, the founder of Hungary. In the 1980's President Carter returned the crown of St. Stephen to Hungary. I ended up at the fairytale-inspired turrets and ramparts of the Fishermen's Bastion, built in the 18th century in honor of the fishermen who defended Buda from the Turks during the Middle Ages.

Hungary has a population of 10 million and Budapest houses two million. Coffee is a part of Budapest's culture. There are many thermal springs in the city and people come from all over to enjoy the baths and play chess while being treated by the healing waters.

The singer Madonna was the subject of conversation wherever I traveled. She was doing a southeastern European tour. Her concert in Budapest began at midnight and 100,000 people attended. Hungary has a problem with the gypsy population, and Madonna opened her concert with a gypsy band, which was applauded. She then proceeded to tell the Hungarians they needed to deal with the gypsies in a fairer manner. She was booed. She continued to follow me, and the same events happened in Bucharest and Belgrade.

Over 80 percent of the city was damaged during World War II. The Germans destroyed all of the Danube bridges, and in 1956 Soviet tanks rolled into the city center. During the ensuing 13 days, over 2,000 Hungarians lost their lives.

Following a day of walking and touring the city, I went up to the Citadel for a dinner of beef gulyas, made of beef, onions, red peppers and paprika powder, and listened to some gypsy music. A white dessert wine, Tokay, was served.

Having seen enough of the cities and monuments, I took a trip across the landscape of the grassy plains called the Hungarian Puszta to Domonyvolgyi, an equestrian park. The Lazar brothers are champion cowboys and the trophy room was filled with medals and awards from all over the world. A demonstration of their horsemanship was quite dazzling, with archery and riding feats. A traditional lunch of chicken paprika followed. The return trip took me through Godollo, where Sissi, the beloved Empress of Austria, had her summer residence.

The guide told some very humorous stories. I had never heard jokes about how bad it was under Communist rule, and it was refreshing to hear about the Trabant, a car made of paper and plastic in East Germany. The Trabant had a two-stroke engine and oil had to be added to the gas. In order to purchase one of these cars, the buyer had to tender the purchase price and wait four to five years for delivery.

As the story goes, a Texas millionaire didn't believe it could be that bad, so he sent the money to East Germany. The East Germans immediately sent him a car to demonstrate their efficiency. The Texan bragged to his friends that the East Germans were so capable that they sent him a sample.

The Hungarian alphabet has 42 letters and is unlike any language other than Finnish. I couldn't make heads or tails of the signs.

The plains of Hungary are cultivated with sunflowers, corn and wheat. The sunflowers furnish cooking oil, and the corn is used for ethanol and livestock feed. Hungary is a member of the European Union, and one of the criteria to join is that the country has to produce 30 percent of its own biodiesel.

The boat docked early in the morning in Osijek, the capital of Slavonia, an eastern province of Croatia and its fourth largest city. It was heavily shelled during the Serbia/Bosnia conflict of the 1990's and has been mostly rebuilt. Osijek was a part of the Roman Empire in the third century and was then destroyed by the Huns in the fifth century. In the seventh century it was a Slavic kingdom, and from the 11th to the 16th century, it was part of Hungary. The Turks conquered the area in the 17th century and ruled for 160 years.

Later, Austria defeated the Turks and Croatia became part of the Austrian empire. After World War II, Croatia became a part of Yugoslavia and achieved independence in 1991. What followed for the next four years is known as the Balkan Wars. At first the Serbs occupied the Croatian province of Slavonia. Then in 1995 the Croatians re-conquered the area, and as a disputed territory, Slavonia was overseen by the U.N. until 1998.

We stopped in the small village of Laslova for lunch at a local home. The village was occupied from 1991 until 1998, with 90 percent of it being destroyed. I talked to the woman of the house. During the war, she had fled with two small girls, was pregnant and lived with relatives in Greece until the fighting was over. Her husband fought in the war. When they returned to their village, only a few walls of the house were standing. They rebuilt the home, orchard and garden. She fed people in her home for extra income. One of the daughters was married and the other worked in Osijek. The boy born during the war and now in high school spoke good English and translated. The village was a contrast in reality. Next to the bombed shell of a home was a new white home.

Before lunch, a glass of plum brandy was served. The lady of the house served paprika chicken with rice, a cucumber and tomato salad and sponge cake with a sweet icing. The custom with the local drink is to swig it down in one gulp. It is very strong; they called it slivovitz.

The area around Osijek is known as the granary of Croatia, one of the most fertile areas in Europe—a landscape of walnut trees, wheat fields, vineyards and corn. They also grow rapeseed for biodiesel. They do not eat canola oil but rather use sunflower oil for cooking. The fields were full of sunflowers ripe for the harvest.

As we left the village, I saw signs along the road forbidding entry to fields where the mines had not yet been cleared. As we entered the town of Vukovar, signs of the recent destruction were visible—rubble, bullet-pocked buildings and bomb craters. It was difficult to imagine the hardships the people suffered. I was thankful to be an American.

Vukovar is a city dating back to 2000 B.C. It was a major trading and transport center and after Croatia's independence in 1991, it became the main administrative center of Slavonia. It also has the dubious distinction of being the city in which the Balkan conflict of the 1990's began. Serbian troops laid siege for three months, shelling many of the buildings and killing thousands.

The city of Vukovar was elated to have tourists, though there were only 30 or so of us. They presented a musical concert in an airport hangar, where we were served once again a shot glass of slivovitz and crackers with ajvar—a Macedonian relish made principally from red bell peppers, garlic and chili peppers. Most households can their own ajvar for use throughout the winter season. After refreshments, we were seated, and I noticed that the backdrop for the band playing traditional instruments was a giant photograph of a fly, the exact same photo on the small spiral notebook that I had purchased at the HEB grocery store in Uvalde. The thought occurred to me that I wasn't that far from home, no matter how far I had traveled.

The first song the band played was "Take Me Home, Country Roads" by John Denver. The second song was "Oh, Susannah, Don't You Cry for Me" and the third song contained the lyrics, "Rolling on the River." Then they played some Croatian folk music and told a few jokes.

One joke went as follows: A villager was given some Russian vodka and then asked how many chairs do you see? He replied five. He was then given American bourbon and asked how many chairs he could see. He answered 10. Then he was given some slivovitz and asked how many chairs he could see. He replied with the question—In which row? Their humor was refreshing in spite of the ravages of war that had torn their country apart.

The boat docked in Belgrade, Serbia, early the following morning. Belgrade is one of the oldest cities in Europe, located at the confluence of the Danube and Sava Rivers. It started as a Celtic settlement, but the rivers continuously brought infamous invaders—the Huns, Sarmatians, Ostrogoths, Avars, Slavs, Romans and the Ottoman Turks.

Despite this turbulent 2,500-year history, Belgrade has a vibrant character and is rich in culture. Since the Greek historian Herodotus first mentioned it 25 centuries ago, the city has been completely destroyed 44 times, has witnessed 115 major battles, has had 40 different names and has served as a capital of five different states. During the centuries when Christians fought against the invasion of Islam into Europe, the city was burned many times. The two world wars were devastating. In 1941, Nazi bombs killed 25,000 people in one morning.

Belgrade means "White Town," and it is located in a beautiful position with the greatest amount of light and sunshine. The city was filled with parks, fountains, monuments, cafés and attractive views of the Danube. Belgrade today is the capital of Serbia. Its strategic position at the junction of two rivers makes it a crossroads between the West and the Orient, being always on the border between the eastern Byzantine-Turkish influence and the western Habsburg tradition.

The day began with a tour of the region's Roman and medieval past at Kalemeggdan Fortress. We then rode through the upscale living area where the high-ranking Communist leaders once lived and visited Tito's Memorial and mausoleum. Josip Broz, known as Tito, both united and divided the citizens of Yugoslavia, which was formed in 1918 after World War I.

Honk if you married Sonja

Yugoslavia and Macedonia said no to Hitler, and Tito supported the American and British forces. In 1948 he sent 800,000 soldiers to fight Stalin. Churchill and Truman were both friends of Tito, who, as the leader of Yugoslavia, was the only barrier to the Soviets. It has been said that during World War II the Yugoslavs were the fiercest resistance fighters.

The country flourished under Tito, who was a benevolent dictator. He also allowed Albanians and Muslims to settle in Kosovo, which later caused major problems. The U.S. provided aid to Yugoslavia during those years. Tito died in 1980. When Germany and Austria recognized Croatia and Slovenia in the 1990's, contrary to international law, war broke out. Kosovo was a province of Serbia. NATO bombed Serbia.

The Serbians tell jokes on themselves. They say that nothing is successful in Serbia; even the economic crisis is not successful. U.S. Steel and Phillip Morris have investments in Serbia, where everyone smokes. Cigarettes are less than $1 per pack. Israel is also invested in Serbia.

Another Serbian joke: Since I read alcohol is bad for my health, I don't read anymore.

Gasoline is $7 per gallon. Unemployment is at 20 percent. The Serbians used to have free medical care under socialism. Now it's not free, not medicine and they don't care—another Serbian joke. Karl Malden and Johnny Weissmuller, the original Tarzan, were also born in Serbia.

I visited St. Sava Cathedral, a massive domed church that began construction 85 years ago. It still is not finished, but when finished it will be the 15th largest in the world and will accommodate 15,000 people.

From Belgrade, we cruised down the Danube to Kostolac, another Serbian city, where I visited Viminacium, a former Roman outpost with wide streets, luxurious villas, extensive baths and an amphitheater. In the fifth century A.D. the Huns destroyed Viminacium, called the Balkan Pompeii. The site, which is spread over 800 acres, was the civilian and military capital of the Roman province of Moesia Superior and was settled by two Roman legions, a legion being between 5,000 and 7,000 soldiers.

Viminacium has well-preserved structures, frescoes and more than 32,000 artifacts. There wasn't a Roman emperor who did not pass through Viminacium. Hadrian hunted here. The emperor Septimus Severus, Gordian II, Phillip—the Arab, Trebonium Gallus, Hostilian, Diocletian, Constantine the Great, Constans I, Julian and Gratian all spent time in this important ancient city.

The site was discovered when a coal mine and plant were built. The closest village to the site is inhabited by gypsies and refugees from Kosovo who work in the power plants.

Returning to the ship, we cruised down the Danube to the small village of Donji Milanovacs, where the whole town had turned out to greet us. Women were selling embroidered cloths and blouses. The men were peddling home-brewed slivovitz. I strolled into town and purchased some lovely hand-embroidered linens and a blouse, and as I visited the grocery store, enjoyed a modern supermarket with a great variety of fresh fruits, vegetables and well-displayed meats.

At the outdoor bar and restaurant across the street, I encountered some of my fellow travelers—the rowdy Aussies—and joined them drinking local beer and wine. The red wine was quite good. I refrained from drinking the slivovitz. One of the earlier guides had informed me that the Romans drank only red wine, and it was somewhat true in most all of the countries I visited. Red wine was most commonly served; white wine was more of a dessert drink. The owner of the restaurant came out to greet us, happy to have the tourist business. He sent out complimentary bottles of slivovitz, and as the rowdies became more so, I walked back to the boat. Safety was not an issue here or in any of the towns I visited. I later heard that some of the Aussies barely made it back on their own two feet. They were very quiet that next day.

The main attraction this day was not a church, fortress or museum, but the river and the gorgeous landscape it created with the help of the Carpathian and Balkan Mountains. The Danube breaks dramatically through the Carpathians forming a 100-mile sequence of gorges named the Cataracts. The gorge of the Iron Gates acts as a natural border between Serbia and Romania and is one of the most dramatic natural displays of beauty in all of Europe.

The Romans left their mark here. On one side of the river is the country of Romania, which bears their name. We sailed past the Trajan plaque, a reminder of the hanging road anchored in the steep cliff side over the treacherous rapids and built by Roman engineers around 103 A.D. We also viewed other Roman remains, including an ancient fortress and Severin Castle as well as Golubac Castle, built in the 14th century. Over time, the Serbs, Magyars and Turks attacked it. The Turks won the castle in 1458 and held it until 1867, when it was abandoned.

Honk if you married Sonja

We then approached the engineering marvels of Iron Gate 1 and Iron Gate 2, locks created in the 1960's and 70's as joint Romanian-Serbian projects designed to harness the hydropower of the Iron Gate Gorge, where the mountains close in to form a narrow valley. The gates are enormous locks that lowered the ship for the continuation of the trip down the Danube. The high lock lowered the boat almost 90 feet in 60 minutes. It was quite an experience.

As we continued the cruise down the Danube, the first major Bulgarian town was Vidin, founded in 300 B.C. by the Romans. The country of Bulgaria was formed in 681 A.D. by Slavic tribes. The country has a population of eight million. Sofia is the capital. The communists ruled Bulgaria for 50 years, beginning at the end of World War II in the 1940's. The religion is Greek Orthodox and the country is 86 percent Christian and primarily agricultural. Deer, fox, wolves and bear inhabit the countryside. Fishing is popular and ski resorts are a destination in the mountains.

The town of Vidin has a long history since the Romans built forts along the river, and the town has been a port of prominence and briefly the capital city of a kingdom. In 1371 the son of the Bulgarian king defied the Ottoman Empire, which was poised to invade Bulgaria. He declared himself the ruler of Vidin. In 1396 Turks invaded and ruled Bulgaria for almost 500 years. The Turks built a city wall around Vidin, and by the 16th century it was the largest town in Bulgaria. Although heavily taxed, Bulgarians were not forced to convert to Islam or to abandon their language and customs. The town prospered from the river traffic and became a center for traders and artisans. In 1878 Turkey ceded 60 percent of the Balkan Peninsula back to Bulgaria.

I visited the medieval fortress of Baba Vida overlooking the river. From the 10th to 14th century, 400 years were spent rebuilding the ancient fortress.

A fairytale stone world surrounds Belogradchik, a short distance from Vidin. The weathered sandstone formed fantastic formations, and the site has been declared a national landmark. The Ottomans built the Fortress of Belogradchik in the early 1800's on the remains of a first century Roman fortress.

The following day we arrived in Rousse, the largest Bulgarian city along the Danube. It was founded in the first century as a Roman military and naval center and was called Sexaginta Prista or the City of

60 Ships. The name was changed during Ottoman rule beginning in 1388. The city contained a beautiful square, theater and concert hall, as well as the Church of Sveta Troitsa (Holy Trinity) built in 1632 and the Battenburg Palace. Today there are shipyards, a petroleum refinery and factories making machinery, leather goods and textiles.

I rode a motor coach through the countryside to Veliko Turnovo, built on three hills. It was here that in 1187, two brothers, Asen and Peter, declared an end to Byzantine rule. The town became the cultural center and the strongest Bulgarian fortress in the Middle Ages until the Ottoman takeover. I walked through the ruins of Tzarevetz Castle and the remains of its walls and towers and parts of the Royal Palaces as well as Baldwin's Tower, the 13th century prison of Baldwin of Flanders, once Latin Emperor of Constantinopole.

Strolling through the village below the castle, I discovered rose oil. The valleys of Bulgaria grow roses for rose oil, used in perfume, cosmetics, food and medicine. Bulgaria produces 60 percent of the world's rose oil. It takes 6,000 pounds of petals to make 2 pounds of oil. The Damascus Rose from Syria is favored in the production of rose water for skin hydration and for cooking. I tasted rose brandy, rose jam and jelly. They tasted like roses.

The town of Veliko Turnovo is considered the spiritual center of Bulgaria. The population is 70,000 with 10,000 of them being students. The name means either great throne or thorn; no one knows which. The coach clipped the bumper of a taxi, and we were left with time to spare in the town while the coach driver was taken to the hospital for a blood test. He passed and we continued on to Abanassi for lunch at an outdoor restaurant. Since it was Saturday, local music and dancing made the afternoon quite festive, and as I looked around I had that moment of illumination that appears unannounced on every adventure.

I didn't know where I was. I could have been in Chile, Ecuador, Tajikistan or Lebanon. The thought did occur that maybe I had traveled too long and too much. Memories were running together. Thankfully that moment passed as I enjoyed the chicken stew, vegetable soup, cucumber salad known as Shopska Salad, a mixture of tomatoes, cucumbers, onions, roasted peppers and topped by sirene (white brined sheep cheese) and good bread.

After returning to the river boat and a welcome rest, the next day began with a coach drive to Varna, the largest city on the Bulgarian Black

Honk if you married Sonja

Sea coastline with a population of over 300,000. Varna is famous for the beaches along its Gold Coast. I cruised the harbor and enjoyed fish soup on the beachfront before wading in the Black Sea and getting quite wet because of the strong undertow—a big mistake.

The museum in Varna had many gold artifacts dating from 500 B.C. Bulgaria is the poorest member of the European Union, with many social problems. The pensions are low, the funds having been spent. The country has a negative birth rate. Unemployment is high. There are problems with the gypsies and school dropouts. The health care system needs reform; dental care consists of two free fillings and one extraction. The schoolchildren are not prepared for life, and theft is common.

The Black Sea is so called because of the danger and treachery of the waters. It is blue and roughly 600 by 1,200 kilometers and is 2,470 meters at its deepest. Little lives below 150 meters due to the hydrogen sulfide content. Salinity is 17 percent. The countries of Bulgaria, Russia, Georgia, Ukraine, Turkey and Romania are on its shores. The waves are large and the waters contain sharks, dolphins and seals. The water was originally sweet water, but 7,400 years ago it was flooded by the Mediterranean. Mt. Ararat in Turkey on the Black Sea is said to be the final resting place of Noah's Ark.

The city of Varna was originally settled by the Thracians. Sparticus was a Thracian. Gold and silver treasures have been found in the royal tombs all over Bulgaria. Bulgaria is the third country containing the most archaeological sites. Italy and Greece are the top two. The area was settled 500 years before Christ. The Romans invaded in the first century. Wine was a sacred drink and the raising of grapes was quite ritualized. When the workers gathered in the fall to prune the vines, wine was poured over the trimmed vines as part of the rituals.

I found the port and harbor of Varna quite busy. As I had lunch I saw ships being loaded with scrap metal and wheat destined for unknown ports. The Bulgarians joke about life under the Communists, much like the other countries I visited, and I found it refreshing to know that their spirit had not been subdued.

I left the boat in Biurgiu, Romania. The town was quiet with no industry. Visible were 14th century ruins of a Wallachian fortress built to defend against the Turks. I traveled through the cultivated countryside to Bucharest observing corn, sunflowers and wheat ready for harvest. The countryside was abundant with apple, plum, cherry, apricot and peach trees. The area was known as Dachia, the population being members of the greater tribe known as the Thracians. The Roman emperor Trajan conquered the country in the 100's.

The language is Latin rather than Slavic, and for the first time in weeks I could clearly read the signs, the language closely resembling Spanish. After the fall of the Roman Empire, other tribes attacked the country; in the 14th century Transylvania, Moldovia and Wallachia were combined. They were then conquered by the Hungarians and became part of the Austro-Hungarian Empire.

In 1859 Romania was created by joining Moldavia and Wallachia, and in 1918 Transylvania became a part of Romania. During World War II Romania fought on the German side and the Allies bombed the oil fields of Ploesti. In 1944, Romania split with the Germans and sided with the Allies. The communists ruled from 1947 until 1989, when they became independent. Ceausescu ruled as dictator from 1965 until 1989, when he and his wife were executed.

I toured the colossal palace of the Parliament, the second largest building in the world. The Pentagon is the largest. Nicolae Ceausescu commissioned 20,000 laborers who worked three shifts a day for five years to build it. It was not finished when he was executed. The dictator destroyed much of the old historic part of Bucharest to erect this magnificent palace. It was unbelievable, with thousands of rooms. In addition to the palace, he erected buildings with 24,000 apartments surrounding it.

I spent the afternoon strolling through the main part of the city, where the customs are changing. There are many fast food restaurants as well as sidewalk cafés where Turkish coffee, dark and sweet, is enjoyed.

The city of Bucharest is only 60 kilometers from the Danube and hosts a population of over two million with more in the suburbs. The city is old but progressive. In 1857 Bucharest had oil lamps before Paris or Vienna, and the city was known as the Paris of Eastern Europe. My guide, Violet, told me that one of the president of Syria's wives was from Transylvania.

Of course, there were more Communist jokes: A man ordered a car, and when they informed him that he could pick it up in five years, he asked if it would be morning or afternoon. When asked what difference it made he replied that the plumber was coming in the morning. Another joke: Policemen always travel in threes: one who can read, one who can write and one to protect the intellectuals.

In the last 15 years, 3,000 new churches have been built. The Greek Orthodox priests are allowed to marry but the monks are not.

Romania is not a rich country. Salaries are about $750 per month. Another joke: Of the $750 salary, they spend about $1,000 per month and put the rest in the bank. The spending and generosity of the Romanians does not match their income.

Madonna continued to follow me, having a concert the evening before, the tickets selling close to $200; 70,000 attended. Again she made the inappropriate comments about the gypsy problem and was booed. The gypsy population is about 6 percent.

The following day I traveled through Ploesti, aiming for the Carpathians and the castle of Dracula. On the outskirts, I stopped at the equivalent of Walmart; only it was a French chain, very modern and full of tempting merchandise.

Ploesti is a town of 300,000 founded in the 1600's. Evident is the Soviet block construction, the architectural style humorously called by the Romanians as brutalism. Driving in Romania is chaotic. The guide said there were no rules for driving, only suggestions. I believed him.

Leaving Ploesti, the Carpathian Mountains rose ahead. These mountains are home to over 5,000 brown bear. The Carpathians contain sufficient salt for the entire world for eight years. Their vineyards are 8th in the world for wine production. On the outskirts of Ploesti I crossed the 45th parallel and passed apple and cherry orchards as well as a Michelin tire factory. Half of the electricity in Romania is produced by their rivers and water. Coal and oil are also produced. Along the road, vendors were selling jars of local honey.

I passed through the town of Sinaia, named after Mt. Sinai. I visited Peles, a 19th century palace of King Carol, the most modern palace in Europe at the time. The town of Sinaia is a ski resort, closely resembling the ski resorts in Colorado. The Orient Express stops here and had come through the day before. The town also hosted elegant casinos and was a playground of the rich and royal of Europe. It still is from what I observed.

Another joke: We waited over 40 years for the Americans to come. We don't know the roundabout route they took, but they finally came.

Sonja Klein

One more: The Romanian army can destroy any enemy in the world in 10 minutes. They just need eight hours to start the engines. The only vessel of the Romanian navy is a World War I submarine. The jokes were endless.

I visited Bran Castle, where the elevation was about a mile high. The Transylvanian Alps are bordered on the east by the Himalayas. The movie *Cold Mountain* was made near Bran Castle, the home of Dracula's grandfather, Vlad the Impaler. Bran means gate, and the valley is a natural border protecting Transylvania. The castle was built in the 1300's and was manned by 500 soldiers to protect the area from the Turks. Vlad was a patriot, as was his son Dracula. Dracula was captured in 1462 and imprisoned in the castle for six years before being released to help the Hungarians fight the Turks. He was assassinated in 1476.

The castle was a favorite retreat for Queen Mary of Romania in 1920. She was the granddaughter of Queen Victoria and a royal beauty. Modern ski slopes surrounded the castle. Here I experienced a touching moment. As I approached the gates of the castle, the loudspeaker was playing my mother's favorite song—"You Picked a Fine Time to Leave Me, Lucille" by Kenny Rogers. Tears flowed; my mother died in January, but she was in Transylvania with me and let me know it.

Bram Stoker, who wrote about Dracula, never visited Romania, Transylvania or Bran Castle. The medieval castle was in good condition, with lots of stairs, secret passages and courtyards—quite impressive. In the village at the foot of the castle, I enjoyed one of my best meals—baked chicken with lots of paprika, vegetable soup, rice and divine apricot crepes for dessert.

I found it interesting that several of the coaches I traveled had Native American dream catchers hanging from their rearview mirrors. As I returned to Bucharest, I heard my last Romanian joke. An ancient blue rust train was moving parallel to the highway at a reduced speed. The guide remarked, "Look, you must see our Romanian bullet train."

My conclusions from the trip: Our country is blessed for not having been invaded many times, and the human spirit is strong and resilient. I admire the citizens of southeastern Europe for their will to survive and lastly their great sense of humor and good nature. On top of that, the Aussies are fun loving and great fellow travelers.

41

Prejudice

Look around. If the people in sight are different than you, how do you judge them? A different skin color automatically qualifies them as a different race, most likely a lesser race than you. Fat people are to be pitied. Poor people are judged by their lack of ambition. Physically or mentally challenged people are candidates for prayer.

Outsiders in small communities are often accepted but remain outcasts. I purchased a ranch from an elderly man who at the real estate closing admonished me, "I lived there for 17 years, and the locals never accepted me."

Contributing to community organizations in a remote close-knit culture is an exercise in futility. No matter how much time or money is added to the local coffers, the natives run the show as they please, taking care of their own kind with a "screw you" attitude.

As for the immigration controversy, one only needs to visit a Walmart or large grocery chain in south Texas to discover that English is not the spoken language. Gringos wait longer in line while the Spanish-speaking clerks visit with friends and family as they tie your flimsy plastic bags in vicious knots. And don't ask directions because they would rather give wrong directions than admit they don't know.

Recently encountering construction on my remote road, I was subject to a flagman who directed me to halt and wait for a pilot car. He could not speak one word of English, yet the construction company was based in Waco. Our only form of communication was hand signals, which indicated that I would only wait for a short while.

Law enforcement officials often stop the luxury speed cars for violations; if not the luxury cars then the junkers crammed with poor people—the philosophy being, "If you're not like me, then you should be locked up." The most intelligent people in this country are either in insane asylums or in prisons.

The educational system discriminates equally. If you are normal and average and of the sheep mentality, then the American public school is for you. However, if you are halfway bright or an independent or analytical thinker, then you will be separated, disciplined and set aside for other regulations, such as suspension, isolation or expulsion.

Prejudice is conveyed not by words but by motions, gestures, expressions and animation. Words are the lowest form of communication. Rank yourself; we are all objects of prejudice. Forget politically correct and endorse common sense.

42

The ditch

The roads in Texas lie between ditches, and the goal of the driver is to stay between the ditches. The same could be said for life's journey, "Avoid the ditches and stay on the road."

Ditches reveal the vagaries of Mother Nature. "Hi, there, looks like y'all have had some rain. The ditches are full."

The ditch is a common euphemism among women. "I ditched that cowboy in the last small town we passed. He was good in bed but wouldn't work a lick, and I figured I'd better ditch him before he ditched me."

The decorated walls of beer joints and even sophisticated bars often echo, "Hey bartender, give me one last one for the ditch."

While the ditch is often to be avoided, there are times when the ditch becomes a refuge, the best way out. "He was coming at me, and I took to the ditch. Good thing it was dry and not very deep."

"My stock trailer came loose with a load of sheep for the auction. I was lucky it drifted right into the ditch and dug the tongue in the dirt. Could have lost my animals or flipped the trailer."

The incline of the ditch is used to facilitate loading in the absence of ramps, an aid and tool for cowboy engineering, a dying skill.

Ditches are often treasure troves; many useful items are found in ditches—buckets, water bottles, wire, string, rope—useful to fill an overheating vehicle, to make minor repairs or to secure a load.

People frequent the ditches, adopting highways and picking up trash that becomes the treasure of aluminum can collectors who supplement their income mining the light metal.

In eastern Texas it is not unusual to see fishing enthusiasts seining the ditches for bait, especially after a good rain.

The dry ditches in west Texas provide food and bedding habitat for the abundant wildlife that grazes the long pasture, the strip of grassland on either side of the rural roads that dissect the sparsely populated areas.

Sonja Klein

"Late last night I was coming home from the dance, and that deer just jumped right out of the ditch into the front of my pickup. Luckily the grill guard protected my truck from the son of a bitch. Wish the county would mow the ditches."

Springtime and the abundance of wildflowers draw the city people to the ditches, where they can be seen crossing them to pose in colorful clusters of blooms with their families for future Christmas cards. The chiggers, red bugs and mites hitch a ride home with them, happy to leave the ditch.

The Texas Department of Transportation excavates ditches for archaeological artifacts, attempting to preserve the integrity of sites that have a historical significance. Biologists examine the flora and fauna of the ditches to preserve endangered species, anxious to leave no weed unexplored.

Springtime in Texas fills predominately dry ditches with abundant blackberries that are ardently picked by natives and sometimes sold in gallon buckets under a shade tree by the side of the road or taken home to be made into cobbler served warm with ice cream.

The primary purpose of ditches is to provide drainage to prevent flooding, but the soil from the ditches also provides the dirt foundation for the roadbeds.

The common toast heard in bars all over Texas invokes stories that are only limited by the imagination of the speaker and his ditch experiences. "Here's to the ditch."

43

The Cactus Affair

I have a relationship with the cactus plant and though my relationship has not been graced with longevity, it has been quite intimate yet not dysfunctional.

The cactus affair began 10 years ago, starting slowly, as we initially became acquainted after the death of my husband. I was alone at the ranch we had aptly named Ambush Hill. At first the cactus and I were friends during the period of discovery, moving cautiously, not interfering with each other's space. At times we were at odds, as the cactus encroached upon my limited pastureland. As I attempted to manage the ranch I had the cactus plants piled in big mounds, using a unique piece of equipment called a Bobcat that easily scraped and gathered the cactus onto mounds. I was surprised how shallow the roots were, how easy it was to dislocate the cactus plant.

Burning the mounds was another story, almost impossible without many gallons of diesel; and there was the ever-present danger of fire, of wind kicking up in the canyons and a blaze out of control. I delayed the destruction, the confrontation distasteful, until time rendered it ineffective. The mounds remained and grew into large clumps of cactus. Cactus piled does not die, just keeps growing, multiplying and blooming.

A circle of rocks in the middle of my driveway causes visitors to remark on the loveliness of the circle, a perfect spot for a cactus garden. My reply was always the same, that there were adequate cactus plants growing all over the ranch and that I had no desire to transplant any of them. In spite of my reluctance to relocate any variety of the cactus family, my friends, family and guests always managed to find some little barrel cactus plants to extricate, not without a thorn penalty, and relocate in cute painted pots for display on patios in Austin or Dallas or Houston.

As time passed, my relationship with the cactus plant intensified. One hot summer day on the steep side of the cliff, checking my fences, my shin brushed against the common variety of cactus called the prickly pear. I was holding onto the fence, making my way slowly down the steep hill. Every step intensified the pain in my left lower extremity. My leg was on fire. I had no choice but to stop, take off my shoes, socks, jeans and extricate the spines from my leg.

I dress commando, meaning I don't wear underwear, panties or step-ins. I soon found myself naked from the waist down on the side of a cliff, carefully removing cactus spines from my tender shin. The thought crossed my mind that if I fell and was found naked alone from the waist down on the side of a cliff, no one would ever know the truth. Dead, I would become a legend, a story of the canyons, the old widow found dead, solitary and bare below the midriff, not much comfort. I did survive that day, the result being that I had a newfound respect in the burgeoning relationship, and respect is extremely important in any relationship.

Years and seasons passed as I observed the beauty of the cactus plants, the bright pink blooms on the small barrel cactus, plants pretty as a rose, even exceeding the size of the plant itself, the colors vivid and eye-catching. I ate cactus in my salads, leaving the plants on my ranch alone, watching from a distance, not ready to commit.

The relationship once again intensified while cutting grass and weeds with my new riding mower, navigating near but not on the clumps of cactus in the game-proof enclosure surrounding the pink guesthouse and cabin used by the hunters who leased the ranch during hunting season. In the hour required to mow the yard, I had two flat tires, I had to stop and replenish the air in the hissing tires, and the affair with the cactus again accelerated with intense emotion.

The initiative was mine and with a shovel, pitchfork and gloves, I began to scrape up the cactus clumps, piling them in my burn pit. The project took a month, but at the end of the month two giant heaps of cactus plants were built, each one close to a faucet and hose.

Since cactus plants do not die when uprooted and since the piles were contained in my fire rings, I had no choice but to attempt the burn procedure. Cardboard, newspaper and catalogs ignited into a flame that only managed to make a small dent. Cactus plants contain a lot of water, and the fire needed continual maintenance—sputtering and spitting, reluctant to blaze.

Necessity became the mother of invention as I remembered that cedar burns hot; it would intensify the heat and incinerate the cactus pile. The cedar worked its magic, and as I watched, I was shocked, horrified and mesmerized by a trail of green ooze slime snaking up, down and around the cactus in the fire pit. The scene was straight out of a science fiction movie. Except it wasn't a movie; it was occurring here and now. I was fascinated by the trail of the slime and spent two weeks burning and slime-watching before I eradicated the piles of cactus. I spent many afternoons in my old wooden folding chair watching the slime trail while feeding cedar deadfall into the rock-enclosed fire pit.

Winter came and the relationship cooled. The abundant spring rains showered the earth. The cactus plants bloomed more profusely and colorfully than any time in the 10 years I had occupied the ranch.

The cactus and I had come to an understanding, a pact of non-interference, love and respect with no abuse—that is until I purchased a new piece of equipment, best described as a weed eater with bicycle wheels, the more easily to traverse the bazillions of rocks on my ranch.

Nature had delivered so much rain that the yard was waist high in grass, and as I cranked up the gasoline motor of my new toy I was ever mindful of the tiny barrel cactus plants in my yard, careful not to step on or crunch them beneath my heavy-duty tennis shoes, so cautious in fact that I backed into my friend—the prickly pear. A few steps later and I had to stop the machine, pull down my pants and attempt to extricate cactus spines from my ass. Living alone has its advantages, but living solo is not conducive to picking cactus from your behind.

Not being able to sit and drive for assistance forced me to blindly probe my behind with tweezers and allow the pain to guide the hand with the tweezers. The better part of the afternoon was spent accomplishing the removal as I acknowledged that my affair with the cactus was a lifelong commitment to a relationship with passion and respect.

44

The dog was white

J uly 4th was just an ordinary day until the phone rang. I was alone. Barksdale was the nearest town, 16 miles distant.

"Sonja, it's Rosemary. I was on my way home from church between Vance and Barksdale. There's a white dog with a red collar beside the road, looks like a pit bull. He just watched me drive by like he's waiting for someone. I stopped and tried to coax him into the car but he wouldn't come. He's got scabs on his back, like he fell from a truck. Is he yours?"

"No, Rosemary. Both my dogs are here in the yard. I saw that dog a couple of days ago when I went into town. He's still there?"

"Yes, a man stopped when I did. He doesn't know whose it is either. Did you go to church this morning?"

"No, I was just lazy and praised God at home."

"It's a good thing I didn't turn around. I almost went back to Barksdale to get you out of church. I would have been embarrassed."

I chuckled at the thought of Rosemary marching into the small rock church and looking for me among the faithful, and I thought of that poor dog waiting in the heat with no food or water.

Later that evening my neighbor invited me to share some wine and cheese on their deck in the cool of the day. Their foreman joined us as we visited.

"What's new, Sonja? You always seem to know the latest."

"Oh, not much. Rosemary called about a white dog with a red collar beside the road between Vance and Barksdale, wanted to know if it was mine."

"I saw that dog, too. Took it some water and food yesterday and ran into Eddie. He was feeding it too. No one can seem to convince the dog to leave. Seems friendly."

As I drove home I reflected that the small community cared and nurtured its own, even a strange dog beside the road and realized that was community involvement at its best. I jokingly called it paradise when in fact it truly was—a place where everyone was his brother's keeper.

45

Rumor has it

At the post office in Barksdale, I visited with Olen, one of my dancing friends.

He couldn't wait to tell me. "I guess you missed out on the big commotion at Vance last weekend."

"What happened? I'm on my way home from the Terlingua Chili Cookoff out in Big Bend."

"You haven't heard?"

"Heard what?"

"Seems there was a big drug bust at Vance—Texas Rangers, helicopters, the DEA and the Border Patrol."

"No kidding. Where in Vance?"

"Not sure; must have been at that ranch with the airstrip. That's the only place I can figure. There's only six or seven houses in Vance. Had to be there at that airstrip. Must have been a load of drugs flying in."

"Wow. That's hard to believe."

"See what you can find out. . . . How was the cookoff?"

"Great, as always. The weather was the best ever—cool nights and warm days, and the crowd was rowdier than ever."

"Yeah, I've heard rumors that the cookoff is a wild rodeo."

"For some it is. We camp out on the hill and cook and sit around the fire, mostly watch people making fools of themselves. Mainly we go to dance three nights."

"Who played?"

"Some band from Abilene. They weren't very good, but at least they played a few waltzes. It was one of those bands that doesn't know how to end the song and changes the beat in the middle of the music. Hard to dance to that."

"Bet you're worn out."

"Not really. I'm in pretty good shape after my last trip, lots of hiking. But I did manage to dance the rhythm out of my body."

"What do you mean?"

Honk if you married Sonja

"After the second night of dancing, I wasn't too game for that third night and when I did dance, my body couldn't find the beat."

"Never heard of that."

"It's only happened once before, the same thing; after three nights of dancing, my feet still worked but I lost my smooth. What else is new?"

"A drug bust at Vance is pretty much all there is."

As I hung up the phone and unpacked my camping gear, washed clothes and went through the mail that accumulated during my short absence., I smiled, recalling the unseen telegraph system that echoes through the Nueces Canyon, where I've lived since the death of my husband.

John had always said, "Real County is nothing but an open-air insane asylum full of rocks and cactus." It was a good line, one I used often when there was nothing left to say.

The following day I drove to my other ranch on the Leakey highway. Not far down the fence line, I stopped to examine a hole in the fence and saw that it had been expertly clipped and the wires cleanly bent inside my neighbor's fence.

After patching the hole as best an aging woman could do, I drove into town, pondering the fence mystery. I thought it was against the law in Texas to cut the fence, and after posing the problem at the feed store, I received a lot of advice.

"You can't cut the fence. If the fence is on the line, then you both own it and can do anything you agree on."

"If the fence is on your property, no one can cut it."

I didn't know who owned the fence. It was there when I bought the ranch.

"Call the sheriff; he'll know the law."

"I think I'll just call my neighbor."

When I returned home I made the call. "Hello. This is your neighbor to the east of your ranch in Real County."

"Hello, there. How can I help you?"

"I noticed a hole cut in the fence between us and patched it."

"I cut that and wish you wouldn't patch it. I want to leave it open."

"Why?"

"So the baby deer can come through the hole. They can't jump the fence like their mamas."

"It's not a game-proof fence. They can jump it."

"Oh no, I've seen the babies left behind."

"I don't want a hole in the fence."

"It's my fence and I can cut a hole in it. What difference does it make? You don't have any livestock in that trap."

"I plan on getting some goats."

"When you do, let me know and I'll patch the hole."

There was nothing more for me to say until I knew whose fence was cut.

A little research yielded the fact that the fence was on the line and that we both owned it, and the only way to stop my neighbor from cutting holes was to file suit and get an injunction against him to prevent fence cutting.

Over the next few months, I patched the hole twice and both times he removed my patch. After assuring him that I wanted to be a good neighbor, a call to the sheriff's office and the story to the new deputy produced results. The deputy went and talked to my neighbor, who agreed to patch the hole. By the time the matter was resolved, the deputy and I had a working relationship.

One Sunday on the way home from church, I passed a neighbor on the road. He blinked his lights, which is the signal to stop for a cowboy conference beside the road. He was the first to speak. "How's it going? I noticed you've got a lot of projects going. What are you building?"

"A round pen and a barn, and then we're adding on to my daughter's house. She's completed her master's degree and is pregnant. Not the best timing but we're thrilled. Going to be my first grandbaby."

"Yeah, I heard your daughter was pregnant and going to get married."

"Not exactly true. She may get married after the baby's born."

"The new girl at the bank told me her boyfriend's from Egypt."

"I don't think we're on the same page. His name's Israel and he's a Cajun from Louisiana."

"Congratulations on the baby."

"Thanks." I asked him, "Aren't you working at that ranch in Vance, the one with the airstrip?"

"Yeah, building the foreman a new house."

"I heard there was a big drug bust there a few weeks back. Is it true?"

He laughed. "So that's the rumor. The Texas Rangers came to do their arms qualifying at the ranch. There were about 40 of them. Robert

Duval and his wife were there. He autographed a Texas Ranger cook-book for my wife. He's a real nice guy."

"Good to know the canyon telegraph is still working. See you."

Later that week I again drove out to the Leakey highway to check on the fence status. I saw a sign over the hole facing my property. "We're praying for you."

I laughed out loud and spoke to the rocks. "And God bless you."

46

Morocco

T he afternoon flight from Houston to Paris was easy. I arrived at the
Paris airport refreshed and willing to follow the signs to the
adjacent terminal. There, I made the connection that delivered me and
my baggage intact to Rabat, Morocco, where a guide from the Cross
Cultural Learning Center met me. A short ride delivered me to the
luxury hotel, where I had a few hours to stretch the tired body and have
a power nap.

The next thing I remember is that I woke up and looked at my
watch—6:30 P.M. I rushed to the lobby and managed to convey to the
concierge that I had missed the coach to the Cross Cultural Learning
Center, and with the help of intermediaries, a taxi transported me to
join the others. With profuse apologies, I slipped into the rear of the
lecture hall and attempted to collect myself in Morocco. It was difficult.

Introductions had already been made, but there was ample time in
the next three weeks to get acquainted. I found myself in the courtyard
of an old Moroccan palace. Three stories above was an elaborately tiled
roof. Balconies from the rooms above overlooked the courtyard. There
were 12 of us intrepid travelers, well-educated academics. Among them
were attorneys, doctors, a dentist, librarians, college professors and
authors of university textbooks. I was probably the most uneducated
with a simple bachelor's degree. Most of them were over 60 but healthy
and vigorous in appearance. Their clothing was vanilla, the nondescript
garb of seasoned adventurers. Their hair was utilitarian, not much
individualism displayed. Martha Stewart was definitely not on this trip.

I soon discovered that our handler and leader was Rachid Qasbi, a
young, single Moroccan in his early 30's who was somehow related to
the King of Morocco and was employed by the Cross Cultural Learning
Center. Farah Cherif, an impassioned woman in her early 40's, whose
energy had contributed to the formation of the Center, delivered an
overview lecture on Morocco. I was later to discover that her husband

was a law professor and equally impassioned about the center and the dissemination of cultural information.

We learned that Rabat is the capital and the second largest city in Morocco with a population of over one million when combined with Sale, its sister city across the Bouregreg River. The French selected Rabat as the administrative center of the country in the early 1900's. The city has been influenced by all of Morocco's civilizations—Roman, Medieval Muslim and French. The modern quarter of Rabat contains many beautiful and inspiring, as well as sobering, reminders of the past. In its 2,500 years Rabat has twice been the imperial capital and twice a maritime trading power; in-between it has existed as a humble village. The 12th century city walls are still obvious, along with its medieval medina (walled city) and the royal necropolis in the Garden of Chellah. In addition to one of the many royal palaces, the city is home to the Parliament and government offices and the Mohamed V University, the oldest and largest of the Moroccan universities.

Africa, the Middle East and Europe converge in Morocco. The focus of the trip was to study the diversity of culture and daily life as expressed in concepts of religion, spirituality, secularism, patriarchy, human rights, beauty and pleasure—a giant menu.

What little I saw of the city that first night was impressive— boulevards, cultivated flower gardens and a mild temperature to warm the weary traveler's soul.

While the lecture was inspiring, the meal was a dream to be treasured—pastille, a fine thin pastry layered with chicken, almonds and eggs. The main course was preceded by an eggplant salad and completed with fresh fruit—melon, apples and dates—and mint tea. A wonderful custom was introduced following the meal. The chef, with a smile on his face, sprinkled rose water on our hands and heads. The custom followed us through most of Morocco.

The capital city of Rabat was home for the next two days. The drive to the cultural learning center was more revealing in the morning light. Mimosa trees, blue plumbago, bougainvillea, oleander and hibiscus lined the streets. The Almorids settled Morocco in the 12th century. A large influx of families also settled in Rabat following the expulsion of the Moors from Andalusia.

The day began with a lecture on the veil and Moroccan costumes. Women are not required to wear the veil but do so out of respect for their husbands. Liberal women were seen on the streets in modern dress, and billboards advertised women in lingerie and shorts. There was little Christianity in evidence. Women were police and office workers as well as students. The coffee shops on the outside were filled to overflowing with men smoking and drinking coffee. The women drink and smoke inside the shops.

Private schools exist where the women are forbidden to wear scarves. Private medical insurance is available for a price, and government and business employees are furnished with medical insurance. Free medical care is provided for the impoverished. Power is obtained primarily from hydroelectric dams and wind. The annual income is about $1,600–$1,700. Most of the doctors, pharmacists and 25 percent of the judges are women. There are 57 Muslim countries in the world.

Following a lunch of zucchini and carrot salad, meatballs with tomato sauce, eggs and potatoes, and fresh fruit, we were driven around the city to a partially constructed project along seven kilometers of the river—shopping malls, an entertainment complex, office buildings and hotels. The United Arab Emirates is financing the ambitious development. Only Phase I is being implemented due to the worldwide recession.

No matter where I travel, movies and movie stars are always mentioned. *Black Hawk Down, Babel* and *Body of Lies* were all shot in Morocco. The town across the river from Rabat, Sale (pronounced Sally), was famous for the pirates that populated the town in the 1600's.

That evening we returned to the center for a lecture on religion and Moroccan identity, learning that Morocco is a Sunni country and has no diplomatic relations with Iran or Hezbollah because of the Shia Muslims. Sunni Muslims are the most conservative and follow the old ways of Mohammed. Sunni Muslims comprise 82 percent of the world's Muslims. Iran is 100 percent Shiite. Since the 2003 terrorist bombings in Casa Blanca, Morocco has reformed its religion. The King of Morocco is known as the Commander of the Faithful.

Only 54 percent of Moroccans live in the cities. The rest of them are tribal and still wear the costumes. In the past a sheet was wrapped, the origin being a Roman man's customary robes. The dress and headwear have nothing to do with religion. The first time head coverings were related to religion was 30 years ago during the Iranian revolution.

Following a series of lectures the following morning, I chose to walk through the souk, which means market, and the casbah, which means fortress. Morocco is mostly sounds—donkeys, sheep, goats, drums and horns and muezzins calling the faithful to prayer. Smells of cedar burning, animal dung, rotting garbage and people living too closely were some-times fragrant and sometimes not so pleasant. The two-mile walk furnished the opportunity to clear my mind with all the information I had received over the past two days.

That afternoon, more information was given. Muslim society constrains women with modesty in order to avoid chaos and social disorder. Only women, they believe, can cause social disorder. A woman's choice of wearing the hijab or veil is her statement of freedom. In Morocco it is against the law for a Muslim to drink in public.

More than 50 percent of the population is Berber, or descendants of the original inhabitants. None of the Moroccans think of themselves as African. The caftan or robe comes from Andalusia in Spain. Moroccans don't speak standard Arabic but instead their own dialect. Family law is Muslim and the rest of the law is the Napoleonic Code from the French.

Following a dinner of salads, smothered chicken with lemons, quince and olives, cushaw (an Arabic word for squash similar to butternut and pumpkin), cabbage, green beans and Moroccan pastries injected with almond paste, we were entertained by a performance of traditional Moroccan music. I found it discordant but pleasant. Green tea with mint and biscotti with raisins completed the evening—and as always a splash of rose water.

Day three began with a lecture on Moroccan architecture and the French and Spanish influence and history. We learned that doors are very important and are arranged so that when the door is opened nothing inside is visible.

Of the more than 200 countries in the world, about 20 are monarchies, and 57 countries—about 1.5 billion people—are Muslim. The Arabic League is comprised of 22 countries. From 700,000 to 800,000 Israelis are of Moroccan descent, after being expelled from Spain to Morocco and then immigrating to Israel. There are 33 million inhabitants of Morocco and the monarchy is the longest existing monarchy in the Arab world, the Alawite dynasty having ruled since the 1630's and having descended from the prophet. Mohammed V refused to sign the Jews over to the concentration camps. Morocco was the first country in the world to recognize the independence of America in the 1700's and has always been closely allied with America.

The people elect the Moroccan parliament. The king appoints the prime minister who appoints the cabinet. The parliament approves the cabinet by a simple majority and the king has veto rights.

The chef treated us to a delightful lunch of fresh tomato salad, lentils and baked sea bass followed by a dessert of bananas and tangerines.

We spent the afternoon at a modern art exhibit at a French Villa and returned to the center for a cooking demonstration on how to prepare couscous with raisins and lamb, which we enjoyed for dinner, followed with fruits, tea and cookies and an amazing concert of Andalusian music developed in the 10th to the 15th century.

Following is a quote from the musicians: "We feel overwhelmed by a mystifying pleasure when a perplexing idea, a vague feeling or a powerful experience is grasped in words, an image or a sound. We feel equally overwhelmed when we discover the ability to preserve for hundreds of years, as is the case of Andalusian Music, the passions of love, the sufferings of separation and ecstasies of Sufism." The poetry that accompanied the music was passionate and sensuous.

Tangier, gateway to the African Continent, was the next destination, and I was ready for the road after days in the classroom. The highway was smooth. The Shell gas stop was clean, with adequate restrooms. As we traveled along the coast we observed the fertile soil and fields as well as Roman ruins and abundant pine trees. Stands along the roadside were piled high with honeydew melons, which we enjoyed every day.

For the first time, I saw cork oak trees, which furnish the cork for the wine bottles throughout the world. Cork oak trees achieve production after 25 years and live to be 150 years old. The bark is harvested every 12 years, and there were piles of it along the roads waiting for shipment.

Bananas and strawberries are also produced for export in Morocco, which is primarily an agricultural country. Numerous dams—128 of them—are scattered throughout the country, providing power and water.

We stopped along the way at Asilah, a seacoast town, and strolled within the old medieval walls to view the murals amid the alleyways. A lunch of fresh seafood was served, so fresh it did not smell, and I was overwhelmed by the variety—sardines, bass, shrimp, lobster, tuna, squid, trout and herring—boiled, steamed, grilled and fried. I do not believe I have ever had a meal so tasty.

Honk if you married Sonja

We resumed the trip to Tangier, one of the world's largest ports, and arrived to look across the Mediterranean at Europe from the shores of the Atlantic and Mediterranean alike. Its strategic position has made it a crossroads of two civilizations. As a meeting point of routes to so many different destinations, Tangier has inevitably been marked by the history of Phoenicians, Berbers, Portugese and Spaniards, all of whom have left their influence on the city before it passed into Moroccan hands.

That evening we had an adventure through the souk of Tangier, walking through the twisted walkways and paths of the market, taking a few wrong turns until we arrived at the famous Hammadi Restaurant, where we were serenaded by "When the Saints Go Marching In." The meal far surpassed the music—eggplant and tomato salad with beef and meatball shish kebobs, followed by mint tea, fresh fruit and cookies with that wonderful almond paste—marzipan.

Leaving Tangier following a sumptuous breakfast buffet, we traveled towards Chefchaouen via Tetouan, journeying through the Rif Mountains, which were splendid and scenic. Lunch in the coastal town of Tetouan was beef tagine, a seasoned stew, with sweet apples, fruit and Moroccan pastries followed by the ever-constant mint tea. As we left our lunch, the music from the movie *Ghost* was playing, not long after the death of Patrick Swayze.

With about 45,000 inhabitants, Chefchaouen is one of the most beautiful towns in Morocco. Located about six hours north of Fes, it is completely surrounded by the Jebala Mountains. The altitude is about 2,000 feet and it often snows. It was founded in 1471 as a fortress by Moorish exiles from Spain and was known as one of the main concentrations of Moriscos and Jews who sought refuge in this mountainous city after the Spanish reconquest in medieval times. Religious tolerance has always been a part of Morocco's past. The only Jewish museum in an Arab country is in Morocco.

The town preserves centuries-old lifestyles, architecture, music and poetry. Populated since the 15th century by Andalusian Muslims driven out of Spain, the town is a place where the past still echoes. The medina, with its red tiled roofs, whitewashed walls and architectural detail looks largely unchanged from the 15th century. The evening meal at the hotel consisted of Moroccan salads, delicious tagine with beef, veggies and dry raisins, followed by lemon pie.

Sonja Klein

The following morning we were treated to a walking tour of the city, led by a guide who sniffed a tobacco combination from his wrist. We learned that, through the labyrinth of alleys and walkways, the cobblestones that were painted indicated a dead end. There were no roaming dogs because the Moroccans believe that barking dogs scare away the angels and that touching a dog required ablutions before prayer. Cats were okay and many were lurking in the alleyways.

As usual, our guide was a wealth of information and misinformation. He informed us that half of the world's cannabis or marijuana was grown in Morocco and that it was illegal to grow or possess it. Illegal immigration is a problem; African emigrants travel through Morocco to arrive in Europe, which is only eight miles across the Mediterranean.

Lunch was again a combination of the vegetable salads, roasted chicken and rice and fresh melons. The afternoon was free to shop the many stores that lined the streets in front of the hotel, and that evening we again tasted a beef tagine, this time with potatoes and olives.

Fes was the next city of destination as we passed through groves of olive, fig and orange trees. Donkeys were numerous along the roadside, and sheep and sheep dogs dotted the hills. A pleasant stop at a rural Saturday market provided an array of sounds and smells. I purchased a kilo of fresh dates for about $1.60 and a bag of large acorns for less than a dime. Our guide showed me how to peel the acorn shell and eat the white meat inside. The acorns were not very tasty, but the dates were delicious.

We stopped in route in the town of Ouezzane, a city of about 56,000, and had lunch in the home of Farah, one of the lecturers at the cultural center in Rabat. She and her husband maintained a residence there on the hillside overlooking the fertile, cultivated valleys. We were served dried bean soup, briouats (salted Moroccan appetizers), chicken and vegetable dishes. Mint tea and cookies completed the meal before we continued on the road to Fes. Following a lecture on Sufism, our hostess Farah reminded us of the importance of education. When you educate a man you educate an individual; when you educate a woman, you educate a nation.

Cultivated fields and orchards lined the road as we approached Fes (pronounced with a soft "s" rather than a "z"). We stopped at a roadside stand. I was surprised to find that my learned companions could not recognize a cushaw from a pomegranate.

Honk if you married Sonja

One of them asked, "What are those things?"

I was quick to answer. "Those are cushaws. The cushaw is a member of the squash family. You bake them with either chili powder or brown sugar and butter, very low in calories and high in potassium."

Another inquired, "What are those?" She pointed to a stack of very ripe pomegranates.

Again I answered, "Those are pomegranates. They are a very healthy fruit." I purchased a sack of them and showed how to peel them. We ate them as the coach continued.

We entered the city of Fes as the sun was setting in northern Africa. Fes was founded in the ninth century and is regarded as the cultural capital of Morocco, located inland on the original trade routes linking the Mediterranean to the Sahara. The Atlas Mountains furnish Fes with abundant water for its 1.3 million inhabitants. It was the largest city in the world in the 1200's, and Old Fes is surrounded by 14 kilometers of medieval wall. The Royal Palace is the oldest in Morocco and the grounds contain 30 acres of buildings and over 40 beautiful parks.

On the first morning in Fes, we walked through its medina, an amazing souk (market) and living museum, a labyrinth of narrow alleys and covered bazaars where centuries-old traditions and crafts continue to be the livelihood of thousands of artisans and shopkeepers. The old walled city through which we walked is classified as a UNESCO World Heritage Site.

Dodging donkeys and hand-pushed carts, we spent hours visiting galleries, a tannery and food and spice stalls. At the tannery, we watched workers pulling hides out of large vats with limestone and pigeon droppings. The smell was overwhelming.

After the presentation at the tannery, shopping was almost compulsory. A salesman helped me select a leather vest for my daughter's fiancée. After the usual bargaining, I made a deal for less than half the asking price. As I began the effort to pay he asked, "Do you have a tip for me?"

I answered, "Do you have a tip for me?" I received two nice leather billfolds.

As we left the market, I made the observation, "I've spent thousands of dollars avoiding mules, people, donkeys, animal droppings, garbage and cats to walk behind a guy wearing a bathrobe and pointy-toed shoes. And on top of that I could have just brought a couple of bathrobes and house shoes instead of my heavy suitcase."

Sonja Klein

A lunch of lamb with prunes, cauliflower, eggplant, sweet carrots and fava beans, followed by fresh melons, was a welcome relief. That afternoon I visited a gallery and admired a small carved wooden duck. When I asked the price I was told $600. Not wanting the duck, I offered $100. The salesman replied, "You bargain like a Berber woman, wanting to buy a camel for chicken prices." We had a good-natured laugh, and I left the gallery and went on to visit a ceramic factory, where the clay was baked in giant kilns fired by wood with no thermostat. The workmanship was beautiful and colorful. The prices were more than a Berber woman could pay.

The evening meal of salmon, lentil soup, carrot quiche and French pastry was enjoyable, and a soft bed felt wonderful.

The following day I was back on the road, traveling to the magnificent site of Volubilis, the best-preserved Roman ruins in north Africa. Volubilis was designated a UNESCO World Heritage Site in 1997. Archaeological evidence suggests initial settlement occurred in 40 A.D. upon a preexisting Carthaginian site dating back to the third century B.C. Volubilis emerged as the administrative center in Roman Africa until an earthquake caused the city to be abandoned in the fourth century A.D.

Many of the columns were still standing, as were the baths and mosaic floors of once-elaborate homes. The main boulevard was cobbled. The setting was picturesque with the valleys and fields surrounding the city ruins. The Romans never built a city where grapes could not be grown. The Romans captured the lions, bears and elephants of Africa and took them to Rome for the games. Lions and bears are now extinct in Morocco and the monkeys reside in such great numbers in the mountains that they are now posing a threat to the trees. The lion was their natural enemy.

Leaving Volubilis, we crossed the mid-Atlas mountains, passing through Berber towns. The landscape was changing from cedar forests and monkeys to partial dessert. The road was lined with tamarisk and eucalyptus trees, with olive groves on the hillsides. The argan tree is indigenous only in Morocco and the oil is used to treat wrinkles and for cooking. It was expensive.

We stopped in the town of Meleadres for a lunch of lamb tagine with quince and continued to Moulay Idriss, where I observed one of the most impressive buildings I have ever seen, the largest structure in North Africa. It was a granary that stored adequate grain for 12,000 horses for three years. The building was three acres under roof and 36 feet high. And even though the afternoon sun was hot, inside the granary the temperature was cool and pleasant. Our local guide was charming; no wonder he had been married eight times. He was a Berber.

On the return to Fes, we passed through Meknes, where the treaty recognizing the United States as a nation was signed. George Washington sent a letter asking the King of Morocco to protect U.S. naval ships from the Barbary pirates and then sent a second letter requesting the king to recognize the United States as a sovereign country. Morocco recognized American independence and donated a palace for the American Embassy.

We returned to Fes and a dinner of salmon, potatoes and vegetable salads and a final night in Fes before heading south to the Sahara Dessert.

Leaving early, the coach paused in the Alpine college town of Ifrane. When the Arabs had an oil spill off the coast of Morocco, they gave millions to clean it up, and with the leftover funds, the king of Morocco built the University of Two Brothers, where Christians, Muslims and Jews could attend college together.

The Sahara was making its presence known as we continued south. The roads were deteriorating and the landscape was changing. The road was lined in places with tamarisk and eucalyptus trees. We encountered semi-nomads along the road tending their sheep. Semi-nomads travel less than 120 miles, whereas the nomads travel more extensively. They control their animals with dogs and restrain their other livestock with hobbles. Most of the sheep were Suffolk. Semi-nomads do not dock their tails and shear only once a year.

The majority of the nomads are of Berber origin and illiteracy is high among them. There are three main Berber tribes in Morocco, those of the north, middle and southern Morocco. The Rifi in northern Morocco are known for their honor and their drug dealing, though I did not understand how there is honor in drug dealing. I did not catch the name of the middle tribes, but they are known for their fun-loving habits, folklore, entertainment, music and prostitutes. They inhabit the Atlas Mountains. The southern tribe called the Tshelhiyat are greedy and sloppy and are good businessmen. None of the tribal attributes make sense, but this is what the guide said.

Reforestation of the Atlas Mountains with the thuya tree is being done by the government. We saw evidence of this as we traveled via

Errachidia. We stopped in Midelt for a lunch of couscous with apples, fresh fruit and salads and drove through oases that went on for miles. The dates were ready for harvest. We observed women walking along the road with and without headscarves. Married women wear the scarves; unmarried women go without them.

The sun was setting over the desert as we arrived in Erfoud at one of the most beautiful hotels, the Hotel Chergui, and a delicious buffet dinner. Dinner was followed by dancing to Dekka and Jorfi music.

Erfoud is largely a French-built administrative center with a frontier town atmosphere, and the following morning we visited a fossil factory where furniture was constructed from slabs of granite. We viewed the ruins of the town of Sjilmasa, the ancient port for caravans traveling north from Timbuktu. Our guide was half Berber and half Tuareg. He was quite handsome and charming as we walked through the market and visited the Ksour of Tafilalt, a medieval city settled in the eighth century. No rain had fallen in six years. A lack of rain posed no problem for the numerous date palms that can exist and produce for 10 years without rain. There were 800,000 date palms in the area.

Morocco has been conquered and visited by the Phoenicians, Romans, Vandals, Byzantines, Arabs and Europeans, and they all mixed with the native Berber tribes.

As the desert progressed, dromedaries replaced horses. The Berbers moved at night by the stars. We moved by four-wheel vehicles into the desert and the dunes of Merzouga.

Merzouga is a small village in southeastern Morocco, 20 kilometers from the Algerian border. We set up a tent camp in the dunes and rode camels up the towering dunes to watch the sun set. The camels were well behaved and smooth to ride.

That evening in camp, some Tuareg tribesman arrived. With drums and clackers the seven white-robed men sang and danced, an event worthy of a National Geographic special. They were the first black Africans I had seen on the trip. The music was Gnawa, a sub-Saharan Moroccan music and a dance that fuses classical Islamic Sufism with pre-Islamic traditions. The music strives to evoke a deep hypnotic trance, often aimed at frightening off evil spirits and assuaging scorpion stings.

Chicken tajine was our desert dinner. At last I had arrived in the Sahara. The sand was so fine that I removed my shoes. I was asked, "Aren't you afraid of going barefoot?"

Honk if you married Sonja

"Afraid of what, a good natural pedicure?"

Soon they were all shoeless.

I heard remarks, "Isn't this great?"

Another reminder: "Don't forget to set your alarm to see the sunrise. I hear it's the most beautiful over the desert."

The chill of the desert descended as the Navajo coat again provided needed warmth and my bare feet were covered with warm socks as I slept beneath the same stars that shine over Texas.

I joined them on the dunes in the early morning darkness. As the sun rose, the desert was aglow in pinks, yellows and oranges, just like the cliff opposite my home on the ranch.

Again the wonder of the city dweller, "Look at that, isn't that just the most beautiful sunrise ever?"

The dialog was interesting. "Yes, but did you see the stars last night? I could even see the Milky Way and Orion's belt."

I reflected that the stars composed my ceiling every night. The sunsets were turquoise over the cliff opposite my home. The pastel hues were common.

Another added, "Did you hear the wind over the sand dunes of the Sahara? It was a murmur in the silence."

The caress of the wind was a constant in my life.

After breakfast, we visited Merzouga and observed the irrigation system of the oasis and returned to civilization via four-wheel drive following a visit to a nongovernmental organization dedicated to helping women.

The afternoon provided a pleasant surprise. We visited a Berber co-op, where of course purchases could be made. After having been served tea and cookies we were seated in a large room and the rug presentation began. Huge colorful rugs were brought out and laid before us. One in particular caught my eye. After the presentation the salesman approached. I asked the price of the rug, already thinking of it as mine. The price he quoted was a bit steep, so I offered him less than half the asking price. He pulled a pad and pencil from his robe and wrote down the asking price. Then he handed me the pad and asked me to write down my offer. I penciled my original offer and returned the paper. He wrote a lower price and returned the pad once again. I pointed at my offer and gave him back the pad. He shook his head. I walked away.

He followed. We agreed on my original price. As he was wrapping the rug he asked, "Do you have a tip for me?"

I replied, "Do you have a tip for me?"

He smiled and gave me a bright blue strip of cloth, soft and fine, indicating it was a Berber head wrap and then wrapped my head like the desert tribesman, the ends trailing down my back. The rug is in my bedroom.

As we left the desert, I found that the basic knowledge of my companions was lacking. They didn't know that turnips grew in the ground, had just learned that cork came from tree bark, that olives were inedible from the tree, that there were so many varieties and colors of dates, that oranges were not necessarily orange and that lemons were not always yellow and that sunflowers were pressed to produce oil. As for flowers, most of them could not discern a marigold from a pansy or a petunia from a periwinkle. They could recognize a golf course and a pasture.

The journey continued to Ouarzazate via Tinjdad and Tinghir. Along the road through the desert we stopped to observe the desert divers who maintain the water channels below the desert bringing water from the mountains. The tunnels go from 50 meters deep in the mountains to 10 meters to ground level, delivering water to towns and oases. The desert divers go down into the tunnels to keep them clean from debris and silt—quite a dangerous job.

We stopped in the Todgha Gorge for lunch, a scenic and spectacular setting in the Atlas Mountains, and continued on the road of 1,000 casbahs and on through the Kalaa M'Gouna, the Roses Valley, where roses are cultivated for their oil. We passed through the high Atlas and Tishka Pass down to Ouarzazate, situated below the high Atlas Mountains. Ouarzazate is an ancient garrison town situated on a vast desert plateau. For this reason, the city is popular with filmmakers for its contrasting vistas, where the roads between the Draa, Dades and the Ziz valleys cross.

Ouarzazate is called the door of the desert; the name comes from a Berber phrase meaning without noise or confusion. At present, it hosts one of the largest movie studios in the world, Atlas Studios. Some of the movies filmed here were *Lawrence of Arabia, The Man Who Would Be King, Cleopatra, Kundun, Gladiator, Alexander, Kingdom of Heaven* and *Babel*. It was also the location of a 2006 episode of the television series *The Amazing Race 10*.

We left Ouarzazate, traveling through Tizi-ntichka where we stopped for a lunch of salads and couscous and arrived in Marrakech, known as the Red City, a city of over one million. There is a very large international community of Europeans, mainly French. Marrakech has been known for centuries for its seven saints when Sufism was at the height of its popularity during the reign of Moulay Ismail.

Marrakech was built in the 11th century and was the Berber capital, a place where the nomadic people embraced Islam and an urban culture. It was in Marrakech that powerful Sultans secured the golden Trans-Saharan trade, ruled empires that extended from Timbuktu to Andalusia, and became patrons of Islamic scholars, artisans and poets. Marrakech today is a living melting pot of the Berber, Arabic and African cultures.

The morning was spent touring the city and crowded markets as well as the Kasbah Glaoui, the palace of the last ruling family.

We feasted on an evening meal of barbecued meats on skewers, enjoying the sights, sounds and smells of the famous nighttime market of Marrakech. We saw snake charmers, storytellers, fortune readers, and henna and tattoo specialists and rode a carriage back to the hotel. It was nighttime in Marrakech.

A visit to the Marrakech gardens occupied the following morning, and a free afternoon was a welcome rest before the last leg of the journey, Casa Blanca.

The trip to Casa Blanca was short. We arrived in time for lunch and an excursion to Hassan II Mosque, an imposing structure. And of course we visited the bar featured in the famous movie, *Casa Blanca*.

Casa Blanca (Spanish for white house) is located on the Atlantic Ocean. It is the largest city in Morocco, with a population of over three million, and the 6th largest city on the African continent. Settled by the Berbers in the seventh century, its port serves as the country's chief harbor and is one of the largest artificial ports in the world.

Poverty accompanies any large city, especially along the waterfront. When the government abolished the shantytowns and established social housing, the fishermen, who preferred close proximity to the water, rejected it. Our guide said, "Any system that fails in France is applied in Morocco."

Sonja Klein

And here the journey ended, a sojourn in an Islamic country. I found the people friendly, religious and hardworking. Their religion is one of moderation, not extremism, and they have a remarkable tolerance for other faiths, an example for others to follow.

A final remark caught my attention as we entered the airport. "Oh my goodness, look at that sky. It's really blue."

I couldn't help myself. "But of course, the sky is blue."

47

Bestiality

Being blessed with three siblings, all of whom live on farms or ranches, including myself, we often get together for a visit in our rural settings. The last time was the occasion of my oldest brother John's birthday at his cattle ranch in Crockett, Houston County, Texas.

Early in May, the weather was delightful on his back veranda, high on a hill overlooking the Trinity River bottom. Most of his flowers were in full bloom, and we were all feeling the effects of the excellent wine my brother kept stocked in his wine cellar. My three sisters-in-law were present and I stirred the pot, being the interrogator for a change. My youngest brother was the customary inquisitor, but I took the reins and posed the usual question to his wife Mary: "How are the twins and what is new at the farm?"

Mary replied with a question. "Hasn't David told you?"

We all sat up a bit straighter in our Adirondack chairs.

"No, what's going on?"

"About the bestiality."

"What?"

David couldn't help himself. He kept the ball rolling.

"Arturo, my foreman, came to me and said he thought someone was trespassing and messing with the goats in the shed late at night. We set up a motion-detected video camera and caught him in action."

"Caught who?"

"Well, this is a bit awkward."

"Tell us."

"It seems this Middle Easterner, a Muslim, would grab one of the young goats, take it in the shed and tie it to the post, beat it with a stick and then have sex with it."

"You're kidding."

"No, it's all on the video. I watched it."

David's wife Mary chimed in. "I couldn't watch it all. It was disgusting."

"I guess so."

271

"What did you do?"

"It seems he came twice a week. So Arturo and I waited for him and caught him in the act. He tried to run away when I told him to stand still, so I shot at his feet. He stopped and while I held him at gunpoint, Arturo called the sheriff's office."

"Then what?"

"The deputy came and arrested him for trespassing."

"What about charging him for the other, you know, what he did to the goat."

"You're not going to believe this, but Texas is one of the few states that has no law on the books making bestiality a felony. All they could charge him with in addition to the trespassing charge was animal cruelty, only a misdemeanor. They took him to jail. He's 19 and his parents bonded him out. They live in that fancy subdivision where the houses start at $200,000. They fined him and we thought it was over."

"What happened next?"

"He came back."

Mary couldn't keep quiet. "I don't want him around. The twins are 13."

David continued. "We waited for him again, caught him in the act and called the sheriff's department. They arrested him and sentenced him to anger management and community service."

"I told David just give him a goat," said Mary.

Brother Allan ventured, "You can't do that. What about the poor goat?"

"They can't keep goats in that subdivision anyway," John said. "It's against the restrictions."

I asked, "David, what are you going to do?"

"I called the sheriff's department and told them that the next time I caught him on my property I was going to shoot him in the crotch. I think they conveyed that information to his parents."

Being a world traveler, I mentioned. "When I was in the Middle East I asked my guide what the most troubling social issues were. She replied that homosexuality and alcoholism were major problems and that the women are sequestered and expected to be virgins at marriage, so homosexuality is common and tolerated."

Alma, another sister-in-law, became involved. "But why is alcoholism a problem? I thought alcohol is forbidden."

"It is, but the middle easterners have a desert mentality. They consume everything in case it might spoil in the heat. When they have alcohol, they drink until it's all gone, no matter how much."

"That makes sense."

"I'm on the legislative committee for the water district and will be in Austin lobbying for water legislation in the next session." I said. "I might look into this, maybe get a law passed."

Mary added. "I'm involved in lobbying for geriatric nursing and will be in Austin for the next legislative session too. Maybe we can make this a cause."

John, the birthday man, had been silent. "Better you than me."

Allan closed the discussion. "You girls can lobby all you want. Just shoot him, David. This is Texas. Let's have some more wine."

48

Just for a minute

One of the most pleasurable moments of the day is that moment between waking and sleeping, when the senses are first developing. Daylight is drifting through the windows and the grayness of dawn filters sunlight like the fog in the canyons on a spring morning.

In the recesses of my mind, my mother is still alive, my children are small, my nephew does not have cancer and my favorite husband is beside me in the bed. There is peace in the world; I am young, slim and vibrant faced with the projects of the day.

And then reality grips my thoughts. None of it is true, but as I linger under Grandpa's feather comforter, I resist that perception as long as possible before I reluctantly arise, pad naked into the kitchen and put on the coffee, brush my teeth and return to fix the bed. Then I slog on a pair of flannel drawstring pants and a tee shirt—my usual uniform for a day at my ranch in west Texas. I spend another day alone with the computer and the words that flow intermittently like some of the springs on the ranch.

Though there are goats and sheep to feed and a very pregnant daughter in the canyon below, I hover between the past and present, wishing for what was and anticipating what might be. No longer is my mother available, my husband nearby or my children innocent. But this morning I make them so; and in the exercise, they are as real as ever before. I hold that joy as long as possible, and it is a good day, a day I create as if I own the world. And today I do. I own the world and I choose joy.

Reflections caress my emotions for hours and then I realize that no one is gone, they merely changed dimensions, shapes and energy. The past is the present and the present is the future. They are all the same and I am king of the universe, capable of writing the script, casting the play and directing the movements. What a feeling of supreme elation.

49

Pets

Before my husband died, he gave away his dog. I don't know why he did that, but I guess it was because he wanted his best friend to have his dog. I thought that I was his best friend. Maybe he thought I didn't want his dog because when he gave her away, I remained quiet on the issue. He knew he was dying and I didn't want to argue with a dying man. Besides I had enough to think about, taking care of him and dealing with my own emotions.

In the months that followed his death, I grieved and mourned alone until I was spent. Then I rejoined the world, wounded and scarred but walking.

When a neighbor offered a dog, I took it. She was free, but I learned there was no such thing as a free dog. I named her Yikes because she was going to be a big dog and whenever anyone would see her they would say, "Yikes!"

Yikes chewed up hoses, dug up flower beds and ate a lot of food. I took her regularly for shots, kept her in flea collars and even bought her a doggie bed. She liked to run away, so I bred her to keep her calm. She had eight puppies. I gave them away, except for one male that I named Easy because he was tranquil. His mother wasn't.

My daughter Molly fell in love with Easy and took him home with her. Yikes kept running away. I received calls from miles away, had to drive for an hour to retrieve her. She continued to embarrass me with my neighbors. I bred her again. She taught her puppies to run away with her. I gave the puppies away.

Yikes was a Houdini. She could get out of my fence no matter what I tried. I put chains and heavy stuff around her neck to slow her down. I patched my fence daily. Still, she escaped until one time she never came back. I like to think of her as out there free somewhere.

My daughter chastised me, "You didn't give her what she needed."

"Hell, she didn't tell me what she needed."

"You're just not a dog person."

Sonja Klein

"I tried my best."

"It wasn't good enough."

When my daughter went to Nicaragua for a month, I was given custody of her dog Easy with instructions to play with him. Easy came with his bed and toys. He was the best dog I have ever known. He didn't dig, chew or destroy. He never left the yard or even attempted to flee. He always came when I called. He barked when strangers drove up to the gate. When I told him to stay, he stayed. We had a great relationship. I attributed his good behavior to the training my daughter had given him.

I didn't give him back. "I need a dog for security reasons."

"He's still my dog."

"Okay, but he lives here."

"Just for the record, he's my dog."

"You can keep him when I go traveling."

The agreement worked. He was her dog but he lived with me.

Sometimes she would talk to him on the phone. When she came to the ranch, he stayed down in the creek bottom with her in the house we had remodeled. He was always happy to see her.

Life on the ranch was good; I had security from varmints with Easy. He killed coons, squirrels, rabbits, an occasional hog and skunks, and fought porcupines that entered the enclosed two acres surrounding my house on the hill.

Porcupines posed an occasional problem. From most of the encounters, he only received a few quills around his mouth. I could cut the ends of them to release the air and pull them out. Only once I took him to the vet, had him sedated and the quills were extracted from the inside of his mouth. The bill was over $100. The skunks never managed to totally douse him.

The only thing lacking was rodent control. Mice and rats were enamored with the engine compartments of my car and pickup, as well as the utility room. When a friend offered a cat, I accepted. Easy and the cat became friends. I named the cat Parlay because he was quite vocal.

My daughter insisted that I have him tested for everything and then neutered. She didn't want him giving any diseases to her dog. Parlay received his flea collar, regular shots and ration of cat food. Molly brought him toys and treats just like she did for Easy. She even brought Easy a tire toy that she hung from a tree and put treats inside.

Honk if you married Sonja

Parlay decimated the rodent population, and I no longer had wiring repair bills on my vehicles. I accepted that the vehicle repair bills were less than the cost of the cat.

And then I came home one day to find that Easy was not waiting at the gate to meet me as usual. I found him lying in the grass, barely able to raise his head. After calling my daughter, I drove 60 miles to the vet, where they agreed he was really in bad shape. I was stunned. The day before, I had taken him to the creek. He played in the water, chased fish and was his energetic self.

The blood work indicated that he had a bad infection of unknown origin. I left him there with an IV. After three days he was not better. The vet was alarmed and said to take him to the animal hospital in San Antonio. The bill at the first vet was less than $1,000 but not much less.

I spent the next day at the animal hospital, a large multi-storied facility in the medical center. X-rays, ultrasound and every sort of test were performed on the dog while I waited anxiously in the visitor area. I was allowed to see him, and then the vet came out. Easy had an enlarged prostate, a kidney infection and an elevated white cell count. They kept him.

After a few days and daily phone calls, it was determined that he was getting better, but the edema in his testicles was not lessening. Easy was neutered and I brought him home. The hospital bill was a lot more than $1,000. He had lost over 20 pounds and had an Elizabethan collar around his neck to prevent his licking the staples and sutures.

I kept him in the house with me for two weeks, taking him out several times a day and giving him pain pills and antibiotics in lumps of peanut butter. After two weeks, the collar came off, the staples were removed and he was becoming his old self. We had bonded emotionally and financially. When a friend asked, "How much was the bill," I answered, "A lot. Why do you ask?"

"Just curious. Some of my friends have spent astronomical amounts on their pets and I just wanted to see if you had spent more."

"I don't have to answer that question and I'm not going to. There is no such thing as a free pet. Why do you think they have superstores that sell only pet stuff? Besides, whatever I spent, he's worth it. After all, he's my daughter's dog."

As time passed, Easy moved slower. My daughter finished her education and returned to the ranch to have a baby. Easy stayed close. My grandson

Theiss was born. The dog loved him. By the time Theiss was 8 months old, the two of them had bonded. Whenever we were outside, Easy licked him. The baby laughed, never tiring of touching the big dog.

Early one morning Molly called. "Mother, I think Easy is dying. He won't get up and his breathing is labored. I need to take him to the vet."

A trip to the vet revealed that Easy's white blood cells were high and that he had an infection. The doctor mentioned exploratory surgery. After a family conference we decided to wait and hope that the antibiotics would work a miracle. He remained in Molly's house, on the porch, lying on his bed with a soft blanket.

A follow-up visit to the vet revealed his white blood cells were still too high. We brought him home and kept him warm and comfortable. He died before Christmas with Molly petting him. We don't think he suffered.

The cold night he died, Molly and the father of Theiss, along with his children, hand dug a grave between the peach trees in the yard at her house. They wrapped him in a blanket and gave Easy a burial befitting a great dog.

His grave is a monument—a great slab of stone and a plaque that reads, "If tears could build a stairway to heaven, I would come and visit you."

He was the best dog I ever knew.

50

Alaska

My mother loved Alaska. She visited four times, inviting me to join her every time. "Mother, you know I don't like cold weather. I can't leave the children right now." There was always an excuse.

As the summer heat engulfed the Hill Country, I found a deal—free airfare and no penalty for traveling single. With two weeks to spare I booked a trip on a ship with fewer than 100 passengers for a cruise through the inside passage, the southernmost region of Alaska.

I flew via Seattle on Alaska Airways to Juncau, Alaska's state capital. Established in 1880 as a mining camp, Juneau was originally called Harrisburg, after Richard Harris and his partner Joe Juneau discovered gold. Of the communities that sprouted around the mines, Juneau and Douglas still survive.

Hosting a population of 30,700, Juneau is Alaska's third largest city. Juneau is one of only two state capitals that are not accessible from the rest of the United States by road. The other is Honolulu, Hawaii. The Juneau ice field prohibits the construction of any road into Juneau.

Alaska is one-fifth the size of the entire United States and two and a half times the size of Texas. Juneau lies in a rainforest with an annual precipitation of 120 inches. Only 40 miles of roads exist around Juneau.

As I arrived in Juneau, Celebration was under way—a biannual festival celebrating the native tribes and culture. The city was crowded.

Juneau was the last United States capital to open a McDonald's. On the first day, over 17,000 hamburgers were sold, with planes flying from all over the state to pick up orders. One small community sent a plane to pick up their hamburgers, and the school band serenaded the returning plane.

That first evening, I visited the Mendenhall Glacier, observing the blue glacier chunks (calves) in the lake below. I walked through the wetlands refuge teeming with plant life—lichen, willows, lupine, yarrow and many other medicinal plants. The temperature was in the 50's, and I returned to the hotel in daylight at 10 P.M. The shops along the central city displayed furs, native crafts, smoked salmon, items carved from whalebone and walrus tusks, totems, dream catchers, rocks, expensive jewelry and gems.

As I walked along the street entering the tourist shops, the Navajo coat drew attention. One obvious native Alaskan asked me for my coat. Fellow tourists asked, "Where did you buy that coat?" "Is that a Pendleton?"

Having lost three hours flying time, I awoke to daylight at 3 A.M. During the course of the journey I never recovered those hours.

I joined a native Tlingit from Ketchikan for breakfast. He had flown in for Celebration and commented that it was nice to see so many of his relatives. I questioned him about living in Alaska. He was full of information. Property taxes are low and there is no state income tax. Residents over 65 pay no sales tax. All residents receive dividends each year from the investment fund of oil revenues—from $300 to $2,000. The native Indian tribes own corporations that earn revenue from business, real estate and hotels.

Following breakfast I waited at the dock near the hotel for a jet boat that would take me across the water to a zipline adventure park. There were five of us.

A young man with a clipboard asked, "How old are you?" My fellow zippies replied:

"Twenty-four."

"Twenty-three."

"Forty-eight."

"Forty-seven."

I was the last to speak. "Over sixty."

"Any alcohol this morning?"

A chorus of no's.

"Do any of you have a heart problem?"

More no's.

"Are you able to climb four flights of stairs?"

All yeses.

"Please sign this release and initial at the red X."

We were all in compliance.

"Follow me to the jet boat that will take you across the bay to Douglas Island."

The temperature that June morning in Juneau, Alaska, was hovering at 50 degrees; the skies were blue.

Honk if you married Sonja

The trip across the bay was short. We disembarked on the rocky shore and stumbled through the gravel to a flight of stairs leading to the visitor's center of Zipline Adventures.

Upon entering the wooden building, we were issued helmets and heavy work gloves and were outfitted with harnesses over the upper torso as well as our rears and crotch. Straps and hardware were hanging everywhere. I silently repeated my daughter's words, "Fear is irrational."

We exited the back of the building and boarded an ancient Mercedes that resembled the modern Hummer, except there were no windows in the back, only open-air benches.

Our young driver explained that the rainforest through which we were driving was similar to that which the Ewoks in *Return of the Jedi*, flew through on their airborne vehicles. I was thinking more like *Avatar*.

As we passed the ruins of a gold mine, our informant spoke of the abandoned mine having been the richest in Alaska, with millions of ounces of gold extracted. On a steep incline we left the safety of the Mercedes and began a long uphill climb.

There was a degree of difficulty having to do with the four-story climb as well as the harnesses and gear encumbering my body. I had passed the point of no return.

Meekly following with my head to the ground, I found myself on a platform high up the trunk of an Alaskan spruce. One of the two guides grabbed a hook hanging from me and hooked me to an overhead cable. It was a good thing. There were no sides or rails on the three-foot diameter platform encircling the trunk of the tall tree. The tree began to sway; so did the platform. I didn't dare look down; instead I looked over the horizon and spoke, "Definitely *Avatar*. A good day to die."

After a brief intro by one of our sadistic guides, the five of us were instructed to step up on a three-step stool, put our gloved left hand on the gear next to our chest and our right gloved hand on the cable gear overhead, thus keeping us from twisting. On approaching the platform ahead, a palm up would signal us remove the right hand from the harness equipment and put it on the cable behind our head thus slowing down the speed for the treetop platform approach. A palm in front would result in injury being entangled in the cable.

I went last, stepped off the stool and sped along the cable, twisting from side to side, dangerously close to the giant trees. When I tried to correct the twist, I twisted even more, managing to catch my jacket sleeve in the rigging, thus coming to a complete stop in the most extreme sag of the cable, dangling helplessly 80 feet over an abandoned mine pit. Our expert guide sped down the cable, extricated my sleeve and physically pulled me to the awaiting platform hand over hand on the cable.

He added, "You did great. Roll up your sleeves so that won't happen again and remember to put your feet out straight ahead to keep from twisting."

One of my companions smiled, "Isn't this great fun?"

We were on another swaying tree platform with no sides. The instructor cautioned us, "This leg is longer and you'll get up to 40 miles per hour. If you want to go faster, tuck your legs."

Again I twisted horribly, forgot to brake when signaled and only the expert guide kept me from slamming into the massive tree trunk.

He was encouraging, "Great, you're getting the hang of it. Don't forget to brake and relax your overhead hand. Then you won't twist."

My twist was getting better, but I missed the stool on the landing. Again the competent guide caught me.

"Much better."

My four companions were having a great time, yelling and taking pictures and going perilously close to the edge of the platforms. They trusted their harnesses; I didn't. After the first four zipline segments I felt more confident of my harness, realizing that at no time was I ever disconnected. I even managed to look down a few times.

Hoping above hope that I was at least halfway through the course, I noticed a rope bridge, open slat bottom and a single rope rail. Hooked to an overhead cable, I had to walk across the bridge my evil guide was swaying to make the adventure more exciting. I was the slowest on that bridge and across the even longer one that followed it.

The second half of the course consisted of longer ziplines, but by then I had managed to control the twisting and the braking. My landing still needed refinement and by the last zip, I did everything right. Fear was under control—until I discovered that at the end of the course I was still up in a tree.

Rappelling was the final exercise. I jumped off a platform with two ropes and managed to hit the ground with both feet at the same time. I was still alive.

Honk if you married Sonja

We returned to the visitor center, where our harnesses were removed and we were all awarded a gold medal suspended from a wide red ribbon. We were told, "You are now full fledged Zippies." To me that medal was the Academy Award, a Grammy, an Emmy, the Nobel Prize, the Pulitzer and the Congressional Medal of Honor all in one.

One of my companions spoke, "That was well worth $169. I'd like to do that again. What about you?"

"I'm from Texas. Bring it on."

Having extended myself far beyond any comfort zone, the following morning I boarded the ship as it floated out the Gastineau Channel, observed by eagles atop the light posts of the city.

As the ship cruised the narrow waterway out of Juneau, we dined on salmon, rice and vegetables, only to be interrupted by the sighting of a pod of Orcas, commonly but mistakenly called killer whales, as in the movie *Free Willy*. Actually they are dolphins and perhaps became known as killer whales because they kill whales. We observed males, babies and mothers sounding on all sides of the boat. The captain slowed the engines as we circled and observed them for hours.

When I went to bed after 10:00, only the blackout curtains in my room shielded the sunlight. By 5:30 A.M. I was in the lounge drinking coffee, watching the ship maneuver through icebergs up Tracy Arm, a steep-walled fiord. An occasional iceberg bump rocked the boat. The cliffs and floating icebergs were spellbinding. I watched harbor seals and their pups sleeping on the hunks of ice.

The resident biologist on the ship answered many questions. Harbor seal pups weigh from 25 to 30 pounds at birth and resemble shriveled raisins. In eight weeks their weight doubles and they are on their own. The seals leave Tracy Sound as the food plays out because the waters contain silt from the retreating glacier. The silt prevents the plant growth that attracts the fish on which the seals feed.

Two forest rangers approached via kayak and boarded the boat to explain their role in the Tongass Designated Wilderness Area, 17 million acres of which 43 percent is rocks and ice. They explained the difference between a wilderness and a park—road access. We could not use the PA system due to noise restrictions. The rangers camp nine days and then have five days off. We boarded small boats and traveled across the Sound, circling icebergs and approached the cliffs towering up to 1,500 feet. The waters reached that same depth. Only from a small boat could we understand the dimensions of the Sound.

We retreated from Tracy Sound under blue skies with temperatures in the 50's. While the sun was warm, the wind chill required ample coverage. The afternoon was spent observing humpback whales flaunting their tails and as many as 35 eagles floating on a single iceberg. And what is a group of eagles called? A convocation.

We dined on fresh tuna, wild rice and steamed vegetables and attended a lecture on John Muir, a naturalist who visited Alaska in the 1800's. After retiring to my room in the 10 P.M. daylight, I rested in bed, watching humpback whales blowing.

The following morning we docked in Wrangell, near the mouth of the Stikine River. Wrangell is the only Alaskan town to have existed under four nations—Tlingit, Russian, British and American. The Russians settled the town in 1811 as a fur trading post. The town's industries include logging and canneries. I cruised up the Stikine River in a jet boat, observing eagles and the fertile estuary of the river.

Later that afternoon we passed through the 22-mile Wrangell Narrows, one of the most famous waterways in southeast Alaska. The passage averages only one-half mile wide at high tide so only smaller vessels can get through. The Alaska state ferries are the largest ships able to travel the Narrows.

Grilled shrimp, beet and potato salad and fresh fruit were served for dinner, which was followed by a lecture on photography.

The ship arrived in Petersburg the following morning. Petersburg, on the northern tip of Mitkof Island, has a strong Norwegian heritage. Norwegian fishermen founded the village of 3,200 residents in 1897. Abundant halibut and salmon as well as a unique type of shrimp make this town a fish-canning site.

We were treated to Norwegian cookies and dances similar to "Put Your Little Foot" and other circle dances. We joined in. Again we saw eagles perched throughout the town, feeding on fish scraps from the canneries.

As I walked through the town, I observed the high price of gasoline and that a two-bedroom, one-bath home was listed at $250,000.

That evening while cruising, we dined on haddock and veggies. Out the windows, I observed sea lions and humpback whales.

Honk if you married Sonja

The ship docked in Sitka the following morning. The name is Tlingit in origin. The city is a treasure trove of Russian, Tlingit and U.S. history. The Russians founded the present town in 1804. Sitka functioned as the capital of Russian America for 63 years and was known as the Paris of the Pacific. Cultural events, balls and parties took place in Sitka as the Russians posted to this remote setting, struggled to keep their culture alive.

Castle Hill, where the transfer of Alaska to the United States took place, is right in the middle of town. I spent the day walking the city, attending a Tlingit native dance demonstration, visiting St. Michael's Cathedral and observing the native totems in the Totem Park.

The shopping was great fun, and I had fresh salmon on a stick for lunch. I visited an art gallery and spoke with the owner, a young lady native to Sitka. She enjoyed the tourists and shared some interesting conversations. Some of her customers asked, "Do you take American money? Do you speak English?" The weather was in the 50's. Of course, I purchased some prints.

We dined on Dungeness crab for dinner and attended a lecture on the geology of Alaska, preparing for a visit to Icy Strait.

Icy Strait is the northern entrance to southeast Alaska from the Gulf of Alaska and the Pacific. As a passageway, the region attracts large numbers and many varieties of sea life. Where there are plankton, kelp beds, invertebrates and fish, there will be larger fish, whales and sea lions, and birds to reap the bounty. The area attracts one of the largest congregations of humpback whales. I observed Dall porpoises, humpbacks and tons of sea lions. The boat circled an island full of the massive creatures bellowing and jockeying for position. After a barbecue lunch, we exited the ship in small boats and explored the tidal zone as well as the temperate rainforest.

Later that evening we entered Glacier Bay National Park and picked up the national park ranger and the Huna cultural interpreter for a full day of exploration of the park. After dining on lamb and sweet potatoes, we were treated to a lecture on the native Huna population, who inhabited the area before the advancing glacier drove them out 300 years ago. Years later, when the glacier retreated, they returned. When captain George Vancouver was exploring this area in 1794, Beardslee Island was the farthest navigable spot in Glacier Bay. Later, in 1879, when naturalist John Muir visited the bay, the wall of ice had receded nearly 40 miles.

Sonja Klein

Having been briefed on the possibilities of wildlife visible on the shores, I awoke at 4:30 and while having my first cup of coffee saw two brown bears on the seashore. After watching them for hours through my binoculars, I observed deer. Whales, sea otter, seals and dolphins were in evidence all around. Glacier Bay is a wonderland protected by the park service. Only three ships are allowed in the bay at any time. A park ranger is required to be in residence on the ship.

We dropped our visitors off at Glacier Bay Lodge, a beautiful resort managed by the park service and accessible only by boat or plane. The facilities were first-rate, with a museum, lodging and restaurant—an idyllic vacation for getting away from it all. I took a two-mile hike through the rainforest, still amazed that southeast Alaska is a temperate rainforest.

That final night, we dined on salmon steaks as I reflected on the trip. It had been a sort of pilgrimage to my mother, but in the meantime I had seen the beauty and remoteness of Alaska, the sparse population, the abundant wildlife and the hearty inhabitants. I was impressed by the environmental conservation and the friendliness. The numerous native tribes were preserving their cultural heritage, celebrating their history.

I loved Alaska, but it's not Texas. I don't like the cold, and I love the open road.

52

German

Being full-blooded German, it is hard for me to seek pleasure for pleasure's sake. Every trip I have taken has been a sort of schoolroom experience preceded by weeks of study and reading about the culture and history of my destination.

Traveling for sheer enjoyment is difficult for me. Over the years I have tried to change but to little avail. I hire guides, take notes, make keen observations and on rare occasions actually let go. Most of the moments I indulge myself involve dancing or sitting in silence.

For me a journey is a global course on other countries. Countries that appeal the most to me are those with dry arid climates and expansive lands. Cities all seem to exude the same atmosphere. People, their faces, what they eat, what they do every day, how they dress, their smiles and gestures reveal much.

The more I travel I realize that all is connected. The cultures and peoples of this planet are all the same. Their histories are intertwined. While on a flight to Vladivostock, I found myself reading a book written by an Afghan who quoted a Persian whose children's stories I had recently discovered. A sweet melon, some fresh fish and a good cup of coffee taste good no matter where you are. The pleasures of the senses will always delight.

I have met all types among fellow travelers. Some I have kept in touch with for short periods of time. A rare few have remained in my life. One couple, Ted and Barbara from Canada, shared the ride on the Trans-Siberian, a singular couple who have visited me at the ranch. Their adventures and compatibility are unique. Their visit brought great pleasure. I loved cooking southwestern Texas for them. After the second day, Barbara asked, "Do you have any bread? I would love a slice of bread."

I had no bread. I had been serving tortillas for breakfast, lunch and dinner. This year when they come to visit I will have bread.

Sonja Klein

Perhaps because I live in words and the mind, I am isolated and thus prefer traveling alone. I have no desire to be burdened by another's moods and whims. I guess that's why I'm single and have remained so.

As for my preoccupation with rainfall, crops and livestock I can only say that my roots are of the earth. As to the cost of things, that is German frugality. I think in numbers.

The beauty of a sunset, a rainbow, a thunderstorm or a cloud-filled sky—that sings to my soul. Somehow that seems enough. If my travel stories seem dry, I apologize. After all I'm German.

53

The Texas connection

You may be in Bhutan clinging to warmth by a yak-dung fire high in the Himalayas with Mongolian descendants or amidst the clouds of the Andes at Macchu Pichou with a Mayan remnant guide playing a haunting melody on a wooden flute or on a wild game preserve in Kwazululand with a dark Zulu tribesman in South Africa. But almost always a simple outline of the state of Texas marked with pebbles, scratched in the fertile silt or marked with animal turds gains instant recognition. "Ah, Texas," followed by nods in unison.

Thank you, John Wayne.

A Texan is a rugged individual, a person set apart from any other human being. How the battle of the Alamo and the fight for independence from Mexico captured the imagination of the entire world is a tribute to the power of Hollywood and the actors and actresses that portray the characters of Texas. The vastness of the untamed diverse land creates characters made in heaven for those writers who are limited only by their imagination.

Being a fifth generation Texan has always set me apart. Texas is not all that big. No matter where I go, I meet people who know people I know, and the older I get, the more pronounced the coincidences.

Coincidences are funny, weird encounters that never fail to astound. Back in the 60's I hitchhiked through Europe. Visiting an exchange student from college days at the University of Texas, I partied with some French citizens through a night of carousing, ending with watching the sun rise over the Seine in Paris. Over twenty years later at a party in the fashionable Galleria area of Houston, my brother Allan was attending a reception in the ballroom of a well-known hotel. As he was introduced to a tall handsome Frenchman, the stranger noted his name. "I once partied all night with a girl from Texas named Sonja Klein."

"That was my sister."

Texas is known for its parties. The Terlingua Chili Cookoff is one of those singular events that have been taking place for well over 30 years, a party I try not to miss. I will drive hundreds of miles for a good dance, especially the waltz. On one such year I was dancing with an attractive man and, in the course of the conversation, names were exchanged. "I played dominoes in Houston with Allan Klein."

"That's my brother."

A friend of my late husband was living in Santa Fe and bellied up to a bar in a popular disco, sitting next to an attractive blonde drinking a margarita. She glanced over and asked, "What are you drinking?"

"Whiskey and water."

"What kind of drink is that?"

"It's a Texas drink."

"You're not from Texas; I'm from Texas."

"Where in Texas?"

"Tomball."

"How are you related to Sonja Klein?"

"She's my double cousin."

Coming out of a Porta Potty at the Terlingua Chili Cookoff, a flashlight momentarily blinded me. "Hi, Sonja. What are you doing here?" It was a friend of my daughter's who lived in Austin.

When I was waiting tables at a friend's café in west Texas a scruffy bearded young man in a baseball cap looked up from his menu. "Ms. Klein, what are you doing here?" I instantly recognized James from Houston, a friend of my son Joe. He observed me in my apron and tee shirt and immediately I read his mind.

Poor old thing, she has really gone down hill, waiting tables in west Texas.

On a flight from Memphis to Amsterdam my partner in the cramped seating asked, "Where are you from?"

"Camp Wood, Barksdale, Vance. Do you know where that is?"

"Yeah, I live outside Camp Wood. My name is Charles Sutherland."

"I think I might know your wife. Where exactly do you live?"

"Below the dam on the Nueces."

I asked him, "On the east or west side of the road?"

"On the east."

"I know where you live."

"Small world."

I answered the common phrase, "Yeah, small world."

Honk if you married Sonja

During the legal process of purchasing another ranch in west Texas, my attorney from Tomball contacted the surveyor from Hondo chosen by the sellers. They were cousins and shared a great-grandfather.

At a conference in west Texas I met a man from the high plains who raised goats. I asked him, "Do you know Irby Chandler?"

"He's my best friend."

I replied, "Well, he's my husband's first cousin."

Later that same year I was at a dance. The weather was cold, bitter and windy. I was wearing my colorful unique Navajo coat. An older cowboy walked up, looked me over and asked, "Have you ever heard of Camp Wood?"

"I live 20 miles from Camp Wood."

"There's this lady there that makes coats like that out of mohair. I can't remember her name."

"Dolores."

"That's it."

He asked, "Did she make that coat?"

"No, it's Navajo."

"Well, she makes some beautiful coats."

I replied, "Yes she does. I have some of her shawls."

After serving six years on the local water board, I attended a water conference in San Angelo with Perry, our president. During the course of the trip he mentioned that his wife's family were Missouri Synod Lutherans and that her brother was a preacher. When I asked what her maiden name was, he replied. "Wagner."

I mentioned that our Lutheran church in Houston once had a handsome vicar named Richard Wagner.

Perry said, "That's my brother-in-law."

I recently attended a music festival in Utopia with my friend Linda from Uvalde. While we sat under a shaded canopy, a young man ventured up and visited with us. He was from the Terlingua area and knew my daughter, Molly.

Several months later, at the Terlingua Chili Cookoff, he wandered into our encampment, took one look at me and said, "I know you."

I answered, "Right, from the the Utopia music festival.

I have discovered over the years that Texas is not that big and that you can run but you can't hide. I anxiously await the next coincidental connection.

53

Ireland

Leaving Texas in August seemed like a good idea. I chose Ireland mainly because I had never been there. After a long flight I landed in Shannon at 7 A.M., anxious for a bed and a bath.

The trip from Shannon to Killarney seemed to last for hours. Upon depositing me at the International Hotel, the driver left me with, "I hope you have some craik while you are here." I later learned that craik is the Irish term for fun.

The hotel dated from 1864. It was located on the main plaza, and as I explored the center of town I visited St. Mary's cathedral and noticed the many pubs lining the streets. Horse-drawn carriages called jauntys offered rides through the city and park.

After exploring the pubs, I entered one with music and an inviting menu. Dining on steamed mussels, I listened to a pair of Irishmen sing songs. The pub became crowded as the evening progressed, and we joined in the singing.

I ordered the black and white pudding for my first breakfast. The black pudding was blood sausage; the white was regular sausage. I didn't order it again.

I spent the day traveling the Ring of Kerry, a 112-mile loop along the coast in southwest Ireland. From the guide I learned that Killarney has a population of 16,000 and is surrounded by a national park of 25,000 acres.

The total population of Ireland is 4.5 million people, 6.5 million cows and half a million sheep. Ireland produces most of the beef for Europe. Salmon fishing as well as whale watching and deep-sea fishing draw tourists. The manufacturing of cranes is an important part of the industry as well as computer parts. Sports occupy the entertainment industry—hurling, rugby, cricket, soccer, golf, horseback riding and racing and Gaelic football. There were many beautiful golf courses, all advertising that Tiger Woods played their course.

The Ring of Kerry took me through the heartland of peat or bog land. Peat is a nonrenewable source of energy that takes 1,000 years to grow. It needs high rainfall and moss to grow one inch every 100 years. Ireland has an average of six feet of peat beneath the surface. It is dug up and sold or used in brick-like chunks after drying. Peat contains 60 percent water. The peat is mechanically harvested in May.

The average rainfall is over 60 inches per year. The country has a maritime climate, wet and windy. That is to say, the oceans surrounding the country affect the weather. Ireland at its widest and longest is 189 miles wide and 302 miles long. There are four provinces and 26 counties.

As I traveled the Ring of Kerry, I noticed that the black-faced sheep were painted either red or blue. The colors denote ownership, not sex. The driver spoke, "When I get tired, I close one eye. When I am really tired I close the other eye." I tried not to pay attention to his driving since he drove on the wrong side of the road. Crossing streets was a problem because I was always looking the wrong way for oncoming traffic. Thankfully in the cities the crosswalks had signs: LOOK THIS WAY. It was helpful.

St. Patrick brought Christianity to Ireland in the fifth century. He blended the pagan and Christian religions to make them more palatable to the native population. There are no snakes or reptiles in Ireland. Only red deer are native to the country.

The homes were neat and well kept. Petunias, hydrangeas, fuschia and roses lined the streets of the city and the yards. Ireland is only 8 percent forested. The government encourages reforestation with tax incentives. Sitka pines have been planted in groves.

The gorse was in bloom and my driver said, "You don't kiss unless the gorse is in bloom. Of course the gorse blooms year round."

Students are taught Gaelic until the eighth grade. Most signs are in English and Gaelic. I couldn't make heads or tails of the Gaelic, which is an Indo-European language like Sanskrit.

After a lunch of smoked salmon and salad, we visited the town of Waterville, where Charlie Chaplin had a home. He spent time there and loved to fish.

We stopped at some stone monuments that had been erected in 2000 B.C. The four standing stones were perfectly aligned with the winter solstice.

The following day, I spent walking the national park, which is a biosphere reserve. Yew, oaks and alders are native to Ireland. The yew tree is sacred and the hawthorn tree is the entrance to the fairy world.

Roads in Ireland have been rerouted to avoid cutting down a hawthorn and disturbing the fairies.

A late afternoon jaunty ride provided a wealth of information. Mike, the jaunty driver, entertained with an assortment of facts and jokes. He said that genetic testing has proven that the Irish are most closely related to the Basques of Spain and that the song "Spanish Eyes" is an Irish song.

He continued to tell me that the sea eagle, otter, mink, hedgehog, red squirrel and pine marten are native to Ireland. As the traffic whizzed by the horse and carriage he added, "Undertakers love overtakers."

An Irish joke: "The bishop traveled through Ireland checking on the priests. He asked the priest from Dublin how he decided how much of the offering to keep and how much to give God. The priest told him that he drew a line, threw the offering in the air and what fell to the left went to him and what landed to the right of the line went to God. When the bishop went to Cork and asked the same question, the priest replied that he drew a circle, threw the offering in the air and what fell inside the circle went to God, the rest went to him. When the bishop came to Killarney, he asked the same question. The priest from Killarney replied that he threw the offering in the air and what stayed up went to God and what fell down was his."

That evening I dined on Irish stew and the ever-present potatoes. Over the course of the trip I was to learn that potatoes are served with most meals, often grilled and mashed on the same plate. The potato is not native to Ireland, but the Irish eat more potatoes than any other people. Sir Walter Raleigh brought the potato to Ireland from the Andes in South America around the end of the 16th century. The potato grows remarkably well in the cold, wet Irish climate and feeds more people per acre than any other crop. The disease that destroyed the potato crops of the mid-1840's caused over one million deaths, and millions emigrated to avoid starvation.

Breakfast the following morning consisted of oatmeal, a fresh baked scone, fresh fruit and eggs. Fish and grilled tomatoes were also an option.

I toured the Dingle Peninsula, a beautiful drive along the rugged coastline and observed the Blasket Islands. My driver was a storyteller. "The woman calls her landlord, tells him the house shakes every time the train passes. The landlord doesn't believe her. She tells him to come and lie in the bed. The woman's husband comes home early, walks in the bedroom and asks what going on here. The landlord tells him that he probably won't believe it, but he's waiting for a train."

My driver continued. "Charles Lindberg first crossed the coast of the Dingle Peninsula when he made his famous trans-Atlantic flight. Henry Ford came to Ireland and donated 5,000 pounds for a hospital. The paper published that he had donated 50,000 pounds. When he issued the new check, he stipulated that he could dictate the words on the plaque for the hospital. The plaque read, "I came to Ireland and you took me in."

When I asked my driver about driving accidents and violations, he replied that there are few accidents. Fines are administered by points. A driver is allowed 12 points worth of fines every three years before having his license suspended.

I left Killarney for a swing through northern Ireland to Adare, where I visited a primary school. The children wore uniforms and behaved well —except at recess. If only that energy could be harnessed. The school contained all the modern technology necessary for a good education. The government pays the cost of higher education.

Along the road I noticed wind turbines. I visited Desmond Castle, dating from the 1300's, which Oliver Cromwell destroyed in the 1600's. Cromwell is not well loved in Ireland.

In 1609 the British monarch brought Scottish settlers to Ireland and dispossessed the Irish landowners. A rural society existed with tenant farmers and absentee owners; and by 1841 the population of Ireland was over eight million. The life expectancy was 25 to 40 years.

In 1845, 95 percent of the potato crop failed. The government provided soup kitchens and fever hospitals. Workhouses existed for the destitute. A mass migration to England and the United States resulted. The famine was a catalyst for change. The population was cut in half. England introduced reform. A legacy of bitterness was created between England and Ireland that sowed the seeds of independence.

I climbed the 700-foot cliffs of Moher for a view of the awesome coastline and the Atlantic Ocean. The driver along the road to Galway provided a running dialog. "The Romans never came to Ireland. St. Bridget is the pagan goddess of the Earth. The burren with the karst landscape is the poorest land in Ireland. The bad economy in Ireland is due to Bush, Palin, the English, the Normans, the Vikings and women, all in that order."

Sonja Klein

The hotel in Galway was located in the central district. I walked the old and new city. The ancient walls still stood in some parts. I noticed signs that threatened the cars would be clamped if parked illegally.

Galway was settled in 1250 by Anglo-Normans. I visited St. Nicholas Anglican Church and the chantry chapels inside, where families donated income from rents so the priests would continue to pray for the family.

Many of the meals I consumed were without seasoning and flavor, but in the open market in Galway I found a vendor selling crepes. My choice was a flavorful spinach, garlic and feta crepe.

That evening I dined at Glenlo Abbey, an ancient site that has been converted to a plush resort. During the meal a lecturer spoke of the Irish poets—Yeats and Lady Gregory—and read some of their poetry. Irish poetry tends to the dark side.

The meal was designed in heaven. First course was chicken leg and mushroom Ballotine flavored with fresh rosemary served with fig and cucumber stacked on mustard cress with honey, olive and rosemary dressing. The second course was char-grilled fillet of beef topped with port and Foie gras butter, purple pomme Williams and a mélange of baby vegetables. And if that wasn't enough, dessert was lemon syrup cake, lemon curd and mascarpone lemon ice cream.

Being in Ireland my thoughts naturally compared the country to my own. The cost of living in Europe is more expensive. Housing, food, clothing, hotels, beer, cigarettes and gasoline cost more. Gasoline varies from $8 to $10 a gallon. A mediocre hotel may charge as much as $200 per night for a room. An American-style breakfast can be up to $12.

The Irish worker works less than the American worker. Yet I noticed no beggars or homeless. The cars were all clean and shiny. The cities had clean streets and no litter. Of course all the cars were small and economical. Gas-guzzling clunkers are simply too big for the narrow roads and lanes. When making purchases, if the buyer wishes a plastic bag, the cost is 30 cents per bag extra—a great way to avoid liter. The Irish call plastic bags witches' underwear because before the price was set, the trees were all littered with the bags.

I took the ferry for a 45-minute ride to Inis Mor, the largest of the islands of Aran, where Christian ruins stand side by side with remarkable Pagan relics. The ancient fort of Dun Aonghus, a 2,500-year-old sentinel fort that stands on the cliff's edge, is visible from any spot on the island.

Honk if you married Sonja

It was the day of the hurling championship, the super bowl of Ireland. All eyes were glued to the television. Hurling is a unique Irish sport developed in the late 1800's. Thirty Irish men with sticks and a heavy small leather ball run up and down the field in shorts for 70 minutes. Hurling claims to be the fastest field game in the world. The thousands of spectators who fill the stadium are allowed to drink alcohol only during the intermissions.

The guide refused to be distracted by the hurling event and continued with information telling us that the Aran Islands rank in importance because of the harbor protection for the fishing industry. About 800 people live on the largest island and Gaelic is spoken. The Ogham stones date from the fourth century. The forts on the island date from 1500 B.C., and the cliff top habitats are 3,000 years old. Three thousand miles of stone walls dominate the island, the rocks having been piled into walls to provide pasture.

The rain, which had been falling lightly (called soft weather by the Irish) came down in torrents. I stopped in a pub for shelter wearing the Navajo coat. The man on the stool next to me commented, "It's a shitty day; time for the high stool. Did you hear about Paddy and Mick? They went on their way to do some fishing when a fairy pops out from under a hawthorn tree and gives them a wish. Paddy asks that the lake be turned into Guiness. Mick tells him, 'You idiot, now we have to pee in the boat.' By the way where did you get that coat?"

"The U.S. It's Navajo."

"Very nice."

"Thank you."

Lunch was better, spinach and cheese pannini. The return ferry ride sickened some of the passengers, but the crowd was merry because the underdog in the hurling championship defeated the three-time winner.

Once back on the coach our guide kept a nap at bay by more facts, telling us that Ireland joined the European Union in 1973. The 1990's brought recovery to the country, with payments for infrastructure and free college. Ireland currently suffers from a sluggish economy with the rest of the world. Unemployment is 13.5 percent. Many of the Irish are moving to Australia.

Stephen kept talking. The number of murders in 2009 was 55. Burglary, extortion and kidnapping are on the rise. An identity card is issued for social services. The drinking age is 18. Free public health care

297

is provided, but private health care is available for those who can pay. A health levy of 2 percent of total income up to 100,000 Euros is mandatory. The percentage goes up over 100,000. The Irish do not have to contribute if they make less than 500 Euros per week or if they are over 70. Those over 65 are given a free fuel allowance, free travel and phone units.

Doctor and dental visits are comparable with America, but you must choose a doctor or dentist within seven miles. The Irish live long; life expectancy is 86 to 88 years. Minimum wage is 8.65 Euros per hour. The current exchange rate is $1.32 per Euro. You do the math.

Income tax rates are high—22 percent on total income up to 35,000 Euros, no deductions. Over 35,000 Euros, the Irish pay 41 percent income tax. I gave up on a nap and kept my pen scratching.

I really liked the guide. He was a trivia expert and when I returned to the states I emailed him the titles of books and movies he might find interesting.

The following morning I visited Drumcliffe, the site of the famous Irish poet, W. B. Yeats', grave. His epitaph struck a Texas note. "Cast a cold eye/On life/On death/Horseman, pass by." It was the title of one of my favorite Texas authors, Larry McMurtry. McMurtry is Texan but must have Irish ancestors. We passed by the site where Lord Mountbatten had a home and was blown up by dissidents.

After a tasty lunch of goat cheese baked on tomatoes and lettuce, I inquired about social problems. Racial crime, underage drinking, unwed mothers and foster-care children appear to be the main issues.

Arriving in Killybegs, I enjoyed a dinner of salmon salad, grilled haddock and French fries. The Irish make great French fries.

Killybegs is a small fishing town, and I enjoyed a walking tour of the town along the harbor, a glacial bay. The Spanish and Portugese fished off the west coast of Ireland before the time of Columbus. When England claimed Ireland, they sold the fishing rights off the coast to the Spanish and French and put a tax on salt for the locals to prevent them from selling the fish.

Killybegs is best known for its development of mid-water trolls. Nets made in Killybegs are used in Alaska and all over the world.

The guide was a wealth of information. Mackerel, herring, haddock, salmon and cod are harvested off the coast of Killybegs. The tide rises 17 feet along the harbor. The fishing industry is in decline due to quotas and regulation. The Spanish own the fishing rights off the west coast of Ireland. The European Union controls fishing rights and determined that the Irish do not have historical rights.

Rain and wind dominated the day as I sought the comfort of the local pub, where I was entertained by stories: "An Irish farmer and an English farmer were talking. The English farmer tells the Irish farmer that it takes him all day to drive his tractor over his farm. The Irish farmer replies that he used to have a tractor like that."

A comforting meal of baked monkfish and shrimp in garlic butter and cheese ended a cold and rainy day.

Hotel signs never failed to amaze me. Every city had a different DO NOT DISTURB SIGN. They ranged from LEAVE ME ALONE to GO AWAY.

I left Killybegs after enjoying the small quiet fishing village and crossed into Northern Ireland, which is ruled by the British. The highway signs were posted in miles.

My driver delivered more information. Eighty percent of Irish own their own homes; whereas, in the rest of the 27 countries included in the European Union, home ownership is 20 percent.

The recent war in Ireland was about land, not religion. It just happened that each side was of a different religion. Northern Ireland consists of six counties and according to my driver, the people of Northern Ireland have identity issues. Peace has prevailed since 2000.

The guide Stephen seemed never to be quiet. He was always spouting tidbits of information laced with Irish humor. The Titanic was built in Northern Ireland, in Belfast. The story goes, "The Titanic was fine when it left Belfast, but you know what the Catholics were doing while the Protestants were building the Titanic? The Catholics were building the iceberg."

Davy Crockett, Dolly Parton, Neil Armstrong, Francis Scott Key, Stonewall Jackson, Sam Houston and Andrew Jackson all have Irish roots.

When the Spanish king, Phillip II invaded England and was defeated, he began the return voyage only to be blown off course. Twenty-four ships were wrecked off the coast of Ireland. Many of the sailors remained in Ireland, thus the origin of the term "the black Irish."

Stephen told stories of the fairy world, the wee folk and the Banshee and the headless horseman. I couldn't write them down fast enough.

A rainbow greeted my entry into the city of Dublin. Dinner was salmon salad and baked haddock on a bed of potatoes and parsnips. Irish cheesecake completed the meal—a light tasty confection.

On the way to Dublin I stopped for a few hours at the Ulster American Folk Park. This museum park tells the poignant story of emigration from Ulster to America in the 18th and 19th centuries.

I arrived in Dublin for my last few days. The hotel was centrally located, designed in the décor of a dark bordello, quite an interesting place.

I spent the first morning in Dublin on a walking tour of the city with a Joycean scholar to experience the sights, sounds, streets and monuments that form the city and appear in the writings of James Joyce. I signed up because it sounded interesting. My degree was in English, and I recalled having to read his work while in college but had no memory of it being remarkable. That should have been a clue.

A literary scholar named Jerry greeted our group on the streets of Dublin and led us to a hotel that had seen better days. The lecture began with, "Here the woman Joyce fancied worked as a maid."

The walk continued past the barbershop he frequented. On we traveled to the street made famous by his writings. We learned about his book *Ulysses*, how he wrote about the mundane, his point being that the events of one's life could be made into passionate moments, though sounding mundane.

Jerry spoke of Joyce's life, of his financial difficulties, his personal tragedies and the life he led in Paris. Thirty minutes were devoted to the issue of what side of the street was correct in his book. "Joyce used the directory of Dublin as his source. The directory was not exact. The house to which Joyce referred was on the wrong side of the street in the directory. It was not Joyce's fault that he did not put the house in the correct position."

Three hours spent on Joyce did not inspire me to read his works. Rather, I understood his point that perception is the key to passionate experience—no secret. Artists live emotional lives, whether in action or in their minds.

At the end of the walking tour, I could not resist speaking my mind, "I don't know about you all, but I think if Joyce were alive today, he would never be published. Books today must have dialogue. Roughly only 20 percent of the books published are fiction. Joyce would be an unpublished failure in today's market. Now I know why I don't remember him. I must not have been interested in his work."

A few heads nodded in agreement. I smiled.

I did add some remarks about Jerry, our guide, who was quite accomplished. He had attended many seminars and conferences in America regarding Joyce and was a respected Joycean scholar. He had written a biography of Samuel Beckett.

My conclusion was that I think he had better things to do than guide a bunch of dumb tourists around the streets of Dublin in the rain. I hope he was well compensated for his knowledge.

After a light lunch of carrot and leek soup, I watched a one-person play at Bewley's Café on Grafton Street. Many of the words I couldn't understand. What I did understand was that the words were dark and sad. As I strolled through the shopping district in the late afternoon, I dined on a steak sandwich and pot fries after posing for a picture with a giant leprechaun. He assured me after I donated money to his pot, "If your wish doesn't come true in seven days, come back for a refund." At this point in the trip my only wish was to return home safely. My wish came true. No refund.

My second day in Dublin was spent touring a restored Georgian home from the 1800's. From there I walked to the National Museum, where I viewed gold artifacts and collars from 2000 B.C. I visited Trinity College and viewed the Book of Kells as well as the Long Room of the library, where the old books were stored. It was breathtaking.

The Book of Kells was written over 1,000 years ago. The book contains lavishly decorated copy of the four gospels in Latin and was probably produced in the ninth century by the monks of Iona, working wholly or partially at Iona itself or at Kells.

After my visit to Trinity College I toured the old Jameson Distillery, where the romantic past of Irish whiskey-making was explained. That evening I dined at a local pub, enjoying baked goat cheese on a bed of lettuce and mixed vegetables.

My last day in Dublin was one of the best. I was off to the Hill of Tara and Newgrange, the oldest sacred site in Europe and a UNESCO World Heritage Site. The scenery was one of beautiful greens, rolling hills dotted with the huge mounds that were celestial, that is to say they were aligned with the winter solstice and built before the pyramids of Egypt.

Sonja Klein

A curb of 97 stones, the most impressive of which is the highly decorated Entrance Stone, surrounds Newgrange, the best-known Irish passage tomb. The mound covers a single tomb consisting of a long passage and a cross-shaped chamber. Before we went inside the 5,000-year-old passage and chamber, the guide described the significance of the famous Entrance Stone as well as the Roof Box. Inside the chamber, the winter solstice phenomenon was explained, as well as the burial ritual. The lights in the chamber were turned off and the light at the time of the solstice was simulated. The experience was equal to that of the tombs in Egypt.

Ireland was more than I had expected. I learned that the Irish people love talking. It's a national hobby, especially in the pub, accompanied by a pint of Guiness. Irish people also love to listen. There is a great appreciation for anyone with a way with words.

A Spanish tourist once asked an Irish man if the Irish had a concept of time like the Spanish "manana." The Irishman looked horrified and said, "God no, we've nothing as urgent as that."

Why do the Irish seem so different from the English? The answer Stephen gave was because they are different racially and culturally and have had totally different historical backgrounds. Successive waves of Celtic-speaking peoples settled Ireland in the first millennium B.C. The next settlers were the Vikings, who established Ireland's first towns along the east and south coasts in the 9th and 10th centuries. England was also populated by Celts but became a Roman colony 2,000 years ago. The French-speaking Normans also came to Ireland but not in great numbers. They soon took on the language and customs of Ireland.

The Irish character has been shaped by opposite factors—the continuity of the rural agricultural life combined with the experience of powerlessness under English colonial rule. For now, peace reigns in Ireland, and that is a good thing.

54

Woo Woo

I couldn't wait to announce it to the world. "Molly's pregnant. I'm going to be a grandma."

Most every first response was, "What are you going to be called?"

"Hell if I care. I'll settle for a healthy baby, whatever it is. Twins wouldn't be bad."

My daughter thought otherwise.

With Molly and Israel, the father, living here on the ranch, it was the best of all possible worlds—or so I thought. Towards the end I just prayed a lot, prayed the baby would be healthy, made deals with God so we would be able to get her to the hospital over an hour away in time, prayed she wouldn't die in childbirth or that I wouldn't faint.

Her pregnancy seemed to last forever. We both cried at the ultrasound. The sound of the thumping heart and sight of the outline of the fetus was a moment I'll never forget. She was sick the entire pregnancy and we both worried about everything imaginable.

Names for a boy and girl were left to her and the father. I wanted no part of that choice—just ultimate approval. When we found out it was a boy, she and Israel chose a name, Theiss Aramis. It was a good family name, my mother's maiden name and Molly's middle name. The Theiss's were all good folks.

My cousin Roxanne suggested that the baby call me Wild Woman, which I'm not. I've had some interesting experiences but don't consider myself a wild woman. When I told Molly, she replied, "We'll call you Woo Woo." It stuck.

Theiss is now nine months old, crawling and pulling up. He was delivered Caesarian, healthy but small. No longer tiny, he is more joy than I could ever imagine.

When Molly and Israel planned on attending a four-day water catchment/rainwater seminar I was eager to keep him. They insisted I practice. I thought it was ridiculous but agreed. He was easy; parenting is not a skill easily forgotten.

Sonja Klein

I never thought I would love a grandchild as much as I love that little boy. We have become great friends. At least once a week, sometimes more often, I drive down to their house and just take him for a day. We talk and he sits in his booster chair on the kitchen countertop while I cook. I hand him cucumbers, carrots, let him feel potatoes and tell him stories. He looks at me with so much love that it breaks my heart, makes me teary-eyed.

We play pat-a-cake, crawl on the floor together and I kiss him a lot. He plays with all my plastic measuring cups and spoons, lids and plastic bottles. He smiles a lot and pays attention when I talk to him. He doesn't see my wrinkles. To him I'm beautiful, but he's the beauty in my life. Who needs a boyfriend? I'm Woo Woo.

55

Just when

J ust when I thought my traveling days were over and I could finally relax and quit my adventures around the world and enjoy my grandson, Christmas brought a surprise. My son Joe and his wife Carla gave me some books for Christmas. One was about great driving trips and the other was about great world adventures. Both books come from National Geographic.

Before I even had the courage to open one page, I began to imagine planning another trip, certain that the books would provide the inspiration. I had become lethargic, declining to venture off the ranch, fearful (unfounded) that something would happen and I wouldn't be able to see my grandson grow. I spoke out loud, "Silly old woman. Flying is safer than driving a car."

Another year was ending, a time for reflection. Several of my girlfriends had facelifts. It was an option, quickly dispelled. I had earned my wrinkles but still disguised the gray hair. I felt comfortable in my skin and body.

The coming year, 2011, contained a few plans—a trip to Austin for a family wedding, a trip to California's Pacific coast for another family wedding, combined with a trip along the California coast to San Francisco to eat abalone and explore China Town with my son and his wife. I always looked forward to the annual trip in July or August to my brother's ranch in New Mexico to enjoy the company of my "brothers Grimm" and their wives.

And then there was the book I was having published, a completion but not really, only a beginning. I had already begun converting one of my movie scripts into historical fiction, my next project to be printed.

Yet I felt there was something more out there, maybe the east coast of South America, India or Vietnam and Cambodia. Maybe, maybe Libya or Burma, even Canada.

And then there was my beautiful grandson, Theiss Aramis. I didn't want to miss a day of his life and felt blessed to have him so close at the ranch. I wanted so much to be part of his life and to stay alive to see him grow up and be influenced by his grandmother. What to do, Woo Woo?

There was the dilemma. Was I wild woman or Woo Woo? Perhaps both.

56

On writing

As an avid reader and book lover, I have always been a wordsmith, but the years of marriage, career and raising children had prevented the pursuit of writing. I suppose I was too busy living. "I shall live bad if I don't write, and I shall write badly if I don't live." I don't remember who said it, but the quote is worthy.

The sensuousness of the written word, the feel of the pages turning provided sufficient satisfaction in those middle years. Only when I found myself a widow on a remote ranch in west Texas did I return to my love of writing.

At first I wrote from the position of grief; writing was therapy. And for a while I was satisfied. Once the pain had somewhat assuaged, I began to read about writers, finding that I had a lot in common with their thoughts on the pursuit of putting words together.

I wrote stories about my experiences, essays on topical subjects, several books based on my adventures. I attended seminars on writing, joined a writing group and became informed about publishing and self-publishing as well as the world of agents, publicists and book tours. As soon as I realized the drama and competition of a writing career, I discarded that option. Little money was to be realized; self-marketing demanded much effort. Yet, a person was not a writer unless their words were read. Having someone read my words was scary.

At first I only let family and close friends become intimate with my thoughts. The writer's group helped. We read out aloud to each other. The compliments were void of criticism; we were much too kind.

My community involvement led to the task of writing articles about scheduled fundraising events. I began to travel, picking remote destinations and discovering that I loved traveling alone. I sought even more distant countries and soon found myself taking notes, studying foreign cultures and feeling the passion of adventure—a substitute for the emotions of a relationship.

A friend who owned the weekly free paper in the sparsely populated canyons west of the Hill Country asked, "Why don't you write an article about your travels? I'll print it."

The response was overwhelming. People I did not know well spoke, "I read your article in the *Canyon Broadcaster*. You write well and I really enjoyed it."

I entered a few contests, won some firsts, seconds and thirds. I continued to write about my travels, wrote essays, short stories and even some poetry. Locally I was recognized as a good writer. For a while that was enough.

Then my cousin encouraged me to write a movie script. "That's where the money is," she said. I chose my subject, purchased a book on the format of movie scripts and began to write with addictive passion. My brother John, the Texas historian, intervened.

"You're a good writer. If you write a movie script about the life of Rip Ford in Texas from 1836 to the end of the Civil War, I'll sell it." He fed me books. I researched for a year before I wrote a word. I developed a timeline, had pages of notes and completed the script.

The drive across Texas to his ranch on the Trinity River took a day. We rewrote, edited and spent hours polishing the script. He exposed it to his contacts in New York and California. Their comments: "It's too violent." "It's not politically correct and will be offensive." "Westerns are not popular right now." Still, the manuscript continued to float out there in the world of words and pictures.

John consoled me. "We did it backwards. You should have written the book and then we could have sold the movie rights." Yet, I continued to travel and write. I visited South America, Bhutan, the Middle East—Jordan, Syria, Lebanon, Egypt, Oman and Dubai. I ventured into the Sinai Desert. I traversed the whole of Russia on the Trans-Siberian Railroad from Vladisvostock, down into Mongolia, and on to St. Petersburg. I journeyed to Australia, Tasmania and New Zealand.

My adventures continued to entertain people I didn't know, as well as those I did know. I found myself in social situations where people approached me, "I read your article about Dubai." Or, "I loved your article about the Trans-Siberian Railroad trip." "Where are you going next?" "Aren't you afraid of traveling alone?" "Do you ever get scared?" "You sure are brave." "Could you email me your articles about Australia? My cousin is going there and wants to read them." "I wish I had the courage to do that."

I had written numerous essays, short stories, five books, three movie scripts and even some short poems. The exhilaration of writing was sufficient. Fear of being read dissolved.

A moment occurs while writing a piece that is hard to describe—the instant when the words become not yours but flow through you. Once that something else takes charge, it will not let you write "The End" until the moment is there. The feeling is beyond comprehension and absolutely enthralling. And I don't believe that having a book published could be more exciting than that solitary moment in front of the computer.

I guess I'll find out.

Order Form

Fax Orders: Send this completed form to 1-830-234-3155.

Telephone Orders: Call 1-830-234-3156.

Email Orders: Visit sonja@ambushhillranch.com

Postal Orders: Send this completed form to:
Ambush Publishing, PO Box 192, Barksdale, Texas 78828

Name: _____

Address: _____

_____

City: _____ State: _____ Zip: _____

Phone: _____ Email: _____

HONK IF YOU MARRIED SONJA

Number of Copies: _____ @ $15.00/book Subtotal: $ _____

Add $4.95 for priority shipping in United States. For orders outside of the United States add $5.99 for first class or $11.95 for priority.

Shipping: $_____ Total: $_____

Make check or money order payable to Ambush Publishing.
If you wish to pay by credit card go to www.honkifyoumarriedsonja.com